Mass Appeal

The Formative Age of the Movies, Radio, and TV

Mass Appeal describes the changing world of American popula
from the first sound movies through the age of television.

In short and accessible vignettes, the book reveals the career
of people who became big movie, TV, or radio stars. Eddie Ca
Al Jolson symbolize the early stars of sound movies. Grouch
and Fred Astaire represent the movie stars of the 1930s, a
Benny stands in for the 1930s performers who achieved thei
on radio. Katharine Hepburn, a stage and film star, illustr
cultural trends of the late 1930s and early 1940s. Humphre
and Bob Hope serve as examples of performers who achiev
success during the Second World War. Walt Disney, Woody A
Lucille Ball, among others, become the representative figure
postwar world.

Through these vignettes, the reader comes to understand the
ment of American mass media in the twentieth century.

Edward D. Berkowitz is Professor of History at George Wa
University. He has held academic positions at the Unive
Massachusetts, Boston, and administrative positions at
University and the President's Commission for a National Age
the Eighties. He is the author of six books, including *So
Happened*, his history of the 1970s. He is co-author of fo
books and editor of three, including *A Documentary History*
Security.

Berkowitz has given invited lectures at the European Univ
Florence, at Oxford and Cambridge Universities, and
Netherlands, Australia, and New Zealand. He has publishe
than 100 articles in publications including the *Journal o*
History, the *Milbank Memorial Quarterly*, the *Boston Glc
Washington Post*, and the *San Jose Mercury News*. His medi
has also included appearances on Terry Gross's *Fresh Air*, C-
Washington Journal, and the History Channel. In 2009, he
principal commentator in the AP-TV's coverage of the
inauguration.

CAMBRIDGE ESSENTIAL HISTORIES

Series Editor

Donald Critchlow, St. Louis University

Cambridge Essential Histories is devoted to introducing critical events, periods, or individuals in history to students. Volumes in this series emphasize narrative as a means of familiarizing students with historical analysis. In this series, leading scholars focus on topics in European, American, Asian, Latin American, Middle Eastern, African, and World History through thesis-driven, concise volumes designed for survey and upper-division undergraduate history courses. The books contain an introduction that acquaints readers with the historical event and reveals the book's thesis; narrative chapters that cover the chronology of the event or problem; and a concluding summary that provides the historical interpretation and analysis.

Titles in the Series

John Earl Haynes and Harvey Klehr, *Early Cold War Spies: The Espionage Trials that Shaped American Politics*

James H. Hutson, *Church and State in America: The First Two Centuries*

Maury Klein, *The Genesis of Industrial America, 1870–1920*

John Lauritz Larson, *The Market Revolution in America: Liberty, Ambition, and the Eclipse of the Common Good*

Charles H. Parker, *Global Interactions in the Early Modern Age, 1400–1800*

Mass Appeal

The Formative Age of the Movies, Radio, and TV

EDWARD D. BERKOWITZ

George Washington University

 CAMBRIDGE
UNIVERSITY PRESS

CAMBRIDGE UNIVERSITY PRESS
Cambridge, New York, Melbourne, Madrid, Cape Town, Singapore,
São Paulo, Delhi, Dubai, Tokyo, Mexico City

Cambridge University Press
32 Avenue of the Americas, New York, NY 10013-2473, USA

www.cambridge.org
Information on this title: www.cambridge.org/9780521717779

First published 2010

Printed in the United States of America

A catalog record for this publication is available from the British Library.

Library of Congress Cataloging in Publication Data

Berkowitz, Edward D.
   Mass appeal : the formative age of the movies, radio, and tv / Edward D. Berkowitz.
      p.   cm. – (Cambridge essential histories)
   Includes bibliographical references and index.
   ISBN 978-0-521-88908-7 (hardback) – ISBN 978-0-521-71777-9 (pbk.)
   1. Motion pictures – United States – History – 20th century.   2. Radio programs –
United States – History – 20th century.   3. Television programs – United States – History
– 20th century.   I. Title.
   PN1993.5.U6B385   2010
   791.40973–dc22   2010030171

ISBN 978-0-521-88908-7 Hardback
ISBN 978-0-521-71777-9 Paperback

For my mother, Shalvo Berkowitz, the matriarch of the Schwartz family – with love and affection.

Contents

Acknowledgments   *page* xi

Introduction   1
1   Sound Comes In, Vaudeville and Silent Pictures Go Out   3
2   From Broadway to Hollywood with Groucho, Fred, and Ginger   20
3   Radio Nights   39
4   From the Thirties to the Forties with Kate, Bud, and Lou   57
5   Bogie, Bob, and the Boys at War   76
6   The Postwar Movie Scene   98
7   Make Room for TV   110
8   Putting It Together: Walt Disney Introduces the Baby
    Boom to Television   131
9   The End of an Era?   153

Notes   169
Movie, Radio, and TV Listings   197
Index   199

Acknowledgments

As an only child in the baby boom, I had television as a daily companion. I bonded so closely with the set that I sometimes imagined I had been chosen at birth as the national television child. In this conceit, everything I did and every program I watched were televised on a special channel, something like the setup of the Jim Carrey movie *Truman*. That fantasy led to this book.

My parents also helped. My father bought a television set just before I was born, which meant that I was never without one. My parents took me to Broadway shows and other New York cultural attractions and shared their love of movies with me. On my thirteenth birthday, I received a ticket to see radio and television star Jack Benny perform live in a one-man show at the Ziegfeld Theatre on West 54th Street in New York City. After the performance, I got Benny's autograph as he left the theater, a fleeting but still direct connection with one of radio's greatest stars.

Like any kid who came of age in the 1960s, I played the radio all the time. Although I missed Jack Benny and radio's golden age, I caught a glimpse of the medium's potential by listening to Dan Ingram on WABC and John Gambling and Jean Shepherd on WOR.

My children have also helped. Before the birth of my first child, I went out and, in an unconscious homage to my father, bought a VCR. Its presence enabled me to share old movies and classic TV shows with my daughters, Sarah and Rebecca. Their enthusiasm reinforced my desire to write this book.

This project lies far outside my scholarly comfort zone. I am grateful to Donald Critchlow and to Lew Bateman of Cambridge University Press for giving me an opportunity to write the book. As always, George Washington University provided a supportive environment, from Dean Peg Barratt to my departmental chair Tyler Anbinder. Tyler very generously arranged for Chris Cullig and Bruce Rushing to help with some of the research and other tasks related to the book. Michael Weeks presided over the department with his usual efficiency and good grace. My friend Bill Becker took over as chair at the end of this project and lent his sympathetic support. I always had the feeling that he and all of my colleagues were rooting for me.

I am particularly indebted to three of my colleagues who took the time to read drafts and discuss this project with me. Richard Stott read the entire manuscript and gave me the benefit of his encyclopedic knowledge of the history of popular culture. Our discussions greatly improved the book. Leo Ribuffo, who encouraged me to write what he called my "crazy" book, also took the time to read the manuscript and to make perceptive and helpful comments. Both Richard and Leo would have done a much better job if they had written this book themselves, but both lent gracious support to me. My Trachtenberg School colleague Chris Sterling allowed me to tap some of his considerable expertise and generously read the manuscript with great care.

Family members Emily Frank, Elizabeth Frank, Julia Frank, Naomi Graber, Michael Jerison, and Susan Grant all made it easier for me to write the book, as did friends Howie Baum, Peter and Dale Demy, Gareth Davies, Frank and Ann Hubbard, and Kim McQuaid. James Baughman of the University of Wisconsin helped out at a critical time, and Ronald Cohen did a superb job of editing the manuscript and easing it into print. All have my thanks.

Introduction

Beginning in the third decade of the twentieth century, talking pictures, radio, and then television appeared on the American scene. Along with recorded music available first on phonograph records and then on such devices as compact discs, these three forms of entertainment, each of which relied on the mechanical transmission of sound into homes or movie theaters, dominated American popular culture between 1928 and the end of the century.

Each year, Americans sampled the available movies, radio programs, and television programs. Their choices reflected the categories that divided them, such as gender, region, race, and ethnicity, but the fact that all chose from the same basic menu meant that popular culture united Americans far more than it separated them. Even regional forms of entertainment, such as the country music broadcast over the Grand Ole Opry program from Nashville, reached wide audiences.

What mattered most in the evolution of this wave of popular culture was the essential historical variable of time. Although particular stars and programs retained their popularity over long stretches of time, Americans watched different movies, listened to different radio programs, and viewed different television programs in different eras. Their choices helped to define and differentiate one time period from another.

Mass Appeal describes the changing world of American popular culture from the first sound movies through the age of television. For three basic innovations – sound movies, radio, and television – I explain how each came to be an accepted part of American life. I also characterize the most popular offerings of each medium, and I detail the career patterns of people who became big movie, TV, or radio stars. Charlie Chaplin's life provides a window on the silent film era. Eddie Cantor and Al Jolson symbolize the early stars of sound movies. Groucho Marx and Fred Astaire represent the movie stars of the 1930s, and Jack Benny stands in for the 1930s' performers who achieved their success on radio. Katharine Hepburn, a stage and film star, illustrates the cultural trends of the late 1930s and early 1940s. Humphrey Bogart and Bob Hope serve as examples of performers who achieved great success during the Second World War. Walt Disney, Woody Allen, and Lucille Ball, among others, become the representative figures of the postwar world.

None of these stars is in any way obscure, but they may be figures of interest to students today. This book does not look for hidden aspects of the popular culture experience. Instead, it provides a chronology of movies, radio, and television from sound movies to the VCR. It contains my own "readings," as the academics like to say, of key movies, radio, and television programs. It endeavors to project the history of popular culture against the larger themes of American history and to introduce a new generation to the entertainment figures of the era of their parents and grandparents.

I emphasize that this book gathers together evidence that is available to anyone through personal experience and through the abundance of information stored on the Internet. Libraries no longer close at midnight. Information about nearly any film or TV show lies at one's fingertips. Students now take this technology for granted. Ask them to write a report about the movie star Ginger Rogers and they Google the name and come up with a biography and a list of movies.

Academics worry that information obtained in this way lacks the purity of information mined from a book or an archive. Many of these doubts reflect the usual anxiety that accompanies a significant change in technology. I take the Internet as a given and encourage readers of this book to follow up on the subjects that interest them. The book integrates evidence so as to form a simple narrative and series of biographical sketches that the reader can embellish as he or she wishes.

I invite readers to discover or rediscover the movies of the 1930s, the radio programs of the 1940s, and the television programs of the 1950s and to see how the leading figures of popular culture have changed to reflect the changing times.

Sound Comes In, Vaudeville and Silent Pictures Go Out

On August 15, 1926, the Warner brothers introduced an experimental process to New York audiences that brought synchronized sound to movie theaters. Movies were already a thriving business. Although the early movies did not talk, the audiences made vocal comments on the picture before them and cheered, clapped, and laughed in appropriate places; live or separately recorded music accompanied the film, so silent films were not really shown in quiet settings. The Warner brothers put the sound track directly onto the film and thereby offered something new to an already lively medium. The August 1926 program included a filmed speech from former postmaster general Will Hays, some music recitals, and a silent performance by distinguished actor John Barrymore as Don Juan with a recorded orchestral accompaniment. Audiences marveled at how clearly Hays's words came through and how faithfully the sound process reproduced the musical tones. "The resonance and clarity of the tones seemed to put life into the shadows on the screen," gushed the *New York Times*. It was as though the audience "had a front row seat at the Metropolitan Opera." The upscale audience was reportedly spellbound: "Only those who had to catch trains to go to their summer homes left before the feature came to an end."[1]

THE WARNER BROTHERS AND THE MOVIE INDUSTRY

The four Warner brothers were typical of the men who made the movie business. They were Jewish, the sons of a Polish cobbler who immigrated to Baltimore, Maryland. The peripatetic family eventually settled in Youngstown, Ohio, where the father worked first as a cobbler and then as a grocer, with the sons doing what they could to help. The second son,

Albert, went on the road for the Swift Company selling soap. In Pittsburgh in 1904 he saw his first movie at a "nickelodeon," an early storefront movie theater so-called because of its cheap admission price. The family decided to go into the movie business, obtaining a motion picture projector and a print of a short film called *The Great Train Robbery*. They showed it in halls near their home base as part of a complete program that included a piano solo by Rose Warner (a Warner sister) and songs from Jack Warner. Then they opened their own nickelodeon in Newcastle, Pennsylvania. Starting without enough money to buy necessities for their small storefront operation, they had to borrow chairs from an undertaker down the street.[2]

The Warner brothers went from film exhibition, to film distribution, to film production in 1917. In 1925, still relatively minor players in the business, they became interested in experiments with sound being made by Western Electric and ATT. Although previous efforts at linking picture and sound had not been successful, the Warners thought that the new system held enough promise to eventually replace the need for an orchestra in movie theaters. The Warner brothers invested in recorded sound.[3]

With or without sound, the movies had become big business by the time of World War I. Their development reflected a typical industrial pattern in which the barriers to entry were low at first, and many different companies and individual entrepreneurs joined the movie business. Over time, as in other businesses, some movie operators, such as the Warner brothers, became more successful than others, and their success allowed them to invest in larger theaters or to expand to other areas of the business. Someone who showed movies in theaters might also decide to produce or distribute them, or a production company might buy a chain of theaters to have a guaranteed audience for its offerings. As these things happened, the size of the typical firm grew larger, making it more difficult for upstart newcomers to compete and absorbing or eliminating less successful competitors. The industry eventually consolidated into five major integrated companies – MGM, Paramount, Warner Brothers, RKO, and Fox. Two large companies, Columbia and Universal, made movies but did not distribute them. Together, these companies dominated the industry.[4]

VAUDEVILLE AND THE MOVIES

Sound movies replaced live variety shows, which were known as vaudeville. This late-nineteenth-century show business phenomenon, which peaked in the early twentieth century, provided good clean family fun (although some acts used double entendres and suggestive actions to skirt the edge of decency – to the discomfort of those who ran the business but to the delight of many audiences). Vaudeville shows, at least in theory, offered something for everyone, including women and children. The trick was to provide wholesome entertainment that did not alienate audiences in search of thrills or laughs. Staples of vaudeville variety shows included acrobats or "dumb" acts with animals that often led the program as people were still finding their seats, comedians who might appeal to adolescent males, tenors whose masculinity attracted the ladies, and even sports figures revered by the men.[5]

The creation of vaudeville depended on two important factors: the availability of an audience with the time and financial means to attend the show and the development of an effective transportation network that allowed performers and scenery to move cheaply and quickly from one town to another. Chains, or wheels, of vaudeville theaters developed along the stops of the streetcar and railroad lines that then linked American cities.[6]

Movies began as junior partners in the relationship with vaudeville. Vaudeville theaters showed short movies to quiet the patrons as they took their seats, or to signal the beginning of an intermission. Movies were also exhibited in urban entertainment settings or arcades, where patrons paid to see movies that were shown through a peephole, one amusement among many games and novelties in the arcade.

The first generation of movie entrepreneurs started with the arcades and moved on to bigger things. Adolph Zukor owned a big arcade on New York's Union Square and ultimately became one of the founders of Paramount Pictures. A Jewish immigrant from Hungary who arrived in this country as a teenager, Zukor had already established himself as a successful furrier before going into the arcade business.[7]

A turning point in the movie industry came around April 1904. A businessman in the Pittsburgh area built an amusement arcade, which then burned down. Rather than going back to the arcade business, the man decided to reopen his business as a movie theater, using a machine, similar to the one already used in vaudeville theaters, that allowed moving images to be projected in front of an audience rather than being shown through a peephole to one patron at a time. On June 19, 1905, this ninety-six-seat nickelodeon opened with a showing of *The Great Train Robbery* and a piano to provide background music.[8]

The early operators cashed in on the nickelodeon craze that swept the nation around 1906. By the end of 1907, a journalist in the popular magazine *The Saturday Evening Post* reported that "Three years ago there was not a single nickelodeon devoted to moving picture shows in America. Today there are between four and five thousand. Two million people attend every day, a third of whom are children." The author noted the small size of the nickelodeons – typically less than 200 seats – and the continuous nature of the performances for the short films – eighteen performances a day, seven days a week.[9]

Marcus Loew also got into the penny arcade business and eventually owned a chain of vaudeville theaters and a film exhibition business. In time, he controlled the largest chain of theaters in New York City, and that suggested the need to go into the motion picture production business. In 1920, he acquired Metro Studios for that purpose, and his efforts ultimately led to the creation of Metro Goldwyn Mayer, the largest and most prestigious film company in Hollywood.[10]

With Loew running his chain of theaters, he received assistance on the production end of the business from Louis B. Mayer, another Jewish immigrant. Mayer had started out in his father's junk business in Canada, then entered the theater business in the raw industrial town of Haverhill, Massachusetts, in 1907, and finally became a Hollywood film producer and head of production for MGM.[11]

THE JEWISH QUESTION

That so many of these early entrepreneurs were Jewish immigrants did not happen by conscious design. One might think of the movie business as simply that, a business. Jews intent on, as the expression went, "making a living" and geared toward the retail trades saw the movies as a business like any other, such as salvaging junk (Mayer), selling gloves (Samuel Goldwyn), selling soap (Albert Warner), or selling furs (Zukor). Few of these businessmen thought it possible to, say, start a bank or a steel mill. Those enterprises were beyond their means and outside their network of connections. Movies – or in the earlier phases, amusement parlors, penny arcades, vaudeville halls, and nickelodeons – lacked the respectability of selling financial securities or practicing as a lawyer. Running a movie theater did not guarantee entry to the local Rotary (started in 1905), much less to the local country club. Instead, movies were cheap marginal businesses that changed hands many times and carried an unsavory connection with the tawdry world of show business.[12]

Because it did not seem to matter, Americans trusted what became the single most important component of their entertainment industry to a group of Jews who did not necessarily share mainstream Christian values. In the early stages of development, it was simply not self-evident that the movies would grow into such a large business. If people had known, more businessmen with deeper pockets and hence more respectability might well have entered the business. Of course, producers who were Jewish did not set out to make Jewish movies, any more than Jewish owners of department stores discouraged their customers from Christmas shopping. In both cases, the Jewish businessmen performed a retail function and set out to give the public what it wanted. The same customers who went to Macy's or Bloomingdale's or Filene's or any of the other department stores owned by Jews to do their Christmas shopping patronized theaters owned by Jewish companies and watched biblical epochs like the very Christian *Ben Hur* without giving it a second thought. The executives did not encourage a Jewish identity among the actors who appeared in their films. Theodosia Goodman, said to be a Jewish girl from Cincinnati, became a famous silent movie star, so seductive to the male audience that she suggested a vampire or vamp. She appeared not as Goodman but under the more exotic and ethnically ambiguous name Theda Bara.[13]

EARLY MOVIE THEATERS

As the careers of Nicholas Loew and Adolph Zukor demonstrated, nickelodeons soon gave way to movies shown in more elaborate settings. By 1908, the nickelodeon craze had largely run its course.[14] William Fox, another of the early movie entrepreneurs who would put his name on one of Hollywood's signature companies, opened the Dewey Theater in the Union Square district of New York in 1908. In these and other ventures, he took the movies to the next step, offering a lot more entertainment for just a little more money. The Dewey Theater cost between ten and thirty-five cents, still within many people's range. The 1,000-seat theater presented a show that lasted for two full hours, with five reels of film and five vaudeville acts.[15]

As the storefront theaters began to disappear, more elaborate theaters of the Dewey variety appeared. That happened not just in places like New York but also in smaller centers. In 1914, for example, Pittsburgh entrepreneurs made plans for a 900-seat theater, with a fancy façade and ticket booth and a lobby decorated with tile imported from France. Here was something that anticipated the elaborate movie palaces of the 1920s. There was to be an electric sign in the front that was three stories high and an elegant fountain in the lobby. Even more impressive than the large bathrooms was the fact that the theater would be cooled in summer, using large blocks of ice, and in this way would beat the doldrums that affected the theater business in the hot weather months.[16] Indeed, the movie palaces were early leaders in air conditioning technology, so that the Chicago chain of Balaban and Katz theaters, which came into prominence between 1917 and 1923, ran newspaper advertisements with icicles drawn next to the names of its theaters. Balaban and Katz, like the other big-time operators, promised a grand experience at the movies in settings that included massive chandeliers, elaborate drapery, unobstructed sight lines, and comfortable seats, all presided over by ushers in red uniforms with white gloves and yellow epaulets. Half of the show consisted of a live musical revue.[17]

Even more elaborate movie houses followed. In 1927, Grauman's Chinese Theatre – the theater where the stars would eventually leave their hand and footprints in front – opened in the heart of Hollywood. An impressive monument to the downtown affluence of the twenties, it cost $1 million to build and seated 2,200. In that same year, the Roxy, with its 6,250 seats, started operations in New York.[18]

By 1914, the movies had become the senior partners in the relationship with vaudeville, and by almost any measure the leading form of entertainment in America. By 1920, some 35 million Americans went to the movies each week.[19] In Sinclair Lewis's *Babbitt*, set in that year, the daughter of the respectable middle-class family at the center of the novel is "movie mad," and the family constantly needs to use the car to go downtown to the movies.

Within a few more years, nearly all of the theaters in America, some 97 percent, showed films. In 1926, only six theaters remained in the East that were devoted exclusively to live variety shows in the vaudeville manner, and only six such theaters existed in all the rest of the country. That number dwindled to four in 1928, which meant that the only places to see big-time vaudeville, the traditional stage show without a movie, were New York, Chicago, Philadelphia, and Los Angeles.[20]

Vaudeville, once at the pinnacle of American entertainment, had become a sideshow, a form of entertainment that took place between the showings of movies. By this time, movies satisfied the craving for entertainment because they put the songs and dances of vaudeville performers on film. Live performers had their limits; they could only do so many shows a day. Movies could be rewound and shown continuously day and night. Furthermore, the setting for the movies could be just as genteel and opulent as any vaudeville theater.

EARLY MOVIE STARS AND CHARLIE CHAPLIN

Vaudeville was nonetheless important to the development of the movies because it served as a recruiting ground for the performers who would become stars in the new medium. The inventors of the motion picture, such as Thomas Edison and his associates, assumed that one movie was much like another.[21] One could sell movies by the foot, rather than by the title or the star. Movies tended to be short, perhaps fifteen minutes in length, and largely forgettable as anything other than a momentary spectacle. Over time, however, circumstances changed. Adolph Zukor had the insight that movies could be more than casual short programs and that they might compete with the legitimate theater and offer a full evening's entertainment. He aspired to offer "famous players in famous plays," a departure from the film-as-short-novelty concept in which the producers did not even reveal the names of the actors. In 1912, Zukor bought the rights to a film about Queen Elizabeth starring Sarah Bernhardt that had been produced in Europe.[22] By 1915, long-running, multi-reeled movies, such as *Birth of a Nation*, had begun to appear with some regularity.[23]

Zukor and others like him developed the first movie stars in America. From being anonymous figures in front of the camera, the actors evolved into recognizable entities whose careers could be followed by the audience from one picture to another. People developed a rooting interest in movie stars, such as the exotic Theda Bara, the sexy Clara Bow, or the innocent Mary Pickford, that expressed itself in business at the box office and that nurtured sideline ventures such as fan magazines.[24]

Charlie Chaplin became the most famous performer from the silent era who was able to sustain his fame into the era of talking pictures, unlike Bara, Bow, and Pickford. His image remained so well known even in the early 1980s that IBM used it to introduce the personal computer to America. Like many of his contemporaries, Chaplin appeared to come from nowhere – a pure creation of the movies – to become one of the most famous men in the world.[25]

In fact, Chaplin came from vaudeville, an early example of how performers made the transition from one medium to the other. Those who eventually became the biggest movie stars of the silent era were, by and large, not the biggest vaudeville or legitimate stage stars, like Sarah Bernhardt, who had no reason to linger in a still untested field. Instead, they were performers who thought they could better themselves in motion pictures. Chaplin made his first movie at the relatively advanced age of twenty-five, showing that it took him some time to find his permanent means of livelihood.

His childhood was something out of a Dickens novel, and his movies would retain a Victorian sense of sentimentality. Born in London, he started out in relatively comfortable circumstances with successful show business parents. Then his childhood began to crumble beneath him. Chaplin's father deserted the family and died of alcoholism. His mother suffered from long bouts of mental illness, a far more stigmatizing disease then than now. Without functional parents, Chaplin spent time in an orphanage. He entered the world of the theater and went on extended American tours with an English group of young acrobatic comics, before stopping in Los Angeles in 1914, where he went to work for producer Max Sennett of Keystone comedies fame. Showing the inventiveness and physical grace that allowed him to stand out in slapstick comedy, Chaplin became as close to an overnight success as the real world allows.[26]

He quickly rose from bit player at Keystone to a famous movie star, with authority over his own pictures and even his own movie studio. A year after his Sennett debut, he signed with Essanay for $1,250 a week. A year later, he was with Mutual at $10,000 a week (with a $150,000 signing bonus). "Fulfilling the Mutual contract," he later wrote, "was the happiest period of my career. I was light and unencumbered, twenty-seven years old, with fabulous prospects and a friendly glamorous world before me."[27] If anything, the world turned friendlier after that. In 1917, he signed a million dollar contract with First National and began building his own studio. Then he signed with United Artists and gained complete control over his films.[28]

In the four years between his 1914 debut and his initial First National production, he made sixty-one of his eighty-two films. He retained his character from picture to picture – the famous tramp with the hat and cane who, dressed in baggy pants and an ill-fitting suit coat with a tie and vest that mocked the costume of a gentleman, maintained his dignity and humanity in the face of the world's outrages. He described himself as a geologist, "who was entering a rich, unexplored field." Meanwhile, "Money was pouring into my coffers. The ten thousand dollars I received every week accumulated into hundreds of thousands. Now I was worth four hundred thousand, now five hundred thousand. I could never take it for granted." He lived in a world of success, different from the rest of the world, which permitted him instant entry almost anywhere. "When I met people, their faces would light up with interest," he recalled.[29]

For Chaplin, time punished success despite the longevity of his career. Some of his problems stemmed from the tensions of the creative process. He appealed to the movie-going public, but also to the intellectuals and opinion shapers of the world. It became difficult for him to maintain both his popularity and his critical esteem. The fact that he created his own material, at first by means of almost pure improvisation, added to the pressures he faced. Many people depended on him and his highly perishable stock of artistic inspiration. Money and power gave him the luxury of being able to slow down the pace of production. He moved to his own rhythm, thinking nothing of shutting down his production company during a period of fallow creativity. After 1919, he made only ten more films and retreated more deeply into himself. "You're not dealing with sausages, you know, but with individual enthusiasm," he said.[30]

By the time he made *The Circus*, a silent film released in 1928 after the Warner brothers had already introduced sound, Chaplin was no longer "light and unencumbered." In the film, the simple plot, in which Chaplin comes to the circus and falls in love with the owner's daughter, belies the complex undertones of the story. Chaplin, accused of stealing a wallet, gets involved in a chase that ends up with his inadvertently finding himself under the circus big top in front of a large crowd. The crowd thinks his antics are hilarious, and once the misunderstandings about the wallet are cleared up, the circus hires Chaplin. Although he trains with the clowns, he learns through cruel experience that people only laugh at him when he is not trying to be funny. The whole sequence underscores the serendipitous manner in which the real Chaplin found his way to the movies and a world of success that he could not quite understand or control. In the movie and perhaps in real life as well, the circus owner takes advantage of Chaplin's ignorance, tricking him into giving impromptu performances while paying him a laborer's wages. Meanwhile, Chaplin's portrayal of a circus performer allows him to show off his physical virtuosity – as when he walks the tightrope with monkeys hanging all over him, a feat he performed himself without a stunt double. In the end, he loses the girl to another handsome performer and ends up facilitating her marriage. She and her husband move on with the circus while Charlie remains behind.[31]

When Chaplin made this movie, his personal life had become very complex. The public liked to be titillated by its movie stars without being embarrassed or offended. Chaplin came close to crossing the line, becoming the object of a sex scandal of the sort that had already ruined other Hollywood careers, such as that of comedian Fatty Arbuckle. In 1921, Arbuckle, who had signed a million dollar contract with Paramount, found his career destroyed after a woman died in his San Francisco hotel suite, supposedly raped by him and crushed by his weight. The mere association of comedian Arbuckle with something so sordid, even though he was never proven guilty, was enough to turn the audience against him.[32] Chaplin flirted with similar danger. During the filming of *The Circus* his pregnant seventeen-year-old wife sued him for divorce, revealing lurid details of their sex life to the general public. His penchant for young girls got him into trouble throughout his career. At the time of *The Circus*, Chaplin also owed back taxes to the federal government.[33]

Despite his predilection for young women, Chaplin remained a big star in the 1930s, his occasional movies released at the rate of one every few years. Critics regarded him as a great comedian, although with a retro style, a tendency to wear his heart on his sleeve, and some nasty personal habits, who every so often came out of obscurity and delivered a masterpiece. Chaplin resisted the use of audible dialogue long after the coming of sound. His films had musical backgrounds and sound effects but no sustained conversations between the characters.

For a man whose acquaintances included H. G. Wells, Mahatma Gandhi, Winston Churchill, and Albert Einstein, Chaplin found it difficult to refuse invitations to comment on the major issues of the day through his movies. He ended up making widely acclaimed films about the depression in *Modern Times* (1936) and the rise of fascism in *The Great Dictator* (1940). In *The Great Dictator*, with its wickedly comic portrayal of Adolf Hitler, Chaplin abandoned the character of the Tramp and sang and talked on screen. These political satires were much more ambitious but not necessarily better efforts than his 1931 *City Lights*, a sentimental and bitter-sweet love story voted the best romantic comedy of all time by the American Film Institute.

In the end, aversion to his behavior overcame respect for his genius, and he found himself exiled. After World War II, his career reached its low point. A prosecuting lawyer in a 1945 paternity suit against Chaplin described him as a "gray-haired old buzzard, little runt of a Svengali, debaucher and a lecherous hound who lies like a cheap Cockney cad."

His political problems added to his troubles and eventually sent him packing back to Europe. Chaplin had never claimed American citizenship, and on one postwar trip abroad, after the 1951 release of his film *Limelight*, the U.S. authorities refused to permit him re-entry privileges into the country. At a time of rising Cold War tensions, Chaplin was accused of being a communist sympathizer, a particularly sensitive subject in Hollywood, which had done its part to boost the prestige of the Soviet Union during World War II, when the Russians and the Americans were allies. Attorney General James McGranery noted that Chaplin "had been publicly charged with being a member of the Communist party, and with grave moral charges and with making statements that would indicate a leering, sneering attitude toward a country whose hospitality had enriched him."

Such publicity doomed the reception of *Limelight* in the United States. By February 1953, the picture had played in less than 8 percent of the theaters into which it had been originally scheduled. The incident ended with Chaplin's settling permanently in Switzerland, and only returning to the United States on one occasion after that. He made only two more films, and neither did well in the United States.[34]

AL JOLSON AND *THE JAZZ SINGER*

By the time of Chaplin's exile, he and the silent film era from which he came seemed almost to be afterthoughts. The coming of sound led to a new generation of stars and different sorts of pictures from the slapstick comedies that Chaplin and his colleagues Buster Keaton and Harold Lloyd made famous.[35] The premiere of the Warner Brothers movie *The Jazz Singer* marked the event that historians would herald as the true arrival of the sound picture in America.[36] In popular memory, the earlier Warner sound presentations were forgotten, as was the fact that *The Jazz Singer* was not what moviegoers would later call an "all talking" picture. Instead, it was a silent movie with background music, audible songs, and a small amount of spoken dialogue.

The Jazz Singer came from Broadway, as did many early sound ventures. The first Warner sound programs were more like vaudeville or variety programs than feature-length films. *The Jazz Singer*, by way of contrast, sustained a single plot over the course of the movie. Neither a variety show nor a revue, it was a filmed version of a Broadway musical.

In June 1925, two veteran producers were working on a play that was to be called *The Jazz Singer*. In the lead, they cast George Jessel, an actor and performer from the Bronx who was on the verge of Broadway stardom.[37] Jessel played the son of a cantor – the synagogue official who leads the musical chanting in Jewish religious services – who breaks out of his father's religious world. Refusing to become a cantor like his father, Jessel's character enters instead the realm of popular culture. Rather than singing religious hymns, he blacks up his face and becomes a jazz singer. In the way of Broadway, which liked the audience to go home happy, the play ends with the son's taking his ailing father's place in temple on the evening of Yom Kippur and singing the Kol Nidre service. On the Day of Atonement, father and son let go of past grievances.

In this way, the play accepted a standard ethnic formulation of the day: by becoming black, a Jew announced his allegiance to America. By singing jazz, a musician showed his affinity for modern rather than traditional culture. At the time, Broadway was full of Jewish composers and lyricists who used jazz idioms to write songs they hoped would be popular enough to become standards and enter the American songbook.[38]

The Jazz Singer, a popular Broadway attraction, was an unlikely candidate to become the first sound movie. In this era, just after the fundamental changes in the immigration law that made it harder for people from Eastern Europe to settle in America, visible signs of ethnicity remained close to the surface of American life. In New York City or any of the nation's large and still growing cities, many people spoke with Italian or Yiddish accents. Whether film producers, many of them immigrants in the process of becoming American, should call attention to their foreign roots and the cultural dilemmas of assimilation remained problematic. Nonetheless, Warner Brothers plunged ahead with *The Jazz Singer*, a Broadway property it believed could be a hit movie. It sought a star for the film, with audience appeal, and they also modified the story. In the play, the lead character ends up as a cantor, but in the movie, the hero, despite singing Kol Nidre on Yom Kippur, achieves his ultimate success as a jazz singer. In May 1927, the company announced that Al Jolson, who had already made some Vitaphone short subjects that were essentially filmed versions of his stage act, would make his movie debut in *The Jazz Singer*.[39]

The production, filmed in Hollywood, opened at Warner's Theatre in New York on October 6, 1927. It was four months after Charles Lindbergh had landed in Paris and become a national hero and two days before Babe Ruth and the New York Yankees completed their four-game sweep of the Pirates in the World Series. People read about the Lindbergh flight and Babe Ruth's exploits in the newspapers. The premiere of *The Jazz Singer* marked another ballyhooed event of the era.[40]

The sheer technological magnitude of the production awed the public, but sound on film was no longer a novelty.[41] At some level, the magnetism of Jolson's performance accounted for the film's acclaim, as the audience listened to Jolson singing several of his own songs and chanting the Kol Nidre prayer. People suddenly realized that legendary performances could now be captured on film and the audience could be transported to the high temples of popular entertainment, such as New York's Palace Theater, just by sitting in a neighborhood movie.

When Jolson made *The Jazz Singer*, he was already one of the big stars of the era, who, like many of his successful counterparts, had worked his way up from singing on street corners and the lower reaches of vaudeville to performing in revues and musicals on Broadway, to become the first big movie star of the sound era. Born in 1886, Jolson was a show business veteran by 1910, but not yet a star. In that year, he performed on a relatively obscure vaudeville bill in Brooklyn, where the headliner was Valeska Surratt, whose act consisted of dancing with snakes. Within a few months, however, he came off the road to become a featured player at the Winter Garden Theater. It became a permanent base of operations for him as he appeared in show after show.[42]

Jolson possessed an exuberance that allowed him to "sell" his songs through what one critic described as "his old-time knee-slapping, breast-beating, eye-rolling ardor." Dressed in black face and sporting a "nappy" wig, he faced the audience directly and often went down on his knees as he appealed for its approval and sang his trademark sentimental ballads, novelty numbers, and jazz tunes. He sometimes sang in full-throated voice, sometimes chanted, and sometimes talked to the audience over the music, always trying to whip up the audience's emotions. He also told jokes such as, "In the south, it was so hot that when a greyhound chased a rabbit, they were both walking."[43] His distinctive style, talent, and energy made him the leading musical comedy performer of his day and helped to sustain a career that would last until the Korean War era.

EDDIE CANTOR, THE BACKSTAGE MUSICAL, AND THE EARLY STARS OF TALKING PICTURES

Seasoned vaudeville entertainers such as Jolson helped to sell the concept of sound movies to sometimes skeptical filmmakers, who did not relish the idea of retooling their theaters and redesigning their productions. The conversion to sound drove up costs, which made it difficult for marginal film producers and exhibitors to survive. Many of the older stars regarded sound with understandable ambivalence. Some, who had discovered the artistry of silent movies, thought that something would be lost in the transition to sound. Charlie Chaplin, the most famous silent film star, worried that the movies would be reduced to photographed versions of plays and thus cheapen the medium. Love expressed in pantomime, Chaplin believed, stirred an audience far more than a man and a woman saying "I love you" out loud.[44] "The hysteria that reigns here at present may mean that so many inadequate talking subjects will be issued that people will eventually long for the peace and quiet to which they have been accustomed with the silent features," said producer Samuel Goldwyn.[45]

At some point, however, it became apparent that the producers either had to incorporate sound into their products or go out of business. By March 11, 1928, a full-length voice film was on its way, and the sound era that would last for the rest of the century had begun.[46] In some ways, the timing was fortunate. Sound came in when the economy was robust, and money for investment, the same money that fueled the big bull market of the 1920s, was relatively plentiful. If circumstances had delayed Warner Brothers' experiment by a few years, the history of popular culture might have been different. Sound movies, like television, might then have had to wait until the prosperous postwar era to reach audiences.

The diffusion of sound, like the later dispersal of television, created a small window of opportunity for the great vaudeville performers, who bore recognizable traits of the New York Jewish community (or derivative communities such as Washington, DC, where Lithuanian-born Jolson grew up), to become the first great sound stars. One performer who fit into this window and emerged first as a movie star and later as a radio star was Eddie Cantor.

Born Israel Iskowitz in New York on January 31, 1892, Cantor saw show business as a possible route out of poverty. He made the rounds of amateur night contests, one of the most common entry points into show business, and moved into vaudeville. By the end of World War I, he had become a mainstay of the Ziegfeld Follies, an annual musical variety show that, unlike the touring vaudeville shows, remained on Broadway for an extended run. In the 1920s, he emerged as a full-fledged Broadway star, the lead in shows written specifically for him. Scouts from the Paramount motion picture company noticed him – he was hardly invisible with his name up in lights – and that led to his making a few silent movies. Cantor found that he could not sustain a movie career in the silent era, perhaps because his act depended so much on his voice and not just on the way he moved on stage. Back on Broadway, he starred in *Whoopee*, a major success of the 1928–29 season that producer Florenz Ziegfeld developed for him.[47]

By this time, the conversion to sound had begun in earnest, and movie producers looked to Broadway productions and Broadway stars as important sources of material. The movie companies conducted a raid on Broadway and to a lesser extent on vaudeville, hoping to tie up stars with good looks and voices to movie contracts. The producers also made an earnest effort to make the movies more friendly to New York–based performers by opening up studios, such as the one run by Paramount in Astoria, Queens, right across the river from the east side of Manhattan. A Broadway performer like Cantor could shoot a film in Queens, hop in a taxi, and be back on Broadway for the evening performance.

The aura of Broadway figured prominently in the early talkies. Many of the movies used the device of the backstage musical to frame the plot. A movie about putting a play on Broadway invited the viewer behind the scenes of one of the nation's most glamorous institutions. The plots soon became clichéd, as in the story of the girl from the sticks who, with a country-bred purity of body and mind, upstages the Broadway veteran, gets the lead in the show, and becomes a star overnight. The story played on one of the great urban legends of the day – coming to the big city and making good without being corrupted by the city's moral hazards. More fundamentally, the backstage musical provided lots of opportunities to insert musical numbers from the show within the show into the movie, without regard to the plot. The songs showed off the new sound technology to best advantage.

In the 1929–30 season, studios geared their output to talking pictures. Movies for silent screens constituted only about a third of the productions for that year.[48] In October 1929, Eddie Cantor struck a deal with producer Sam Goldwyn to make a movie of his Broadway vehicle *Whoopee*.[49] The movie was a hit in New York. It did less well in smaller cities and in the sticks, where audiences had more trouble relating to its Broadway conventions.

BUSBY BERKELEY GOES HOLLYWOOD

Whoopee, an early movie musical, featured glimpses of some future stars and brought an important choreographer and director to Hollywood. The chorus line of beautiful girls, an obligatory feature of a Ziegfeld production that Goldwyn adopted as his own, contained future movie stars Betty Grable, the leading female movie player of World War II, and Ann Sothern, who went on to a solid career in movies and television.

Busby Berkeley, a transplant from Broadway, supervised the choreography. Born into a theatrical family in 1895, Berkeley served in World War I, designing parade drills that inspired his later work as a dance director. After the war, he went to New York and appeared on stage, gradually taking on the responsibility of choreographing shows. He became one of Broadway's leading choreographers, working on the shows of composer Richard Rodgers and lyricist Lorenz Hart, including *A Connecticut Yankee in King Arthur's Court* and *Present Arms*. He also remained a performer, earning plaudits for his rendition of the Rodgers and Hart standard, "You Took Advantage of Me." Broadway hand Eddie Cantor suggested to Samuel Goldwyn that Berkeley be hired for the movie *Whoopee*.[50]

For the next decade, Berkeley – first with Goldwyn, then at Warners, then at MGM – helped the movies realize their kinetic potential. His chief insight was that the camera did not have to be a fixed, impassive observer as if it were taking the place of an audience member in a theater. Instead, it could move all around and in and out, capturing the singers and dancers from all angles and invigorating the screen with a sense of movement. If the sound stage were high enough, the camera could also go above the dancers and observe abstract geometric patterns (but composed of real-live female bodies) that a theater audience could not see.

In backstage musicals such as *42nd Street* (1933, director Lloyd Bacon) or the *Goldiggers of 1933* (1933, director Mervyn LeRoy), Berkeley often began a number as though it were being performed on a stage. Then the camera moved in for closeups, and the action shifted to more intimate settings that only the movie audience (and not the theater audience within the movie) could see. In the Ziegfeld tradition, these musical numbers contained lavish costumes and risqué actions, with suggestions of sex and nudity. Before the censors came down hard on sexual material, Berkeley filled his dances with phallic and vaginal symbols. One critic calls him a lyricist of eroticism, but always in a stylized, rather than a raw, way.[51]

Busby Berkeley became a Hollywood fixture. Although he earned considerable plaudits for his choreography, he, like many Hollywood residents, also made the newspapers for more personal reasons. He married six times, including once to Evelyn Ruh, a dancer in the *Connecticut Yankee* company he had met at rehearsal. He was twenty-eight at the time and she only nineteen.[52] Two years later he wed Esther Muir, a Broadway starlet.[53] That marriage, like his others, did not last long. Myrna Kennedy, a film actress, won a divorce from him on the grounds that he cared more for his work than his home.[54] In 1935, drinking and driving on the wrong side of the highway, he got into an automobile accident in which three people died. He ended up settling a damage suit for $95,000, just part of the collateral damage that accompanied the Hollywood life.[55]

CONCLUSION

Eddie Cantor, the star of Berkeley's first Hollywood project, never became as identified with the movies as did Berkeley. As the sound movies reached beyond the big cities and audiences felt distanced from the inside Jewish jokes taken from the Broadway plays, the characters that Eddie Cantor

played were toned down, and what one scholar describes as the
"de-semitization of Eddie Cantor" began.[56] Promoting his next film after
Whoopee, Cantor endorsed quintessentially generic Wonder Bread. Even
as he reached out to the general public, his popularity in the movies lagged
within a few years, although he remained a radio star with a national
following through the 1940s.

The Jessels, the Jolsons, and the Cantors were big stars but not, at least
after the novelty of sound had worn off, such big movie stars. They found
other, friendlier audiences to reach. For a short time, though, they ruled
Hollywood. If they ended up going back to New York for the stage and the
microphone, other Broadway figures, such as Busby Berkeley, stayed
behind in Hollywood and reoriented their careers to the big screen. A
different group of Broadway and vaudeville stars made the trip to
Hollywood in the 1930s and became major movie stars in the Depression
decade.

2

From Broadway to Hollywood with Groucho, Fred, and Ginger

Coming so close to the advent of sound, the movies of the 1930s provided an opportunity for a new group of stars to make their way from Broadway to Hollywood. Comedians who embodied the wit of the 1920s and dancing stars who conveyed the glamour of Broadway stepped in front of the sound cameras and became big stars in the first half of the 1930s. The career of comedian Groucho Marx, which encompassed vaudeville, Broadway, the movies, television, and radio, showed one such pathway, as did that of Fred Astaire and his dancing partner Ginger Rogers.

THE MOVIES AND THE DEPRESSION

The movie industry, like all American industries, suffered during the Depression, but ultimately proved quite resilient. The innovation of sound helped to protect Hollywood against the initial and long-term ravages of the economic downturn. Profits peaked not in 1929, the last boom year, but in 1930, a Depression year, in which the largest eight movie companies made a combined profit of more than $55 million.[1] Movies, like candy, were a cheap item that delivered a great deal of satisfaction, an affordable indulgence in hard times. Still, as the Depression spread to more areas of the country and more sectors of the economy, it put the squeeze on people's pocketbooks in ways that affected the movies. Someone in the habit of going to the movies twice a week might save money by only going once a week. As a result, film attendance dropped by 41 percent in 1931. The next year proved even worse, with the industry sustaining net losses. Highly paid Hollywood personnel took salary cuts. As a result of the financial disruption caused by the expansion into sound and the contraction caused by the Depression, big studios such as Paramount, Fox, and RKO went into bankruptcy or receivership.[2]

The industry's fragility proved only temporary. It broke into the black in 1934 and remained profitable for the next fifteen years. By 1935, the movies had become California's second most important industry. Thirty-nine studios, worth some $98 billion, employed more than 9,000 people.[3]

THE MOVIES AND THE REGULATORY IMPULSE

The movies were an industry that attracted public scrutiny. Film companies needed to stay on the good side of both local censors, anxious to protect their communities from immoral influences, and federal regulators, interested in protecting consumers and small businesses from the damaging effects of monopoly. Put another way, as the industry became more successful and visible, it became more of a target for people who wanted to regulate it to conform to their own vision of the public interest.

Industry leaders, preoccupied as they were with competing against one another, knew they had to take steps to protect themselves from this potentially confining and profit-reducing regulatory impulse. In the 1920s, they chose the device of a trade association. It brought representatives of the large movie companies together in an effort to generate good will and to protect against threats to the industry's autonomy. In a Republican era, the institution of the trade association had a respectable Republican pedigree. None other than Herbert Hoover, the Secretary of Commerce with a reputation for supercompetence, championed the idea. Hoover saw it as a means of stabilizing chaotic industries subject to cycles of boom and bust and of improving industrial performance. He believed that trade associations, by spreading effective business practices from one firm to another, helped to standardize products and production methods, thereby improving efficiency.[4] In 1922, the movie industry fell into line with the trade association movement by creating the Motion Picture Producers and Distributors Association.[5]

The movie moguls recruited Will Hays to head the new trade association. He made a complete contrast to the largely Jewish crowd that ran the movies. He had the right pedigree, as a former chairman of the Republican Party, President Warren Harding's Postmaster General, and a Presbyterian elder, to lend the industry dignity. Operating out of New York, closer to the business end than to the production end of the industry, he provided a sober public face for what some regarded as a tawdry enterprise. Without a doubt, he interacted more favorably with local censorship boards, such as the one that had watched over the movies shown in Chicago ever since 1907, than did Louis B. Mayer or Samuel Goldwyn. Toward those ends, he oversaw the creation of a motion picture code in 1930 that established guidelines for the content of motion pictures so as not to offend the public's sense of dignity or morality. Perhaps most importantly, he had easy access to the Departments of Justice of the Republican administrations of the 1920s, in order to be on the alert for adverse anti-trust actions. He emphasized the ability of the movies to regulate themselves rather than having the public depend on the government for that purpose.[6]

When Franklin Delano Roosevelt came into power in March 1933, the movies needed a different sort of public protection. Surprisingly, though, the new president took actions that were not much different from those of his predecessor. Roosevelt, himself the administrator of a trade association during the 1920s, presided, if rather loosely, over the creation of legislation that essentially encouraged all industries to form trade associations. Each industry would formulate a code of fair competition that would govern production levels and working conditions.[7]

The movies seized the opportunities offered by the National Industrial Recovery Act of 1933. The Motion Picture Producers and Distributors Association essentially wrote the National Recovery Administration (NRA) code for the movies. Hays and his associates used the code to make formal some questionable practices by which the big movie companies exerted their power over independent exhibitors and other small players. Hence, the NRA code affirmed the legality of both "blind booking," which forced movie theater operators to accept movies they had not even seen, and "block booking," which required the operators to take a whole package of movies from a large producer rather than just the ones they wanted.[8] The effect of the NRA, therefore, was to preserve the existing industrial structure and to reduce pressures for anti-trust action, all for an industry that showed every indication of recovering on its own without this special help. The Act, which did little or nothing to get the country out of the Depression, proved a real boon to the movie industry.

The New Deal as a popular phenomenon influenced the content of the movies but not the management of the industry, even though producer Samuel Goldwyn made FDR's son Jimmy a vice president in his company in 1939.[9] We can see how the election of FDR changed the movies by comparing two Warner Brothers pictures, *I Am a Fugitive from a Chain Gang* (1932) and *Wild Boys of the Road* (1933).

Fugitive, made just before the election of FDR, exudes a sense of fatalism. *Wild Boys*, filmed after the election, contains a much more upbeat view of the government's ability to rectify the situation. Both of these movies used a semi-documentary style to chronicle social problems. "Fugitive," nicely realized by director Mervyn LeRoy and star Paul Muni, provides a powerful exposé of inhumane conditions among prisoners in prison camps in the South. Muni's character, whom the movie makes clear is a man of talent and industry with a good service record in World War I, is punished for a crime he has not committed and ends up serving two harrowing stretches on the chain gang. By the end of the movie, Muni, now an escaped convict, has resorted to stealing as a way of making a living. The system has turned an innocent man into a criminal.[10]

King Vidor's *Wild Boys* tells the story of a group of youngsters who, in the face of Depression conditions, leave their parents and take to the open road, suffering many heartbreaking tragedies that rob them of their youthful innocence. In the end, though, the main characters come into contact with the juvenile justice system, where they encounter a kindly judge who looks and talks like FDR. The good judge promises them a "new deal" that will take them off the road and on their way to fulfilling lives.[11]

THE MARX BROTHERS

Partisan politics affected the movies only at the margins. The process of importing actors, singers, comedians, directors, and composers from vaudeville and Broadway continued from the late 1920s into the 1930s without much regard for who occupied the White House or controlled Congress. Among those vaudeville and Broadway performers who arrived in Hollywood early in the 1930s were the Marx brothers, led by the irrepressible Groucho.

In October 1890, Julius Henry Marx, the third surviving son of struggling tailor Sam Marx and his ambitious wife Minnie, was born into a Jewish family in New York City.[12] Sam, who billed himself grandiosely as "Custom Taylor to the Men's Trade," and Minnie had come to New York from Germany in the 1870s.[13] Neither Julius nor his four brothers lasted too long in school, although each showed a certain amount of precocious musical talent. Julius had a pleasing boy-soprano voice. To take advantage of this perishable asset, his imperious mother, who regarded herself as a show business impresario and managed her brother's successful vaudeville career, urged young Julius, although the third in the family line, to tour the vaudeville circuit in the summer of 1905. Two of his brothers eventually joined him in the act, as did Minnie and her sister. With the addition of another female performer, they became known as the Six Mascots.[14]

In 1910, the family moved to Chicago, since Minnie felt that it was easier to get bookings there than in New York. At this point they began to play for more laughs, particularly when they found an audience unresponsive to their singing. They decided to tour with a comedy sketch rather than with a singing act. Adopting one of the popular vaudeville formats, they put together *Fun in Hi Skule* (1912), an act set in a school. The act overflowed with the ethnic and gender stereotypes that were common to vaudeville, where the quick pace demanded that the audience already be familiar with the type of act in front of them. The audience assumed that a character's ethnicity implied certain traits. Julius, using a German accent that was common to "Dutch" comedians, played Herr Teacher – Germans were considered to be smart, at least until the outbreak of World War I (Julius dropped his German accent at that time). Herr Teacher's class contained Adolph in the role of an Irish boy (known as Patsy Brannigan) – Irishmen were considered to be stupid. Minnie portrayed a dim girl and her sister Hannah, a bright girl, with Milton in support. Paul Yale, the only performer from outside the family, assumed the character type known as the Nance or, in modern parlance, the gay character – gays were considered funny in a weak-kneed sort of way. None of these characterizations violated the precept that vaudeville be a clean entertainment medium.

Making the vaudeville circuit in 1914, the Marx brothers acquired the nicknames that would identify them for the rest of their lives. Leonard, who had joined the act in 1913, became Chico, someone handy with the ladies. Adolph (later Arthur) took the name Harpo, and Julius became known as Groucho. At the same time, they developed the characters they would retain for the rest of their careers in vaudeville acts such as *Home Again* (1914) and *On the Mezzanine Floor* (1921) and in the Broadway plays and movies to follow.[15] Groucho delivered rapid-fire dialogue in his New York accent. In 1925, when he had perfected his act, one newspaper described him as the "racial tradesman" with "the hurried make-up of black mustache, plain spectacles and loose fitting cutaway suit."[16] He looked a little like an upscale and more sophisticated version of Charlie Chaplin. Chico settled on an Italian accent, with humor that relied on mangling the English language. Harpo did not speak at all, and instead played a mute character with a bright red wig who expressed himself through pantomime and musical instruments, such as the harp and piccolo, and who wore a voluminous coat in which he put things like the watches and purses he stole from the other characters in the act.

In 1923, the Marx brothers made the jump from vaudeville to the legitimate stage. They cobbled together scenery and routines from past productions and came up with *I'll Say She Is*, which opened in Philadelphia in June 1923. Under the aegis of the Shuberts, the show came to New York in May 1924. It proved to be a smash, running for more than a year, and the Marx brothers left the road and became part of the Broadway scene of the 1920s.[17] They were now stars on the order of Eddie Cantor and Al Jolson, with a Broadway revue to their credit.

Like these other stars, the Marx brothers would eventually find their way to the movies, but they never completely left vaudeville. Playing to a live audience enabled them to hone and perfect material in a far more forgiving and flexible environment than either the Broadway stage or the movie screen. Groucho worked from a script, even though he appeared to rattle off his long speeches as though he were composing the words in his head. He liked on occasion to interject new physical business into the performance and also to experiment with new line readings and even new lines. Vaudeville gave him and his brothers the chance to ad lib in this manner, and if a joke fell flat, it could always be changed in a few hours before the next performance. Even after a string of Broadway successes in the 1920s, the Marx brothers returned to the Palace Theater in April 1929 and appeared there at least two other times, in addition to giving shows in Chicago and other cities.[18]

In the 1930s, when the Marx brothers were movie stars, they still clung to their vaudeville roots. Before filming their 1935 feature, they made a special tour with their writers to test the material in the picture. They gave four shows a day in Western cities such as Seattle and Salt Lake City, retracing the route of the old Pantages vaudeville circuit. The studio, which liked to preview its pictures and edit them with the reaction of the preview audience in mind, approved of the procedure in part because, with ticket sales, the Marx brothers recouped the cost of the tour. It cost little or nothing to fine-tune the material in the picture in this manner. Lines that did not get laughs were deleted or changed. Musical numbers were chosen according to audience response. Harpo said that the tour made the actual production process much smoother. "We didn't have to rehearse," he said. "Just go onto the set and let the cameras roll."[19]

THE MARX BROTHERS ON BROADWAY

Despite their instinctive trust of vaudeville as the medium through which to test their material, the Marx brothers enjoyed the luxury of staying put in New York and earning a big salary by performing once an evening and on the occasional afternoon that the Broadway stage permitted. They followed up *I'll Say She Is* with a more elaborate musical comedy that was written and directed by the top creative talent on Broadway. *The Cocoanuts* opened in 1925 and ran for 377 performances.[20] In many ways it was a quintessential 1920s' musical comedy, with a book co-written by George Kaufman, a score composed by Irving Berlin, and choreography by Sammy Lee. The play parodied the get-rich-quick atmosphere of southern Florida during the great land boom of the 1920s.

The Cocoanuts was very much a 1920s' production, with its featured Charleston number and its cast of characters bearing stereotypical or even crude ethnic names, such as the police detective named Hennessy, or Chico's Italian character, listed as Willie the Wop. Nonetheless, the play drew raves from the Broadway critics, who noted that for the first time the Marx brothers were keeping respectable company with the likes of Berlin, composer of *Alexander's Ragtime Band*, and Kaufman, already one of America's best known playwrights.[21] It was very much a production for the smart set and a decided step up from vaudeville under which a performer gave two shows a day even under the best conditions. The opening night program for *The Cocoanuts* advertised luxury goods and a new sophisticated magazine called *The New Yorker*, which all four of the Marx brothers personally endorsed.[22]

When *The Cocoanuts* had run its course on Broadway and on the road, the Marx brothers returned on October 23, 1928, with *Animal Crackers*, a new musical comedy with a book by George Kaufman and collaborator Morrie Ryskind. By this time, the expectations for their performances were very high, and people paid scalpers as much as $100 for opening night tickets. As the distinguished theater critic Brooks Atkinson wrote, it was almost as if the crowd expected the Marx brothers to redeem an entire theater season in one evening. Atkinson would not go that far himself, but said that those who realized the Marx brothers were appearing in a routine musical comedy would not be disappointed. The play concerned the visit of Captain Spalding, the great African explorer, to an elegant Long Island mansion presided over by Margaret Dumont in the role of Mrs. Rittenhouse. Various complications ensued, some involving the theft of a priceless artwork to be auctioned off for charity by Mrs. Rittenhouse and some involving the usual musical comedy romance. As the explorer, Groucho got an opportunity to deliver his usual non sequiturs and puns, playing with the language in the manner of his *New Yorker* heroes.[23] Offering to marry two women at once, Groucho is accused of bigamy by Margaret Dumont. "Of course it's big of me," he replies. At another point he tells a South American traveler, "You go Uruguay and I'll go mine."[24]

THE MARX BROTHERS AT PARAMOUNT

During the run of *Animal Crackers*, the Marx brothers made the leap from Broadway to the movies. They did it in a comfortable way by simply going across the East River to the Paramount Studios in Astoria, Queens. By day they filmed *The Cocoanuts* and by night they did *Animal Crackers* on Broadway.[25] It made for hard work but was much easier than traveling to California, as Jolson had to do for *The Jazz Singer*. The Marx brothers were among the New York acts that recorded their performances for the talkies. Most of the acts filmed shorts. The Marx brothers filmed an entire play.

The finished product opened on May 24, 1929, and received the complimentary reviews to which the brothers had become accustomed. Much of the commentary centered on the technical aspects of the production. Groucho's soft voice came through loud and clear, and the movie audience was able to follow all of his puns and other tortures of the language. Some of the singing projected less well, but the movie camera could do things that the stage play could not. One shot featured dancers being filmed from above, which thrilled the opening day audience. Although the movie was very much a copy of the play, the producers did make some concessions to the national, as opposed to Broadway, audience. The name of Groucho's character was changed, and Chico no longer appeared as "Willie the Wop" but simply as Chico.[26]

A year after *Animal Crackers* closed, the brothers set to work on a film version of the play, also made in Astoria. They appeared to take the filmmaking process casually, often disappearing between takes or arriving late in the morning. The director needed to have one of his assistants keep tabs on the brothers so that they would be available for filming. In this way, the Marx brothers received valuable publicity for their zaniness on and off the screen. Their apparent spontaneity was part of their appeal.[27]

The movie version of *Animal Crackers* opened at the end of the summer, 1930. Already reviewers, although delighted with the film, were hinting that the Marx brothers were something of an acquired taste, not accessible to everyone.[28] As with the movies of Eddie Cantor, New York audiences found it easier to get the jokes than did the audiences in more rural places. Many of the ethnic references no doubt flew over the heads of the people in the sticks, who could only interpret what was happening on screen as something having to do with New York. In Groucho's opening number, for example, the company cheers him on, singing "Hooray for Captain Spaulding, the African Explorer." "Did someone call me schnorer?" Groucho interjects, using the Yiddish word for a freeloader to complete the rhyme. At another point, Chico exposes a dignified man, passing himself off as a high-society figure, as the former fish peddler from the old neighborhood. The man looks at Chico and pointedly asks him, "Since when are you Italian?"

In 1931, the Marx brothers moved their base of operations from New York to Los Angeles, a move that signaled a key point of transition in American cultural history. The Marxes, like many others in their Broadway set, were heading west to Hollywood. Revered members of the Algonquin Roundtable, an informal group that met for lunch and conversation at that West Side hotel near the offices of *The New Yorker*, such as writers Robert Benchley and Dorothy Parker, made similar moves, although those with ties to the newspaper trade, such as critic and columnist Alexander Woollcott, tended to stay in New York. The great playwright and wit George Kaufman, an Algonquin Roundtable member in good standing and a hypochondriac with an aversion to travel and a love of the Broadway stage, made only an occasional visit to the other coast. Others, seemingly rooted in New York and the Broadway scene, did not hesitate to pick up stakes and leave during the 1930s. The great composers of Broadway musicals in the 1920s, such as Richard Rodgers and George Gershwin, wrote for the movies in the 1930s. Ira Gershwin, who created lyrics for his brother's tunes, found that he could work in Hollywood just as well as in New York. Indeed, Hollywood was in much better financial shape during the Depression decade than was vaudeville, rapidly fading from sight, or the Broadway stage.

If George Kaufman regarded the open spaces of Los Angeles as intimidating and missed the passing of the seasons, many others, the Marx brothers included, felt as if they had come in from the cold to a sort of suburban paradise. The best aspects of New York, the comradery of the Roundtable or the great ethnic cuisine, could be transplanted to institutions such as the Hillcrest Country Club or Musso and Frank's Restaurant. Groucho never moved back to New York on a permanent basis. For him and many others, it became a nice place to visit and see plays.

Monkey Business, which opened in the fall of 1931, became the first Marx brothers movie to be filmed in Hollywood. It closely resembled its predecessors. The theme of stowaways on an ocean voyage who get involved with gangsters looked back to the 1920s as much as it anticipated the 1930s. George Kaufman relinquished his co-scripting duties to *New Yorker* humorist S. J. Perelman, who knew how to write Groucho's logic-reversing speeches, such as the line about working himself up from nothing to a state of extreme poverty. The movie made only passing references to the current scene, as in Groucho's trenchant observation that "the stockholder of yesteryear is the stowaway of today." Otherwise it functioned as a loose aggregation of Marx brothers' bits, some from vaudeville, some from Broadway, and some of Perelman's creation.[29] *Horse Feathers*, the Marx brothers' send-up of the popular college musicals, released during the Hoover–Roosevelt election of 1932, functioned similarly.[30]

Duck Soup (1933), the brothers' next film, opened in the early optimistic days of the Roosevelt administration, proudly displaying an NRA emblem in the opening credits. The movie marked a departure for the team in that it eliminated many of the vestiges of the earlier films. For example, it omitted Harpo and Chico's musical specialty numbers on the harp and piano, respectively, and concentrated more on plot development. The story concerned international diplomacy and intrigue in the mythical, but clearly European, lands of Freedonia and its great rival Sylvania. With the approval of wealthy dowager Margaret Dumont, Groucho ruled Freedonia and tangled with the ambassador from Sylvania, played by veteran character actor Louis Calhern.

Today's movie buffs recognize the picture as a masterpiece that succeeds because it is free of the old Broadway and vaudeville baggage.[31] It is a purer film, more abstract, less tied to current entertainment fashions than its predecessors, yet with lots of punning encounters between Groucho and Chico, comic bits for Harpo, and terrific pieces of physical business such as the famous mirror scene. Groucho and Harpo, each dressed as Groucho, pretend to be one another's reflection in a mirror, until Chico, also dressed as Groucho, shows up and spoils the illusion.

Contemporaries reacted less sympathetically to the movie. It met with a flat response from a public that could not recognize it as a typical Marx brothers production. Perhaps its subject matter made people uncomfortable. It had none of the innocence of a college musical or an adventure on an ocean liner. Instead, it made fun of a deteriorating international situation and looked back to a world war that had put the world in a financial mess and made it unsafe for democracy. The *Times* found it "extremely noisy" without being as "mirthful" as the earlier productions.[32]

The tepid response to *Duck Soup* almost drove the Marx brothers from Hollywood. Paramount dropped their contract. It was as if they had reached the limits of public adulation for an act with its roots in vaudeville. Movies appeared ready to move on to other things and other performers. At the same time, Groucho, in particular, experienced a real sense of fatigue, realizing that in his mid-forties he was like an athlete on the verge of retirement, unable to sustain the physical intensity of doing the act. He talked about working as a single, away from his troublesome brother Chico, who squandered his money on women and gambling and continued to treat work as if it were a sideline rather than the main event.[33] The team also thought about making the logical move back to Broadway and appearing in a new musical with tunes by Irving Berlin and a book by Kaufman collaborator Moss Hart.[34]

THE MARX BROTHERS AT MGM

As it turned out, the Marx brothers' greatest success lay ahead of them. The famous producer Irving Thalberg recruited them to MGM, the leading movie studio, and personally supervised their next movie. Thalberg believed that they could make profitable pictures by cutting down on the number of laughs and beefing up the conventional items, such as plots that took the romance between the hero and heroine more seriously. Instead of being perceived as in some way menacing, with an edge of cruelty to their humor, the brothers would be viewed more sympathetically. They could still be zany and make fun of Margaret Dumont, but at the same time be less subversive because of their obvious sympathy for the struggling lovers.[35]

For their first MGM vehicle, they brought back George Kaufman and Morrie Ryskind as writers and set them to work on a script that parodied grand opera. The movie fit comfortably into a line of literature that went back at least as far as Mark Twain – the pragmatic folks from the New World showing up the pretentious and decadent representatives of the Old World, with low American triumphing over high European culture. Here was a theme that made the audience comfortable. The Marx brothers took on the role of the comedians in a pleasant musical comedy, something they had done before; this time, however, the brothers receded a little more into the background and the romantic plot came more to the foreground.

A Night at the Opera opened in the Christmas season of 1935 and marked the return of the Marx brothers to the big screen. With this smash hit, the brothers reached the pinnacle of their popularity.[36] The critic from the *Times* called *Opera* the funniest comedy of the winter season. "You may have wondered what the trouble has been with operatic films," he wrote. "You will discover the answer at the Capitol: the Marx brothers weren't in them"[37] The Marx brothers had finally hit upon a formula that utilized their talents in a way that played well in New York and in the rest of the nation beyond Manhattan. They had transformed their performing expertise, honed in vaudeville and on Broadway, and brought it to the movies.

As things turned out, the Marx brothers retained their success for just one more picture, another broad farce with a romantic plot, this one about a sanitarium in Florida and the world of thoroughbred racing. *A Day at the*

Races (1937) featured a hilarious scene in which Groucho, a veterinarian pressed into service as the chief doctor at the sanitarium, performs a medical examination on Mrs. Upjohn, the rich woman, played as usual by Margaret Dumont, whose hypochondrical needs for attention have kept the sanitarium in business during hard times. Groucho's distinguished medical colleagues, who have fancy pedigrees and believe, correctly, that nothing is wrong with Mrs. Upjohn, look on with disdain as Groucho, assisted by his brothers, begins the examination. At first he stalls for time, washing his hands and calling for sterilization, at which command nurses run into the room and give him a new surgical gown. Then he puts Mrs. Upjohn through an unconventional examination, asking her, for example, to wave her hands in the air. In the end, Mrs. Upjohn ends up getting her face lathered and shaved by Chico, the sprinkler system goes off and floods the examination room, and the Marx brothers ride off on a horse.

THE MARX BROTHERS IN DECLINE

After that, the Marx Brothers lost their way. Irving Thalberg, the producer who looked after their interests at the studio and supervised their pictures, died during the filming of *A Day at the Races*. After he left, the brothers became much more vulnerable to the whims of Louis B. Mayer and the studio bosses, who held no particular brief for them. In their next project, on loan to another studio, they appeared in the movie version of *Room Service* (1938), a play that had not been written with them in mind. They kept intact much of the original play, with its static setting of a hotel room, and failed to put a distinctive mark on the material. The result was a disappointment that pushed the Marx brothers further back in the queue of people seeking promotion from the studio.[38] Their next picture also failed to live up to the audience's expectations. One critic described *At the Circus* as "a rather dispirited imitation of Marx successes."[39]

It was clear to the Marx brothers that they were in a process of decline. Groucho was one of his own severest critics. When he went to see *At the Circus*, he told a friend that he "didn't much care for it." "I'm kind of sick of the whole thing," he noted. The only pictures of his that he could stand to watch were the ones produced by Irving Thalberg. Groucho and his brothers nonetheless soldiered on in the period right after the start of World War II in Europe. "The boys at the studio have lined up another turkey for us," Groucho reported.[40]

It turned out to be *Go West*, which did little for anyone's career. The Marx brothers looked ill at ease in the Western setting, which seemed to have little connection with the characters they had developed. Even Margaret Dumont was missing.[41] The team did one last movie, and then lost their MGM contract. "We have been ejected from MGM and are now conducting what little business we have in a barnlike building catty-corner from the Bank of America," Groucho wrote in the summer before Pearl Harbor. Chico, in more need of money than his other brothers, organized a dance band. Groucho looked for radio work. As the movies began to enter their most prosperous period in history, the Marx brothers were down on their luck, their 1941 film *The Big Store* failing to excite audiences.[42]

The decline of the Marx Brothers reflected a number of trends. All acts, particularly comedy acts, eventually wore out their welcome, and the Marx brothers managed to stay movie stars for more than a decade. They seemed out of step with the comedians who would come into prominence during World War II, such as Bob Hope and Abbott and Costello. These new-comers came from the world of radio, which the Marx brothers never really succeeded in entering. Harpo, in particular, had a real disadvantage when it came to radio. The new comedians did not dress up in vaudeville costumes but appeared most often in a coat and tie. Their movie personas did not overwhelm their material because they had not yet established a movie persona. Their characters were much more flexible than those of the Marx brothers and their movies did not need all of the supporting material, such as the musical specialty numbers or the punning dialogues between Groucho and Chico. They carried less ethnic baggage, a desirable trait in an era in which the government stressed national unity. Furthermore, as time progressed, it became harder for the Marx brothers, even with the resources of MGM at their disposal, to find writers who could turn out suitable material for them. More fundamentally, the style of comedy changed, away from the pratfalls and aggressive wordplay of the 1920s toward vehicles that were more situation-driven – a funny plot premise that could be sustained for an hour and a half predominated over a series of vaudeville turns strung together to make a picture. It was the ultimate triumph of the unified concept over the talents of the individual performers or writers in the S. J. Perelman mode.

THE RISE OF FRED ASTAIRE

The Marx brothers were just one of many acts that made the transition from Broadway in the 1920s to the movies in the 1930s. Musical perform-ers also found themselves in demand during the talkie era, as the case of dancer and singer Fred Astaire demonstrated. At the same time as the Marx brothers became a national sensation, so did Fred Astaire.

Both Astaire, whose original name was Austerlitz, and the Marx brothers did a family act, but Astaire, who appeared with his sister Adele and was nine years younger than Groucho, stayed with music and dancing rather than turning to comedy. Born in Omaha, the Astaires, like the Marx brothers, had a mother determined to improve the family's economic fortunes by putting her children on the stage. Fred and his sister went into vaudeville at a young age and then became top stars on Broadway, appearing in shows with music by George Gershwin, Jerome Kern, and Cole Porter.[43] In 1919, the same year in which the Marx brothers were nearing the top in vaudeville, the Astaires performed in a show called *Apple Blossom*, not quite the leads, but clearly on the verge of stardom. In Alexander Woollcott's review of the play, he or the *Times* misspelled the name Astaire but he gave the Astaires a rave. He wrote that Fred Astaire was "one of those extraordinary persons whose senses of rhythm and humor have been all mixed up, whose very muscles, of which he seems to have an extra supply, are downright facetious."[44]

The Astaires appeared in vehicles filled with song and dance that had more universal appeal than did the comedies of the Marx brothers. In 1922, the Astaires went to England and met with a cordial reception from London audiences.[45] The Midwestern pair acquired a reputation for glamour and elegance, something associated with Broadway in the 1920s but somewhat distinct from the wit and wordplay of the Marx brothers and the Algonquin Roundtable. The elegance of the dancing traveled better than did the comedy of the great wits. Over the course of their careers, the Astaires, well-mannered and well-dressed, made many trips to England.[46] Adele eventually settled in Ireland (at least before the death of her first husband, an English nobleman), and Fred made London, as well as Paris and Venice, an important location for his movies. The Marx brothers went to Europe as stowaways in *Monkey Business* and felt uncomfortable in their surroundings at the Italian opera house La Scala in *A Night at the Opera*. Fred acted as if he belonged at the best hotels and nightclubs in London and Paris. There was something sophisticated and cosmopolitan about him, even if the audiences always saw through to his Midwestern roots and understood that he was a sensible, American sort of guy.

In 1924, the Astaires opened in a Gershwin musical called *Lady Be Good*, which was a big hit on Broadway and, with the Astaires in the cast, in the West End in London. "They do difficult tricks," wrote one critic, "as they spin and hop and skip into ballet" … "they are easy and familiar" … and "pleasant to see together."[47] Among other things, the musical introduced the tunes "Fascinating Rhythm," subsequently recorded by the Astaires with George Gershwin at the piano and later by pop luminaries Tony Bennett, Petula Clark, Ella Fitzgerald, Judy Garland, and Benny Goodman, and "Oh, Lady Be Good." In 1927, the year of *The Jazz Singer*, the Astaires appeared in *Funny Face*, another Gershwin musical, with the standard "S'Wonderful," that helped to inaugurate the Alvin Theater on Broadway. Astaire, it was said, took the audience's breath away.[48] As was now standard procedure, the Astaires traveled with *Funny Face* to London. In a moment that might serve as a tableau for the urbanity of the 1920s, they sailed at the end of July 1928 on a ship whose other passengers included a member of the Guggenheim family, the artist Norman Rockwell, and publishing magnate William Randolph Hearst.[49] *Funny Face* did big business in London.[50]

After one last Broadway musical, *The Band Wagon*, Adele left the act to marry her English nobleman. As Lady Charles Cavendish, living in Lismore Castle in Ireland, she participated in a real-life fantasy that seemed to come right out of one of the Astaires' own musicals. Her brother continued as a solo performer. In November 1932, he appeared in *The Gay Divorce*, with Cole Porter music, including the tune "Night and Day." Although the opening night audience responded enthusiastically, the critics lamented Adele's absence.[51]

Fred adjusted to his new situation by getting married to New York socialite Phyllis Livingston Potter and then flying off to Hollywood on July 13, 1933. RKO producer David Selznick, who was soon to leave to work at his father-in-law's studio MGM, had signed up Astaire for the movies, even though Astaire had a light voice and lacked the handsome looks of a movie star. Although he expected to make his debut in the RKO production of *Flying Down to Rio*, Astaire instead did a quick cameo in the MGM musical *Dancing Lady* starring Clark Gable and Joan Crawford. He played himself as a Broadway star who dances with Joan Crawford; the Three Stooges, performing under that name for the first time, also appeared in the movie. Astaire spent most of his first summer in Hollywood filming *Flying Down to Rio*, which had a glamorous premiere at Radio City Music Hall on December 21, 1933. For this picture, his real movie debut, Astaire teamed up with an actress and dancer named Ginger Rogers to dance the Carioca, which became a national sensation. It was a breakthrough performance for his movie career.[52]

Ginger Rogers, some twelve years younger than Astaire, had considerably more movie experience. Yet another child of an ambitious mother who wanted to put her child on the stage, Rogers performed in vaudeville, having won a Texas Charleston championship that came with the prize of a fourteen-week vaudeville tour.[53] By the end of the 1920s, she was a recognized Broadway performer, appearing in *Top Speed* in 1930 and then in the Gershwins' *Girl Crazy*, in which she sang two standards: "Embraceable You" and "But Not for Me." Fred Astaire helped with some of the choreography for his friend George Gershwin. While on Broadway, Rogers began to work in movies at the conveniently located Astoria studios. By the time she and Fred Astaire worked in Hollywood on *Flying Down to Rio*, she had made some nineteen pictures, ten in 1933 alone.[54]

GINGER AND FRED

With both Fred Astaire and Ginger Rogers under contract, RKO decided to create a starring vehicle for them. The chosen property harked back to the practice of making a film version of a Broadway hit, in this case Astaire's latest Broadway show, *Gay Divorce*. After finishing *Flying Down to Rio*, he took that show to London, where an RKO executive saw it and decided that it would be a good property to put on film. The finished movie reflected the Hollywood atmosphere in which it was made. Although the producers followed the basic plot of the play, they also changed it to fit the screen and completely reworked the music, so that only one song from the original remained. Retitled *The Gay Divorcee*, the picture featured Fred Astaire essentially playing himself in the role of famous song and dance man Guy Holden. All of the action takes place in Europe, first in Paris and then in London and a seaside resort, similar to Brighton, called Brightburn.[55]

The Fred and Ginger movies relied on a fundamental trick. They made something that was inherently difficult look easy. The audience saw none of the trial and error that went into creating the routines, or the athletic nature of the work, complete with sweat and tumbles, that went into executing the routines. The fancy dress helped to remove all that and put a polish on the performance, at which the audience could marvel without the sense of anxiety that often accompanies such performances. We know that Olympic skiers or gymnasts can fall and do themselves real harm. In the case of Fred and Ginger, we settle into a state of expectant ease knowing that will not happen and, furthermore, that the couple's quarrels are merely amusing diversions on the way to a happy ending.

The Gay Divorcee established Astaire–Rogers as a movie star pairing and brought together a creative team, headed by director Mark Sandrich, dedicated to turning out movies for this collective star. Although Ginger did other pictures in between her Astaire assignments and Sandrich did not direct every Astaire–Rogers film, Fred devoted himself exclusively to these pictures. He helped to take a story premise and music that had been developed by the studio and create appropriate dance numbers to match the material. Others learned how to write scripts that had to establish the basic plot and character development quickly in order to accommodate the musical numbers that were the reason for the movie's existence.[56]

In the mid-1930s, Fred Astaire and Ginger Rogers had become successful Broadway transplants who emerged as two of the biggest movie stars in America. In 1935, the same year in which the New Deal reached its apex and the Marx brothers released their masterpiece *A Night at the Opera*, Fred and Ginger made *Top Hat*, which was arguably the best of their movies. Directed by Mark Sandrich, the movie featured songs by Irving Berlin. The setting and plot were similar to that of *The Gay Divorcee* in that both movies involved a case of mistaken identity and took place in London and a seaside resort.[57]

Top Hat provided the ultimate summertime diversion in a crazy world. It allowed audiences the luxury of escaping to an exotic and safe place – a world where people expressed themselves through dance and music magically appeared. The picture opened in New York at Radio City Music Hall at the end of August 1935, just a few months before the opening of *A Night at the Opera* and a few weeks after FDR had signed his Social Security Act into law before the newsreel cameras. The *New York Times* gave *Top Hat* its usual strong support. "Fred Astaire," wrote the reviewer, "the dancing master, and Miss Rogers, his ideal partner, bring all their joyous gifts to the new song and dance show at the Radio City Music Hall. When Top Hat is letting Mr. Astaire perform his incomparable magic or teaming him with the increasingly dexterous Miss Rogers it is providing the most urbane fun that you will find anywhere on the screen." *Variety*, the trade journal, agreed. "This one can't miss," it said, and "the reasons are three – Fred Astaire, Irving Berlin's 11 songs, and sufficient comedy between numbers to hold the show together."[58]

The picture marked the very top of the Fred and Ginger craze, one of four pictures the team made in 1935 (Ginger released three others that year) and 1936 (Ginger devoted herself to her Astaire movies that year). The team commanded the talents of the very best composers and the studio's top choreographers and directors. People danced to the Piccolino and listened to songs from the pictures, such as the pop standards "Let's Face the Music and Dance," composed by Irving Berlin and "The Way You

Look Tonight," composed by Jerome Kern. One indication of the mark that the Fred and Ginger pictures left on America could be found in a decision made by future president John F. Kennedy at Christmas in 1935. He and his two Princeton roommates, whom he had met at Choate, sent out a Christmas card that featured a picture of the trio, with Kennedy billing himself as Ken, putting on their top hat, tying up their white tie, and brushing off their tails, just as Fred did in *Top Hat*.[59] Many years later, Barack Obama quoted the lyrics of another Astaire–Rogers number from the movie *Swing Time* (1936) in his inaugural address.

The team worked intensively from 1934 to the beginning of 1937, collaborating with Berlin, Kern, and the Gershwins.[60] Even with the success of these pictures, Astaire and Rogers worried about getting stuck in a formulaic situation that would ultimately harm their careers. The ambitious Rogers wanted to further her career as a comic and dramatic actress capable of carrying a picture on her own. Astaire knew he was primarily a dancer but did not want to get bogged down in another partnership similar to the one he had with his sister. Both realized that it would be difficult to maintain the quality of the pictures and that the audience would eventually get tired of the Fred and Ginger movies.

In response to these real or imagined problems, the team began to work separately, coming together for only two more pictures in the 1930s and one at the end of the 1940s. Both went on to have more than credible careers, with Ginger winning an Oscar and becoming a top star during the war years and Fred making first-rate musicals for MGM and eventually becoming a successful straight dramatic actor.

CONCLUSION

Both the Marx brothers and Fred and Ginger succeeded in making the transition between the New York world of Broadway and vaudeville and the Hollywood world of motion pictures. They did so with the coming of sound, which enabled audiences to hear Groucho's jokes and listen to Fred's singing. As with all movie successes, theirs was a near thing. Fred needed to overcome the thinness of his voice and his mundane looks. His extraordinary agility compensated for his voice and Ginger's exquisite beauty made up for Fred's plainness. The Marx brothers, heavily rooted in vaudeville, needed to get beyond their ethnic humor and their tendency to subvert plot to their comedy routines. The creative talent of MGM allowed them to make movies of wide appeal, even if they never did find a completely comfortable niche in the studio system, and they faded from popularity in the 1940s. For much of the 1930s, Groucho, Fred, and Ginger used the profitable movie business to entertain a nation facing considerable economic hardship. They formed part of a 1930s pattern in which the audience allowed itself a suspension of disbelief to laugh at people in outlandish costumes who spoke in Italian accents, or to marvel at dancers who executed difficult moves with a deceptive ease.

3

Radio Nights

In February 1934, director Norman Taurog assembled an excellent cast on Catalina Island off the coast of Los Angeles to shoot a movie to be called *We're Not Dressing*. The movie, based on the appealing fantasy of a group of rich people on a yacht who get stranded on an island and are forced to rely on a working-class crew member's survival skills, was made in an efficient manner and opened at the end of April.[1] The shoot veered from the routine, however, in that Taurog had to work around the complicated schedules of four of the six principal actors. These folks needed to be on the mainland once a week to rehearse and perform their radio programs.[2] Radio, a comparatively new force in mass entertainment, had begun to intrude on the movies.

BING CROSBY AND THE CROONERS

Bing Crosby, the star of *We're Not Dressing*, represented a new phenomenon in American entertainment. He owed his fame not to vaudeville or Broadway but to singing in nightclubs and on the radio.[3] His first feature film, made in the summer of 1932, highlighted his connection with radio, as opposed to Al Jolson's or Eddie Cantor's first films that played on their Broadway and vaudeville backgrounds. In the *Big Broadcast*, Bing Crosby portrayed himself, a popular singer and a popular radio star. People classified Crosby as a crooner, a term that referred to someone who adjusted his voice to sing in front of a microphone. In the movie, Crosby played a crooner in the same way that Fred Astaire played a song and dance man in his first movie; in both cases they put their already established personas on the screen. They came pre-sold to the audience.[4]

In the past, opera and vaudeville singers had benefited from having "big" voices that could fill cavernous halls. They learned ways to project their voices, either in the controlled manner of an opera singer or in the more unrestrained manner of a Jolson or Cantor, who belted out their songs at the top of their lungs. By way of contrast, Crosby modulated his voice so that it sounded good when amplified by a microphone. That required a different technique of singing, one exceptionally well-suited to the radio and the movies. Bing Crosby soon eclipsed Jolson and Cantor in both media.

If Jolson and Cantor shared themselves with the whole audience, Crosby conveyed a more intimate type of charm that made it easier to establish a romantic connection with individual members of the audience. Women swooned over Crosby and the other crooners, such as popular radio star Rudy Vallee.[5] Norma Shearer, the popular actress married to MGM producer and Marx brothers promoter Irving Thalberg, tried to explain it to reporters after *The Big Broadcast* opened. She said that the radio "means romance to most women.... Look at the popularity of crooners. Women all over the country tune in their favorite crooners and listen to love songs and get romantic satisfaction out of it, too."[6] Apparently, the magic carried over to the movies.

The Big Broadcast started a franchise at Paramount, similar to the series of *Broadway Melody* pictures that were made at MGM in the 1930s. In both cases, the movies featured loose plots that allowed plenty of opportunities for different acts to perform. These pictures continued the tradition of the variety show that came from vaudeville and its upscale cousin, the Broadway revue. One studio used Broadway to frame the pictures, and the other employed the more modern device of radio broadcasting, which also served as a bastion of variety during the 1930s.

Despite the synergy of an effort like *The Big Broadcast*, in which the studio recruited radio stars to be movie stars, radio presented a challenge to Hollywood in the early 1930s. It represented an alternative and possibly competitive way of reaching a mass audience. In time, however, Hollywood came to accept the permanent presence of radio and to use the new medium to its advantage. Beginning in August 1936, movie stars had clauses in their contracts that required them to appear on the radio to publicize their pictures. Movie premieres were broadcast on the radio, with the stars expected to say something to the radio audience as they entered Grauman's Chinese Theatre or some other glamorous movie palace (just as Janet Gaynor did in the final scene of 1937's *A Star is Born*).[7]

Once the technical problems of creating a network hookup to Los Angeles were worked out, it became possible for Hollywood film performers to appear regularly on the radio. In 1934, the CBS radio network launched *Hollywood Hotel*, a new program from Hollywood, featuring gossip columnist Louella Parsons, whose combined roles as journalist and industry booster illustrated another form of media synergy, and hosted by heartthrob tenor Dick Powell. The conceit behind the program was that it was taking place in a glamorous Hollywood hotel – not a utilitarian radio studio, as it actually was. Stars dropped in for drinks or dinner and caught up with Louella Parsons, who interviewed them on their latest doings. Dick Powell sang a song, replicating the variety format popular on radio, and then the stars re-created scenes from their latest pictures.[8] It was radio in the service of Hollywood in the service of radio, and everyone made out.[9]

Completing the circle, Warner Brothers made a movie called *Hollywood Hotel*, released at the beginning of 1938, and starring Dick Powell. He played a saxophone player and singer in Benny Goodman's band who comes to Hollywood to make good. He ends up singing at the Hollywood Hotel, as envisioned by Warner Brothers and director Busby Berkeley, on a radio program featuring Louella Parsons.[10]

THE ORIGINS OF COMMERCIAL NETWORK RADIO

Radio became a national phenomenon at about the same time that sound came to the movies.[11] The invention itself dated back to the nineteenth century. In the late nineteenth century, Guglielmo Marconi, among others, figured out how to transmit sounds over distances without the aid of wires. That facilitated such important operations as ship-to-shore communication. American companies soon took an interest in the new technology. In the era just after World War I, large companies such as General Electric (GE), Westinghouse, and American Telephone and Telegraph companies (ATT), consolidated their hold over the American radio industry. In October 1919, GE bought a controlling interest in American Marconi and that way gained control over most of the ship-to-shore and international radio stations that were based in the United States. At the same time, GE established the Radio Corporation of America (RCA) to operate those stations. By the summer of 1921, General Electric, RCA, Westinghouse, and ATT had agreed to a patent-pooling arrangement that presumably would enable the technological development of radio to proceed more smoothly. Each company carved out a niche for itself. GE, for example, manufactured radio receiving sets that RCA sold to the public. The telephone company, meanwhile, made the transmitters that sent out radio signals.[12]

Much like the early personal computers, radio remained a product with a great deal of recognized commercial potential but without the killer application that would bring it into everyday use. The idea of broadcasting news and entertainment on a regular schedule from a fixed point to homes with radio receivers – the idea that would become the killer application – took time to develop. Someone had to conceive of the idea and then to implement it in a way that it could be sustained. That meant the development of radio stations, which would give people the rationale to listen to the radio, and of radio receivers that were cheap enough and easy enough to use so that regular people, not only technological geeks, would feel comfortable with them. All of that occurred in an ad hoc manner, not unlike the sporadic development of early movies in entertainment arcades and nickelodeons. Eventually, in both cases, a large industry developed that was geared to getting individual consumers to use the product.[13]

Amateurs and others with an interest in radio technology, such as newspapers, department stores, and the companies that manufactured sets or transmitters, started the first stations. Start-ups often involved someone getting intrigued with radio transmission and then, taking a leap of faith in the face of little apparent demand, opening a station. The *Detroit News* initiated its broadcast service in an informal manner in August 1920, and that led to the establishment of station WWJ in Detroit.[14] KDKA in Pittsburgh started as an amateur operation in 1916 with a guy who liked to play records over the air for the benefit of other amateur radio operators. A Pittsburgh department store became interested in this operation as a means of creating interest in radio in order to sell radio sets. A Westinghouse executive suggested that the Pittsburgh company build its own station and offer a regular radio service as a means of further bolstering the weak demand for the new product. KDKA, owned and operated by Westinghouse, went on the air on the evening of November 2, 1920, from a shack built on top of a manufacturing plant in order to broadcast the presidential election returns. Implicit in this choice of program was the idea of broadcasting as an important service to which listeners might want to subscribe by buying radio sets.[15]

The diffusion of radio technology to a big audience depended on easily operated, already assembled radios, the growth of local stations, and the creation of networks to tie together a series of local stations. With the establishment of a network, someone broadcasting on a large New York area station, such as WJZ run by RCA or WEAF run by ATT, could reach people who tuned into the program on a different station in a different part of the country. People everywhere could hear the same thing. The largest early network operator turned out to be ATT, which owned the telephone lines that connected the stations together. RCA relied on telegraph wires that proved less useful for the transmission of radio programs. ATT, which enjoyed the technological edge, could string together a temporary network to carry events deemed of national importance, such as the political conventions of 1924 or the big prizefights of the era. By the end of 1924, ATT had turned those temporary hookups into permanent links over dedicated wires and initiated the first major radio network, offering a regular three-hour block of programs. By the spring of 1925, thirteen stations belonged to this network.[16]

In 1926, ATT, under pressure from the government, decided to get out of the broadcasting business (but not the business of serving as a network carrier running wires from one station to another). This move led to the founding of the National Broadcasting Company (NBC). As a practical matter, NBC took over the key ATT stations, including WEAF, which became the New York–based flagship station for the new network. The network also retained WJZ in New York, and in time developed two separate branches, known as the Red (WEAF) and Blue (WJZ) networks.[17] Like the other big ventures in radio, NBC turned out to be a cooperative one. RCA, itself an amalgamation of other companies, held half of the shares, and the others were split between GE and Westinghouse.

The formal launch of NBC came on November 15, 1926, with a four-and-a-half hour variety show from the Waldorf-Astoria Hotel in New York. This program, broadcast over a hookup of twenty-four stations, reached an audience of some 2 million listeners. A shortwave transmission, utilizing the technology that had originally created interest in the wireless, enabled the program to be beamed to Europe and South America. The entertainers that appeared on this program worked as headliners in vaudeville or as stars on Broadway, such as the vaudeville team of Joe Weber and Lew Fields and Ziegfeld Follies star Will Rogers.[18]

The creators of NBC framed its mission in solemn terms, as if they were more interested in performing a public service than in making money.[19] This rhetoric acted as a form of reassurance to the public and to the government, which continued to keep an eye on the new medium. Radio had important military applications, a natural concern of the government, and it had the potential of becoming a significant carrier of political speech. Therefore, although government did not own the radio industry, it still carved out a role as a regulator of the airwaves. Like a public air traffic controller assisting private planes, the government kept the airwaves clear enough so that one station did not overlap another station's signal. As with the movies, the broadcasters sought to regulate themselves, with the assistance of Secretary of Commerce Herbert Hoover, who excelled at using voluntary regulation to solve public problems. Hoover convened a conference to discuss the operations of the radio industry in 1922 and held regular conferences during his tenure as Secretary.

These discussions gave impetus to the Federal Radio Commission (FRC), which was established as a result of the Radio Act of 1927. The Commission upheld the progressive ideal of an independent regulatory agency that would somehow develop an expertise in the area it was regulating, without becoming beholden to the industry or a particular political party. The idea that animated the Commission was that the radio functioned as a sort of public carrier, similar to a railroad, that needed to maintain commonly agreed upon community standards. The airwaves belonged to the public, but the Commission could license individual entities to use particular frequencies for a specified period of time.[20]

THE NETWORK AND THE SPONSOR

The advent of the network turned the radio into one of the glamorous household appliances of the so-called new era in the 1920s. By the end of 1921, about 1 in every 500 American households had a radio receiver. By 1926, one radio receiver had been sold for every six households, and radio had become a common household device.[21] Electricity in the 1920s functioned something like the Internet today. Radio, a black box that was simply plugged into the wall to receive news and entertainment from all over the world, emerged as one of the most important applications of electrical technology to domestic life. In this regard, it was like many of the consumer appliances, such as the toaster and refrigerator, being sold to Americans in the 1920s that made it easier to run a household and that expanded the range of people's experiences.

Radio fit right into an era of technological progress aimed at the consumer. People could have their own home entertainment centers, complete with radio and phonograph. On those evenings when they did not care to go out to the movies, do crossword puzzles, or play canasta, they could stay at home and listen to the radio. In their classic survey of life in Muncie, Indiana, in 1924, the Lynds recorded the thoughts of one housewife, who told them, "My husband is very busy all day and when he gets home at night he just settles down with the paper and his cigar and the radio and just rests."[22] Radio was in the domestic picture.

Radio, a growth industry of the interwar era, greatly expanded the audience for public events. By April 1, 1940, of some 35 million families in the United States, nearly 29 million had radios in their homes. In some of the more urban and affluent states, such as Massachusetts, effectively everyone had access to a radio, some 96.2 percent of the Massachusetts population in 1944. Many people had more than one radio in their house, and another for their car, so that in 1939 there were some 44 million radios in the United States, more radios than families.

For events broadcast on all the networks, including NBC, with its two subnetworks, and the rival Columbia Broadcasting System (which began with a sixteen-station hookup and ten hours of weekly programming on September 18, 1927), the size of the audience was truly staggering. Some 62 million people, more than half the adult population, listened to President Franklin Roosevelt's "Day of Infamy" speech after Pearl Harbor. It was one of ten occasions on which the President had drawn an audience of more than 40 million people. Some of the more popular entertainment programs had 30 million listeners. The Joe Louis–Max Schmeling prizefight of June 1938 attracted more than half of the radio audience.[23] Smaller, more specialized events also drew in listeners on an unprecedented scale. More people listened to a single Sunday afternoon broadcast of the New York Philharmonic than had heard the orchestra in its 103-year history playing in concert halls.[24]

By the 1930s, radio had become the most widely used household appliance next to the kitchen stove, and in the 1940s, Americans owned more radios than automobiles or telephones. From 22 stations at the beginning of 1922, the industry grew to some 933 stations by the beginning of 1945. At the end of the 1930s, a *Fortune Magazine* poll reported that radio was the public's most enjoyable form of recreation. They preferred it to movies, reading, hunting, or watching sports events. Asked to make the choice, people said they would give up movies before they would give up radio.[25]

The potential size of the audience attracted the advertisers who sold their products to American households. The sponsor turned out to be an important factor in the development of radio, solving the problem of financing the programs that went out over the air. Other solutions were possible, such as taxing all Americans who owned radios and using that money to fund radio entertainment, or somehow getting interested Americans to subscribe to the radio the way they subscribed to *The Saturday Evening Post*.

The key decisions were made in the 1920s. New taxes were always a hard political sell, and few precedents existed for a national radio service.

Other key inventions, such as the telegraph, telephone, and railroad, remained firmly under private control, with some government oversight and regulation, and there was no reason to expect radio to be any different. In the highly partisan political setting of America, both parties worried that a national radio service would somehow work to their disadvantage, rather than serving the abstract ideal of public service. User fees of any sort presented difficult technological problems. Once a signal went out over the air, it was difficult to design receivers that would allow only subscribers to pick up that signal and exclude non-subscribers.

Over time, as the audience grew and the possibilities of reaching large numbers of people increased, the radio industry began to sell broadcast time to those who cared to purchase it.[26] Radio therefore developed more like the newspaper industry than the movie industry. Newspapers were essentially given away, using the very small purchase fee to subsidize a distribution system that included home delivery, newsboys hawking papers on the corner, and individual entrepreneurs selling the paper at newsstands. Newspapers earned their profits and financed their operations through paid advertising. The movies charged an admission fee, but audiences, once inside the theater, could expect to watch the picture in relative peace, with no advertising once the movie started. Radio had two profit centers. Manufacturers such as RCA sold radios in the same way that all consumer products were sold and expected to make money on the trans- action. Once a person got a radio home, he or she could listen to all the programs on the dial for free, in particular the programs on the NBC networks that were controlled by RCA. The only catch was that the programs came with commercials.

Just as the radio industry grew, so did radio advertising. An industry that billed advertisers some $4.8 million in 1927 expanded to nearly $392 million in billings in 1944.[27] Between 1928 and 1934, from growth year to Depression year, radio advertising grew by more than 300 percent. In that same period, newspaper advertising dropped 30 percent and magazine advertising 45 percent.[28]

The growth of radio also affected the sale of phonograph records and the diffusion of popular music. In 1919, Americans bought more than 2 million phonographs; in 1921, they purchased more than 100 million records. As the radio became popular, people stopped buying records in such great numbers, since music was available at the flick of a switch. The record industry was therefore perfectly positioned to suffer during the Depression, hitting bottom in 1933. Five years later, only 37 million records were sold. Even with fewer records being sold, music diffused much more rapidly across the nation than it had in the sheet music and phonograph eras. A song could become a hit overnight. By the late 1930s, the phonograph, piano, and sheet music industries experienced something of a rebound. For the same price as a radio used to cost, people could purchase a combination radio and phonograph.[29]

Sponsors became so important to radio that, by the early 1930s, they had almost completely reoriented radio production. The networks sold air time to advertising agencies. In a crucial development, the advertising agencies themselves, rather than the networks, began to produce the shows. The development took a process begun in the print media a step further. Newspapers and magazines accepted advertisements that had been designed in the creative departments of advertising agencies. The advertisers picked their spots as best they could, such as by putting advertisements for women's clothing in women's magazines or in the section of the newspaper that contained features that appealed to women. Unless advertisers could afford a full-page spread, ads for similar products often ran right next to each other, which was sometimes a less than desirable circumstance. Of course, the newspapers and magazines retained control over the news and features in their publications. Things were different in radio, where creative departments in advertising agencies produced whole programs. For thirty or sixty minutes, no other advertiser intruded on the listener's consciousness. In a sense, the whole program, not just the advertisements within the program, was part of the commercial message. Canada Dry, the dry beverage, could sponsor a program with dry humor. Many programs worked the commercials right into the entertainment segments; a character in the show might stumble upon a person who would suddenly start to tout the new Chevrolet.[30]

AMOS 'N' ANDY

Amos 'n' Andy, early radio's biggest hit, was broadcast five nights a week for fifteen minutes in the early evening. If we count its predecessor program that was broadcast on a Chicago radio station, its run lasted from 1926 until 1960.[31] At the height of its popularity in the early 1930s, its audience consisted of a third of all the people in the country, one of the first indications of just how deep an impression the radio would make on America. Between 1930 and 1932, it was the number one program on the air.[32] An often-repeated story about the show told of how movie theaters learned to accommodate their patrons by piping *Amos 'n' Andy* into the theater so that moviegoers would not miss an episode. That mattered because it was a program that the audience followed episode by episode, a comic soap opera that tried to leave people in a state of suspense that would induce the audience to tune in the next day. The seven o'clock time period proved perfect for the program. It became a regular early evening habit, just like the evening newspaper. In fact, the program mimicked the daily comic strips, short but continuous from day to day, easy to understand, with broadly drawn characters whose personality quirks helped to generate the humor.

Freeman Gosden and Charles Correll, the creators and performers of *Amos 'n' Andy*, began their radio careers in 1925, with a weekly broadcast on Chicago station WBEH that originated from the Edgewater Beach Hotel. Gosden and Correll sang in harmony to the local radio audience, just a part-time gig that offered little or no remuneration. In the fall of that year, the pair found out about a paying position on the staff of WGN, the powerful radio station of the *Chicago Tribune*, whose strong signal reached much of the Midwest. There they developed a new show they called *Sam 'n' Henry*, which debuted in the late evening of January 12, 1926. They performed and wrote the ten-minute show, which they always broadcast in a studio without a live audience, six days a week. The show featured Gosden and Correll's voice talents as they each played multiple roles by modulating their voices.[33]

Gosden and Correll, themselves white, played black for the program. All the characters spoke in recognizably black dialect that was full of humorous malapropisms in which, for example, the word disgusted became "regusted." In this manner, the program continued the tradition of ethnic humor that was prominent in vaudeville and becoming prominent in the movies.

Sound movies had come in with a Jewish man performing in black face. Big-time radio now came in with two white performers, one Southern in origin and the other Midwestern, performing in black voice. Jolson adopted black face as a mask, but everyone knew what was underneath. He was the quintessential urban man creating a false sense of nostalgia by invoking a rural tradition that lay completely outside of his experience. On the stage, he felt free to fall in and out of his black character. Gosden and Correll performed a comic drama, not a variety show in the manner of Jolson. Their black voices masked their true identities far more effectively than Jolson's black face did his. Radio gave them the necessary cover to stay in character. The characters they played, unlike Jolson's stage character, had an urban rather than a rural orientation. After the first episode, all of the program's action took place in the North. Sam Smith and Henry Johnson had come from Birmingham, Alabama, and went by train to Chicago.

Gosden and Correll put on an immigration saga instead of a minstrel show or its vaudeville successor. Jolson was his own immigration saga. No one needed to remind the audience that this man, made up in black face, was in fact Jewish, part of the great wave of late-nineteenth- and early-twentieth-century migration to America from southern and eastern Europe. Although Gosden and Correll had deeper American roots, they portrayed immigrants from the rural South on the radio. Jolson's immigration saga included his own ethnic background; Gosden and Correll's created their immigrant personas through their performances.[34]

In 1927, the *Chicago Tribune*, as the parent of station WGN, boosted Sam and Henry by running a Sunday feature that included a script from a recent program and illustrations based on the characters in the program.[35] Gosden and Correll started to franchise themselves as Sam and Henry, making personal appearances and having their likenesses used on a toy. Despite the wide reach of the newspaper and the radio station, they thought they could do even better if their radio program were broadcast over an even wider area. Their ambitions made them receptive to an offer from another Chicago station and another Chicago newspaper as part of an experiment in chain broadcasting. The team made recordings of their programs, which were then sent to stations that agreed to subscribe to the program. It took two records to record each ten-minute program. As Gosden and Correll broadcast live in Chicago, the participating stations played the records on a turnstile and sent them out over the air. The names Sam and Henry belonged to the *Chicago Tribune*, so they needed to rename the characters. They settled on Amos and Andy and gave their first broadcast with their new names on March 19, 1928.

Amos 'n' Andy became a big hit in Chicago and in the other cities with stations that subscribed to the program. In this formative period of network radio, advertising executives kept an eye out for promising local talent that might be ready for a network program. At the time, the advertising industry had a large presence in Chicago. In the course of things, William Benton, who worked at the Lord and Thomas advertising agency, noticed *Amos 'n' Andy*. He consulted Albert Lasker, the head of the agency – who had, among other things, figured out how to get people to forgo handkerchiefs and use a disposable tissue that he named Kleenex – on the prospects for Gosden and Correll. Benton thought that *Amos 'n' Andy* might be a good fit for Pepsodent, the toothpaste that made yellow teeth white. He offered the team a lucrative contract to appear over the NBC blue network for Pepsodent, which Gosden and Correll did starting on August 19, 1929. The two also gave personal appearances that allowed them to do their broadcast on the road and added greatly to their income.

The back story of *Amos 'n' Andy* was similar to that of Sam and Henry. Amos and Andy first worked on a farm outside of Atlanta and then moved to Chicago. There they ran a taxicab company that, because of the cab's missing windshield, was known as the Fresh Air Taxi Company. Many of their adventures involved the activities of a friendly society (or burial society) that they called the Knights of the Sea. Correll played Andy, who spoke in a deep voice; Gosden voiced the higher-pitched Amos. They shared the other characters, as many as ten different voices on a given program. They worked very hard at their craft, taking no vacations during the first six years of *Amos 'n' Andy* and doing a daily show for a decade and a half. They only switched to a weekly show, and a more conventional situation comedy format, in 1943. When they broadcast from their empty studio, reading the scripts they wrote each day, they brought a sense of concentration to the task, which allowed them to remain in character and helped to sustain the illusion of two white men passing for a whole group of black men. If the script called for a character to drink a glass of water, for example, Gosden or Correll drank a glass of water in the studio. Like other network radio performers, they did two versions of each broadcast – one for the East coast and the other for the West coast.[36]

THE RISE OF JACK BENNY

Jack Benny became the biggest radio star of all. His background closely resembled that of many of his contemporaries in show business.[37] His father, Meyer Kubelsky, emigrated from a shtetl in Lithuania to New York in 1889. He did not settle, as many others did, on the Lower East Side but instead purchased a ticket to Chicago. In the northern Chicago suburb of Waukegan, Meyer made a living as best he could, doing things like running a bar. He secured the services of a matchmaker to find a wife. On Valentine's Day in 1894, his wife gave birth to his son Benjamin (there would also be a daughter). Young Benjamin showed promise on the violin, enough to encourage the family to pay for violin lessons in Chicago. A musician, at least one who mastered the classical violin, commanded respect within the Jewish community.

Benjamin continued to practice, showing more interest in music than in his schoolwork. As a teenager, he got a job in the pit orchestra of the local theater, accompanying the vaudeville acts that came to town. He apparently impressed the visiting Marx brothers, themselves Chicago residents at the time, enough that Minnie Marx offered him a job playing for the act. He refused that offer but did enter the vaudeville circuit in 1912.

Early in 1918, Kubelsky enlisted in the Navy. Instead of being sent overseas to fight in the war, he remained at the Great Lakes Naval Station near his Waukegan home and became a musician in the military. He toured in a production that he helped to create known as the Great Lakes Revue. He gave himself some speaking lines in the Revue and discovered he could deliver them in a humorous way that got laughs from the audience. When he was discharged, he decided to go out as a single, doing an act relying on his newfound comic patter that he called "Ben K. Benny – Fiddle Funology." When headliner Ben Berny complained that the names were close enough to create confusion, Kubelsky yielded and eventually became known as Jack Benny, doing acts such as "Jack Benny: Aristocrat of Humor." The fiddle became an incidental part of his act, a prop that he brought on stage because it gave him something to do with his hands.[38]

In 1926, Benny garnered good notices and favorable publicity for his performance as master of ceremonies in a Broadway revue, putting him on a higher ledge in show business, closer to the top Broadway performers such as Jolson and the top vaudeville performers such as the Marx brothers. His material contained little hint of the comic character Benny would later develop on the radio. Instead, it depended on droll delivery of jokes such as the following: "This fellow was living out in Los Angeles. He heard that his mother, who had been visiting in New York suddenly became ill. Hopping on his bicycle, he rode day and night until he arrived in New York. The doctor informed the son that only California air would help his mother and that she was too ill to travel. What was he to do? He let the air out of his bicycle tires, and his mother, breathing that California air, promptly became well again."[39] This was humor of a very gentle kind, and Al Boasberg, who created gags for such luminaries as the Marx brothers, wrote it. In this sort of joke, Benny was truly the master of ceremonies, an observer of the passing scene with a light touch that helped the program get from one point to another. Unlike Chico Marx or Charlie Chaplin, he had no well-developed comic persona of his own.[40]

The next step was the movies. Benny appeared as one of many stars in a 1929 MGM movie, similar to the *Broadway Melody*, called *The Hollywood Revue*. It was simply that, a revue, rather than a movie with a plot. Its notoriety stemmed from its status as the first song and dance movie made in California rather than in New York. The studio put nearly all of its talent into the effort, including twenty-three songwriters and such

stars as Marion Davies, Joan Crawford, Lionel Barrymore, and Buster
Keaton. The *Washington Post* acclaimed the picture as "another smash hit
with the first audible screen entertainment ever executed in true revue
form." In such a crowded field, Benny, in his customary role as master of
ceremonies, struggled for notice. Mostly he introduced other acts and had
a few short comic bits of his own, such as his efforts to play the violin.[41]

The movies brought Benny some notoriety, pushing "him up toward the
front," according to the *New York Times*, but clearly not to the top.[42] He
continued to ply his trade in New York, appearing at the Palace, and in the
summer of 1930, in a Broadway revue, *Earl Carroll's Vanities*. Although
the producers billed the production as a "superspectacle of sixty-eight
scenes," distinguished critic Brooks Atkinson found it "merely degrading"
and lamented that Jack Benny had "hardly a chance to show how subtle a
comedian he can be when his material is skillful."[43]

By this time, Benny became actively interested in the radio as the next
step in his career. He realized that it was getting harder to obtain billings
in vaudeville and on Broadway, and he saw that many of the performers
with whom he shared bills, such as singer Kate Smith, were finding
success on the radio. On March 29, 1932, he made an appearance over
the CBS radio network on a fifteen-minute program hosted by columnist
and man-about-town Ed Sullivan that came on at 8:45 in the evening, just
after Kate Smith's program.[44] Benny did a monologue on the program
and received his usual favorable comments. He then continued the vaudeville grind while arrangements were being made for him to have his own
radio program, two nights a week over station WJZ and the NBC Blue
Network, beginning on May 2, 1932.[45]

THE JACK BENNY SHOW

The role that Jack Benny played on the radio was an extension of his role on
the legitimate stage. He served as the program's master of ceremonies, a
droll and dry comedian for Canada Dry Ginger Ale, which was marketed as
a sophisticated and dry soft drink. He appeared regularly on the program,
but it was not *his* program. The orchestra leader, George Olsen, received top
billing, and most of the program consisted of musical numbers played by
Olsen, with songs by a Kate Smith–like female singer whose major claim to
fame was that she had starred opposite Eddie Cantor in the Broadway
production of *Whoopee*.[46]

Jack Benny failed to achieve immediate success on the radio. As in the
other branches of show business, he remained employed but was not quite

a major star. He switched time, sponsors, networks, and casts between May 1932 and October 1934, working on short contracts that were renewed. Only in the fall of 1934 did he settle into the 7:00 time slot on Sunday nights, first on the NBC Blue, then on the NBC Red network, and in the late 1940s, on CBS, which would be his radio home until 1955.

Over the years, he built up a stock company that appeared with him for many years on radio and, later, television. Sadie Marks, Benny's real-life wife, joined the cast in August 1932, appearing under the name Mary Livingstone. Her role was to needle Benny, as well as to sing an occasional song and do an occasional bit as a dizzy dame in the manner of fellow radio performer and close family friend Gracie Allen. Don Wilson started in 1934 and served as the announcer; pitchman for the products the show was selling, such as Jello, Grape Nut Flakes, or Lucky Strikes; and also as an actor in the sketches that were a regular part of the program. The program always had a resident orchestra, with orchestra leader Phil Harris as an important member of the cast beginning in 1936, and a tenor, most notably Dennis Day, who joined the show in 1939 and remained, with only a brief time off to do his own show, for the duration. Eddie Anderson, in the role of Jack Benny's black cook, butler, chauffeur, and valet Rochester, joined the cast in 1937.[47]

Over time, the program became less of a conventional variety show and more of a situation comedy with variety elements. As that happened, the show became Jack Benny's show, with him, rather than the band-leader, receiving top billing. The writers developed distinctive person-alities for each member of the permanent cast, changing the nature of the jokes. At the beginning of the run, Jack Benny told political jokes that could have been performed by almost any comedian. In 1933, he remarked that President Roosevelt had taken the country off the gold standard and three goldfish turned gray. In that same year, he made frequent joking references to the Indian patriot Mahatma Gandhi and his penchant to fast for the cause of Indian independence – for example, Gandhi ended his twenty-one-day fast and was now wearing a cigar band. In the original show, characteristics that would later be attributed to the character Jack Benny, such as his stinginess with money, were given to the bandleader.[48]

Each of the characters had a chance to interact with Benny in a way that highlighted his comic foibles. The manservant Rochester had many oppor-tunities to belittle his boss. In January 1939, he telephoned Jack to tell him that a telegram had arrived at the house, with charges of $8.80. Urged by Jack Benny not to accept the telegram because it was sent to him as a gag by his nemesis and fellow radio star Fred Allen, Rochester and Benny engaged in the following dialogue:

Rochester: "Well, he must be laughing now. I paid for it!"
Jack: "Paid for it? Where did you get the $8.80?"
Rochester: "I ripped open the mattress and dipped into your reserve fund."[49]

At a Halloween party that fall, Jack dressed up as Romeo, but Rochester could not recognize the costume, producing the following exchange:

Jack: "Look Rochester, I'm wearing a red jacket with a lace collar, a plush hat with plume in it and silk tights. Now, who am I?"
Rochester: "I don't know."
Jack: "I'm Romeo! Romeo!"
Rochester: "The great lover? Say boss, aren't you pressing a little?"[50]

Jack's lack of prowess with women was a frequent topic on the show. In a poignant New Year's episode broadcast at the end of 1939, Jack's date with Gladys gets canceled. Dejected, he decides to get a cup of coffee and then go home. As it turns out, none other than Gladys, who has been called in to work at the last minute, serves him at the coffeehouse. She says that she will be through with her shift by three in the morning, but Jack says he'll be asleep at that time. He never does get the girl.[51]

Although ethnic and racial references abounded on the show, Jack Benny himself maintained his ethnic neutrality. His personality traits rather than his ethnicity defined his character. Benny, who liked to ad lib and let the audience know that the broadcast was being done live with the possibility of mistakes, never alluded to the fact that he was Jewish. With his Midwestern accent, he sounded like any other American who had been born between Chicago and Milwaukee. The show's calendar included New Year's Eve, New Year's Day, St. Patrick's Day, Easter, the Kentucky Derby, summer vacations in Atlantic City, Halloween, Thanksgiving, and Christmas. Benny always did a Christmas show that featured his gifts to the cast. Even the fact that Benny played a miser went unremarked. It was clear that Benny was no Shylock. He was just an American comedian who played upon his haplessness, with the audience fully aware that in real life, which lay somewhere beyond the skits and the situation comedy on the program, he was a different sort of guy – happily married, so far as the public knew, and generous to a fault. Jewish listeners took pride in the fact that he was Jewish, but for most people, this trait went unnoticed. Benjamin Kubelsky had morphed into Jack Benny.

Benny's popularity marked a change among comic stars from the ethnicity of the 1920s and 1930s to the Americanism that would be popular in the 1940s and 1950s. He was a very different character from someone like Chico Marx. The audience had met Chico first on Broadway or the movies, and they knew what he looked like. He always remained in his vaudeville character, with his funny costume and Italian accent. Jack Benny played a character, but it was a flexible one that could be put into many different situations and did not require a special accent or special costume. His character flourished on the radio, and Chico Marx's character languished.

By 1934, Jack Benny had emerged as a major star, one of the first created by radio, with only a small assist from vaudeville, Broadway, and the movies. As a major star, he shuttled from coast to coast, doing his radio show and making movies. In the summer of 1934, he went to Hollywood to make a picture called *Transatlantic Merry Go Round*. He did most of his broadcasts that next season in New York, but left for Los Angeles that April, finishing up the radio season in Los Angeles and working on a film called the *Broadway Melody of 1936*, which was a solid success. By 1935, his program, increasingly dominated by the new show-within-a-show format, led the radio ratings, and he received some 2,000 pieces of mail each week. Broadway producers and writers such as George Kaufman wanted him for plays, and Hollywood continued to offer him pictures.[52]

Beginning in the fall of 1936, his program moved its base of operations from New York to Hollywood, an important moment of transition in the history of radio entertainment.[53] In the show, he became a resident of Hollywood, and the guest stars who appeared often were prominent movie stars. Although an occasional program, such as *Major Bowes Amateur Hour* or *Edgar Bergen and Charlie McCarthy*, edged above him in the ratings, he maintained a strong hold over the American public, signing a $1 million contract to perform on the radio in 1937.[54] His best years on radio lay ahead of him, with skits about the vault in which he kept his money, the Maxwell automobile that he retained well beyond its prime, and his interactions with comic voice artist Mel Blanc (the voice of cartoon character Bugs Bunny) announcing the train to Anaheim, Azusa, and Cucamonga. Only the rise of television, another medium in which he achieved considerable success, slowed down his momentum on radio.

Jack Benny owed his success to the comfort level he brought to the audience. The audience delighted in entering a fictional world, often tinged with the glamour of show business, to meet characters with whom it was familiar and whose company it enjoyed. Jack Benny offered escape and did not require the audience to work very hard to understand the plot. Instead, the program acted as a constantly reassuring presence. In this regard, it was not unlike the Fred and Ginger movies and other cultural landmarks of the 1930s. It was a less elaborate means of escape, without Fred and Ginger's virtuosity (but with top-flight musical talent), but it was a cheaper, more accessible, and equally satisfying form of entertainment.

CONCLUSION

The creation of the network and the prime roles of the advertising agency and the sponsor assured that American radio would develop differently than radio in other countries. In America, the radio industry became big business. The specific content of the radio programs were, however, largely independent of these business developments. Crooners such as Bing Crosby brought the radio to prime time. *Amos 'n' Andy* established that radio could become a daily American habit and not the plaything of technically minded geeks. Jack Benny invented the variety/situation comedy show in a rapidly evolving medium. Because of Benny and his colleagues, radio constituted a major form of American entertainment in the 1930s and through the war years.

4

From the Thirties to the Forties with Kate, Bud, and Lou

In the spring of 1939, Phillip Barry's *The Philadelphia Story*, a play about a rich Philadelphia family about to hold a wedding in an elegant Main Line home, became Broadway's hottest ticket.[1] Katharine Hepburn, whose career had lurched like a roller coaster across the 1930s, played the lead. She enjoyed a spectacular initial success in movies, then was humbled by a series of mid-decade setbacks, and finally reclaimed her prominence in the entertainment world with *The Philadelphia Story*. Her precarious path illustrated the pitfalls that the studio system of the 1930s' movie industry contained for ambitious artists who wanted to control their careers. In Hepburn's case, she overcame adversity and positioned herself to become a big movie star of the wartime era.

The comedy team of Bud Abbott and Lou Costello, also major stars of the early 1940s, appeared on Broadway during that same 1939 season. Although they lacked the sense of refinement that Katharine Hepburn brought to her acting, they received a cordial reception from critics, who appreciated their skills at broad physical comedy and their ability to put over the routines they had learned from performing in burlesque. Like Hepburn, they managed, against considerable odds, to establish themselves as leading movie stars in the period just preceding World War II. In their case, not only Broadway, but also radio, figured in their rise to stardom.

THE RISE OF KATHARINE HEPBURN

Katharine Hepburn was one of the crop of Broadway actresses recruited to Hollywood during the early days of sound movies. Her background differed from that of a Ginger Rogers or other actresses who saw the theater as a means of upward mobility. Hepburn came from an upper-middle-class family in Hartford, Connecticut, with a secure sense of its place in the hierarchy of American society. Her childhood was not a story of dancing for pennies on an East Side street corner or begging for notice on amateur night at the local theater, but rather one of finding her place within a large upper-middle-class family in one of those sprawling Victorian houses. There she lived with a professional father – a respected doctor – and her namesake mother, who, like the mother in the Mary Poppins stories, took part in social causes, such as votes for women and, later, birth control. The senior Katharine Hepburn looked after her large family while also giving speeches about why less fortunate women should refrain from having large families.[2]

Much as Theodore Roosevelt's family looked askance at his plans to enter politics, so the Hepburn family dissuaded Katharine from the theater. In no way did Hepburn have a stage mother, in the manner of a Mrs. Marx or Mrs. Rogers, who pushed her child into performing. Instead, Katharine's upbringing reflected a mixture of passion and restraint, according to the rules of upper-class life. One competed in athletic endeavors and amateur theatricals, but always with a sense of decorum and a strict adherence to the rules. As Katharine came of age in the early 1920s, respectable women did not make a career in the theater any more than they became professional athletes.

Against the better advice of her parents, Katharine Hepburn decided to try for work in the theater after she graduated from Bryn Mawr in 1928. She owed what jobs she obtained to perseverance, and even then often got into conflicts with directors, which led to her being fired from more than one production. In 1932, she managed to get a good part in a Broadway production of *The Warrior's Husband* that allowed her to show off her long shapely legs. She then came to the attention of a film scout who helped her to secure a part in a motion picture.

For a complete beginner, she received prominent billing in *A Bill of Divorcement* (1932). John Barrymore had his name above the title in large print, but just one place below the title appeared the name Katherine [sic] Hepburn. Ads for the movie called attention to Hepburn's "striking and auspicious film debut."[3] In the picture, Barrymore played a shell-shocked soldier who escapes from a mental hospital and returns to his family, eager to resume his role as a husband and father and unaware of his wife's plan to remarry. His daughter, played by Hepburn, forms a bond of sympathy with her father but worries about the insanity in her family that she fears will make it inadvisable for her to marry and have a family.

The film, a transplanted Broadway play in the manner of the era, and the director, stage veteran George Cukor, received strong notices.[4] According to the *New York Times*, Hepburn played her part "in a fashion that will not easily be forgotten." The paper expressed no surprise over the fact that RKO hastened to sign up its promising new talent to a long-term contract.[5] The paper also commended Hepburn on her excellent diction.[6] She spoke with a New England accent that hinted of money and sophistication and sounded, to the ordinary American ear, vaguely English. It gave her a sense of class that Americans associated with high-toned drama in the early sound era. It was also clear that the camera liked her, with her tall, thin, athletic body, and that the long planes of her cheekbones photographed exceptionally well. She did not have the fleshy, voluptuous look of a 1920s' chorus girl, but rather the well-defined features that photographers would capture in the documentary photos of the 1930s.

Such a promising beginning at a time of new beginnings in the movies brought attention to Katharine Hepburn. Arriving back in Hollywood after her movie debut, taking the usual train from Chicago, Hepburn received a welcome from a host of studio officials, press agents, and photographers who traveled some sixty miles to meet her in San Bernardino. Hepburn lapped up the attention.[7]

The studio had no intention of putting her through a long development process. It did all it could to put her name before the public and to turn out pictures with her in them. In *Christopher Strong*, released in the spring of 1933 at the same time as Warner Brothers came out with the Busby Berkeley musical *42nd Street*, Katharine Hepburn had the lead. Directed by Dorothy Arzner, one of Hollywood's few female directors, the picture capitalized on Hepburn's androgyny.[8] She played a sexy and alluring woman who was also an accomplished aviator. Hepburn was "thorough and believable and sometimes fascinatingly beautiful."[9]

The studio knew it had something, even if it was not quite sure what. It tried her out in *Morning Glory*, a movie released in the summer of 1933, with a mundane plot about a country girl who goes to New York and tries to make good on the stage. Like its predecessors, it enjoyed good box office and garnered good critical notices.[10] Next the studio reunited her with director George Cukor in a film version of the novel *Little Women*, released in November 1933, an indication of how quickly the studio followed one Katharine Hepburn picture with another. Hepburn, as the high-spirited Jo, fit right into the New England setting and dominated the ensemble cast.[11] At the end of a busy year, Katharine Hepburn made one Hollywood insider's list as one of the ten "brainiest" women on the screen, women who "know what they want, they know how to get what they want, and they know what do with what they wanted when they get it."[12] As if to confirm the impression that Hepburn was a rising star, she won an Academy Award for her work in *Morning Glory*, her second film.[13] Few people had wowed Hollywood so completely, so quickly.

THE FALL OF KATHARINE HEPBURN

Hepburn wanted still more, true validation as an actress, which she thought had to come on Broadway. At the end of her busy round of activities in 1933, she took the lead part in *The Lake*, which had been a hit in London the previous season and which producer Jed Harris hoped to bring to New York. In Washington, performing before an audience filled with Bryn Mawr alumnae, the audience greeted her enthusiastically, calling her back for repeated curtain calls.[14] The New York critics, who considered themselves the real arbiters of dramatic talent, were much less kind. Brooks Atkinson noted bluntly "Miss Hepburn is not a full-fledged dramatic actress yet. Her rocket-like success in the talking pictures has set too high the standards by which she has to be judged in the more coherent world of the stage." Her accomplishments in the movies only "call attention to her present limitations on the stage." The play closed in seven weeks and made no national tour.[15] It was as if a speculative bubble in entertainment futures had burst.

The Lake became a constant reference point in her career. When the critics reviewed her 1934 picture *Spitfire*, they felt compelled to mention her unfortunate performance on Broadway.[16] Hepburn began to get bad notices in pictures such as *Break of Hearts* (1935 with Charles Boyer) and *The Little Minister* (1935). One unkind critic noted that Hepburn's performance in *The Little Minister* was full of "elfin whimsies likely to cause minor teeth-gnashing among unsympathetic moderns."[17]

Despite the setbacks, Katharine stuck with the movies. When Hepburn tried something truly unusual as she did in *Sylvia Scarlet* (1936, George Cukor director, with Cary Grant), critics slammed her for her audacity. In that film, Hepburn put on trousers, just as she often did in real life, and played a girl passing for a boy in an effort to blend into her surroundings and make it easier for her roguish father to evade the police. The gender-bending aspects of the role made people uncomfortable, even though Hepburn as Sylvia Scarlett lets her heterosexual nature declare itself in her attraction for bohemian artist Brian Aherne.[18] Although the characters were supposed to be lower-class knockabouts, the movie reinforced

Hepburn's upper-class screen identity. Her cross-dressing on screen matched her brother's cross-dressing in a play at Harvard, a time-honored tradition of Ivy League theatrics.[19]

In the era of Fred and Ginger and Groucho, it was difficult for Katharine Hepburn to find her place. She became an unintentionally comic figure, considered haughty and above the rules of ordinary life, with a voice that comedians loved to imitate and mannerisms that critics ridiculed. "Miss Hepburn," one critic admitted, "gives me, personally, the jitters."[20]

AN EXCURSION INTO SCREWBALL COMEDY

The studio, trying to find different and better material for her, put her in a series of three pictures, all of which have been acclaimed as classics and none of which made a great deal of money.[21] The second in the series was the 1938 movie *Bringing Up Baby*, now considered a masterpiece of screwball comedy but then regarded with relative indifference. It was pulled after only a week at Radio City, and RKO ended up losing $365,000 on the film.[22]

Screwball comedy, a significant cinematic trend of the mid- to late 1930s, depended on the humor inherent in absurd situations, with actors putting on a comedy rather than vaudevillians performing their specialties in a variety show. Ensemble-driven plot mattered more than individual star turns; situation-driven wit predominated over physical slapstick of the Harpo Marx or Charlie Chaplin variety. As historian Robert Sklar notes, screwball pictures were comedies of manners.[23] They fit well into the atmosphere of a Hollywood that, in the face of pressure from the Catholic Church hierarchy and local censor boards, had decided to soft-pedal nudity and sex.

The screwball form went back to Restoration comedy, but in the 1930s it received a distinctive twist. It satirized the manners of the idle rich at a time when many people were struggling to feed and clothe themselves. It therefore featured the sort of escapism to an opulent world characteristic of the Fred and Ginger movies, and at the same time contained a satiric edge. Unlike the Fred and Ginger pictures, the setting was almost always America.[24]

Hepburn and her studio decided that screwball comedy would allow her to rehabilitate her image by showing that she could make fun of herself. She was certainly aware that pictures such as *The Thin Man* (1934) and *My Man Godfrey* (1936) had made money for their studios. The urbane William Powell, who appeared in both of these pictures, showed how it was possible to retain upper-class mannerisms but still signal to the audience that he was one of the boys. In *The Thin Man*, he played a former police detective, now married to the rich Myrna Loy, who was a sort of supersleuth. He mixed easily with the police and the criminal element yet enjoyed an elegant life of large hotel suites, a steady supply of martinis, and frequent parties. In *My Man Godfrey*, he portrayed a Boston blue blood slumming in a hobo camp to see how the other half lives, a sort of *Prince and the Pauper* scenario. In the course of the movie, he becomes a butler in an upper-class family and meets and marries pretty Carole Lombard (to whom he had recently been married in real life.)

In *Bringing Up Baby*, Katharine Hepburn's entry into the screwball realm, she plays an upper-class heiress type who is trying to lure Cary Grant from his staid fiancée to marry her instead. They go on many adventures on suburban golf courses, swank Manhattan restaurants with European servers and customers dressed in formal wear, fancy Riverdale mansions, and eventually, in an unintentional reference to Hepburn's real life, a rustic summer retreat in Connecticut.[25]

HITTING BOTTOM

Bringing Up Baby boosted Katharine Hepburn's reputation in the long run but did little to reverse her declining popularity at the time.[26] She hit bottom in May 1938, when the Independent Theater Owners Association took out an ad in a Hollywood trade paper that labeled Katharine Hepburn and a number of other stars as "box office deterrents." "Hepburn turned in excellent performances in ... 'Bringing Up Baby,' but [the picture] died," the advertisement noted. Hepburn found herself in the company of such early sound movie stars as Greta Garbo, Mae West, and Joan Crawford. All of them were supposedly washed up.[27]

There was a subtler implication in the ad that had less to do with Hepburn and more with the movie industry. The independent theater owners wished to call attention to the practices of the studios, such as forcing them to take an entire slate of pictures, or block booking, that forced mediocre movies on the public and kept it from seeing the pictures it wanted to see. If the independent exhibitors were given a freer hand to choose, then the public would benefit by being forced to sit through fewer turkeys and getting a steadier diet of popular pictures. Hepburn, a contract player who held no particular brief for the studio system, found herself held up as an example of its worst practices.

She responded by negotiating and buying her way out of her RKO contract. Always adroit at gathering publicity, Hepburn tried to project a new image: that of the good-natured actor rather than an eccentric diva. According to one Hollywood reporter, she was the "first to admit she has certain eccentricities, especially her dislike of strangers on the movie set," but she wanted people to judge her by her film work alone. In her efforts to please, she even allowed Hedda Hopper to take tea with her on the set and did her best to charm the influential columnist. Other journalists lauded her willingness to break with her dramatic past, despite the fact that she was "one of the earth's finest actresses."[28]

At liberty, Hepburn went into full retreat. In the summer of 1938, she was back at her parents' summer home on the Long Island Sound, a star in seclusion in a proper New England setting in which the residents felt sorry for her mother because her daughter was in pictures. Hepburn swam, went on ten-mile hikes, and played golf and tennis in the company of her family, which the newspapers portrayed as similar to the eccentric family in Kaufman and Hart's *You Can't Take it With You*.[29]

As always, there was a buzz around Hepburn, centering in this case on her possible romantic relationship with aviator Howard Hughes. He sometimes flew over the golf course, signaling his presence to Hepburn, and then landed at a nearby airport. The Hepburn family had even done a little remodeling on its house to make its somewhat spartan accommodations habitable for the fastidious Hughes. Hepburn also figured in a mild way in the gossip over who would get the prize part of Scarlett O'Hara in the upcoming production of *Gone with the Wind*. Rumors circulated that Margaret Mitchell, the author of the novel, wanted Hepburn in the picture, which was to be directed by her good friend and collaborator George Cukor.[30] Although Scarlett might have been the one role to rehabilitate her career, she was an unlikely choice. Producer David Selznick, as it turned out, preferred a fresher face.

THE REVIVAL OF KATHARINE HEPBURN

Staying away from Hollywood, Hepburn commissioned a play that might serve as a vehicle for her comeback. In February 1939, Philip Barry's *The Philadelphia Story* began out-of-town tryouts in New Haven, before an audience that included Hepburn's father and mother. One of her stronger journalistic supporters wrote at the time, "Hepburn never looked prettier nor more vital than she does today." As for her unkind reception at the hands of the Hollywood critics, Hepburn said, "I asked for it." And the critics now appeared to be in a penitent mood, describing her as "the victim of more feather-brained scribbling than ever has been showered upon the innocent head of any prominent young star." One out-of-towner noted the strong notices that *The Philadelphia Story* had been receiving and said that the New York critics who had been "malicious" to Hepburn in her previous stage appearances would find it "difficult to defend a like stand" for the new play.[31]

Back in Los Angeles, Hedda Hopper said that Katharine Hepburn "did not need Hollywood." Her rival Louella Parsons noted that Katharine Hepburn could not get a job in motion pictures, but quoted a prominent producer as saying that "she is such a success in the Philadelphia Story that it will become a legend of the stage."[32]

Hepburn decided to risk bringing *The Philadelphia Story* to New York. She won her gamble. Brooks Atkinson gave the play, which opened on March 28, 1939, a rave and put a stamp of approval on Hepburn by calling her, at long last, "a professional stage actress." Author Barry had "whisked away the monotony and reserve" that had previously kept her acting "within a very small compass." Now she performed with "grace, jauntiness and warmth," just the sort of performance to soothe a public "lost in the whirl of world affairs."[33]

The play became, in the words of one Broadway observer, "a thumping hit" that ran for 416 performances at the Shubert Theatre, not closing until March 30, 1940. Hepburn then toured in the show for a month before coming back to Hollywood to make the film version. By this time, Hollywood was caught up in the war in Europe that had begun the previous September, complicating the problem of casting. The producers nonetheless secured the services of George Cukor to direct and of Cary Grant and James Stewart to appear in the supporting roles.[34]

At the beginning of the picture, we see Cary Grant shoving Hepburn out the door, illustrating the end of their marriage. Undaunted, she gets engaged to a rich but shallow and inexperienced man who sees her as something of a trophy. Two journalists, one of them James Stewart, come to her house to write about the wedding for a popular magazine. Stewart spends a drunken evening with Hepburn that reveals that beneath the perfect but forbidding exterior of a goddess lies a fun-loving girl. Together, Stewart and Grant, who still lives conveniently nearby, bring Hepburn down from her pedestal, so that she is no longer a goddess but rather a real woman. She learns to appreciate people for what they really are, rather than holding them or herself to impossibly high standards. In the end, she leaves her fiancé and impetuously decides to remarry Cary Grant, secure in the knowledge that she will allow men, who might occasionally drink or philander, to be men. She herself will be a woman of warmth and compassion. The picture implies that she is now a "real" woman capable of finding fulfillment in romantic love.

When the movie opened at the end of 1940, it got excellent reviews and, in a reversal of Hepburn's previous luck, did smash business. The picture, wrote Bosley Crowther, had "just about everything a blue-chip comedy should have." Someone had once rudely labeled her "box office poison," but, according to Crowther, they must have been wrong. Indeed, as the picture set records at Radio City Music Hall and became MGM's top grosser of the year, Harry Brandt of the Independent Theatre Owners of America recanted his previous statement and complimented Hepburn on her fine performance. MGM eagerly signed her up for another picture.[35]

As Hepburn's career illustrated, success and failure both fed on themselves; one produced a snowballing positive effect, and the other started a cascading decline. Something was right about *The Philadelphia Story*, just as something was wrong with *Bringing Up Baby*. In *Bringing Up Baby*, Hepburn's character converted Cary Grant to her daffy but endearing point of view. In *The Philadelphia Story*, Grant's character schooled Katharine Hepburn in the lessons of life. By reversing the genders of the dominant characters, making Hepburn more submissive, *The Philadelphia Story* functioned as a redemption narrative for Hepburn and her career.

It was not exactly a feminist tract, and that was the point – to chastise Hepburn for her previous arrogance and to signal that she had gotten the message so that she could now marry, or remarry, Prince Charming and live happily ever after without the audience feeling resentful about it. The picture worked, not only as a self-contained melodrama but also within the context of Hepburn's career.

The public now tolerated, even appreciated, Hepburn's eccentricities, such as her unabashed support of liberal causes. One could see her picnicking with the President and the First Lady on the grounds of Eleanor Roosevelt's Hyde Park retreat, or hear her giving speeches of support for the President in his 1940 re-election effort. They admired her independence as she sat in sessions with MGM head Louis B. Mayer and took a much more active role in picking and casting her movies than she had previously been able to do at RKO. They applauded when she took over Robert Montgomery's dressing room – he was away on a wartime mission – just above that of Clark Gable himself, in what had previously been an all-male enclave at MGM.[36] As the war got closer, she exemplified the new woman who could handle new responsibilities in the absence of men, but who would not surrender her femininity in the process. She had done what was

nearly impossible in Hollywood: re-invent herself, using her old self as the
basic building material.

HEPBURN IN THE 1940S

Her next picture confirmed her success by repeating the basic narrative in a
new context. In *Woman of the Year*, which opened just after the beginning
of American involvement in the war, Spencer Tracy takes the part of the
strong male who helps Hepburn find her inner female. In the screwball
tradition, they are opposites who attract. They meet cute when Tracy goes
to his favorite bar and hears her over the radio as a guest on the program
Information Please. She wows the audience with her knowledge of
American history, but does not know the first thing about sports. As it
turns out, both Tracy and Hepburn work for the same New York newspaper. Tracy, a man's man with one year of college education, writes
sports. He lives in an American context, convinced that people need the
diversions that sports offer. Hepburn, a high-strung and extremely well-
educated woman, writes a political column. Her beat is world affairs, and
she lives in a global context, convinced that the American public must
understand the complexity and fragility of the international situation. He
has occasional problems with subject-verb agreement, and she speaks an
endless array of foreign languages. He pushes out copy on a manual
typewriter. She dictates to a prissy personal secretary and makes frequent
use of the Teletype, telephone, radio, and other modern means of communication. She receives awards as an outstanding feminist and associates
with the world's great leaders. He seems most at home hanging out in the
press box, a traditional male preserve, and drinking with his buddies.

Like Tracy Lord in *The Philadelphia Story*, Tess Harding gets schooled
in *Woman of the Year*. The lessons begin when Spencer Tracy takes her to
a baseball game, and she is unable to separate the nuances of baseball from
those of football. In an impulsive moment, the two get married, and the
marriage soon buckles under the strain of Tess's active life and her lack of
time for her husband. She does things like inviting the staff of the
Yugoslavian consulate into her bedroom without telling her husband,
who has made a special effort to get home from a game in Chicago to be
with her. Also without consulting him, she adopts a Greek orphan and
brings him to live with them, without making any provision for taking care
of him. Like Eleanor Roosevelt, she seems to lack the maternal instinct.
Eventually, she learns her lesson – that it is one thing to win an award as a
woman of the year but quite another to be a real woman. That requires her

to devote herself to consummating her marriage in more than the sexual sense and to become a true helpmate to her husband.

In the end, Tess Harding learns to be a woman in the contemporary sense of the term, but the audience gets the sense that she is not simply going to put herself on the shelf for the duration. For one thing, she lacks domestic skills; she puts yeast in the waffle batter and drops eggs on her shoes. For another, someone of Tess's considerable abilities will be needed for the war. It's just that she will no longer be a goddess in the Tracy Lord manner.

Spencer Tracy and Katharine Hepburn, who complemented one another in looks and temperament, became one of the great screen couples. It gave them an additional weapon in the arsenal of devices that they used to sustain their careers through the war years and into the 1950s and 1960s. By the end of their careers, they could make a picture together that played upon the image they had established, on and off the screen, as a loving couple. They battled one another but always came to recognize that they needed each other.

The path of Hepburn's career traced one route through the 1930s and into the 1940s. She was a recruit from Broadway who made an instant success in pictures, winning the Academy Award for her first starring role, and secured a place for herself as a leading dramatic actress in a studio stable. When she tried to replicate her screen success on the stage, the New York critics punished her by saying that what was good enough for movies was not good enough for the legitimate stage. At the same time, her screen assets became liabilities. The problem was that her very strengths, such as her upper-class New England accent, became weaknesses, and the studio found it increasingly hard to find the right vehicle, the one that would continue to bring in box office receipts, for her. It tried costume dramas, gender-bending dramas, and rural dramas, and then asked Hepburn to step into the entirely new realm of screwball comedy. At first, everything worked; then nothing did. Eventually, Hepburn, with the compliance of the studio that was glad to get rid of her, pulled herself out of the system and fashioned her own comeback vehicle that enabled her to reconnect with her audience on the stage and screen. In this way, she made it through the 1930s and gained momentum entering the 1940s.

ABBOTT AND COSTELLO

Not all of the future wartime stars took this complicated path. Some, like the comedy team of Abbott and Costello, auditioned on radio during the late 1930s and made it as screen stars in the 1940s.[37]

In 1934, when Hepburn was already a glamorous Hollywood star, Lou Costello, the former Louis Francis Cristillo, was performing in burlesque at the Gayety Theater in Washington.[38] He had already been to Hollywood and back. He grew up in Paterson, New Jersey, the son of an insurance broker in an Italian-Irish family. The record was never very clear on his date of birth. He liked to claim 1908, but the real date might have been 1906. Like many future performers, he did not do particularly well in school, playing the role of the class clown and excelling only in sports as a proficient free-throw shooter and later a boxer. After his junior year in high school, he set off, much as near contemporary Lyndon Johnson would do, to make it in California. He got work in the movie industry, mostly as a stunt man, but found it difficult to secure steady employment as sound came in. He headed back east, taking jobs in burlesque along the way.

At some point he met Bud Abbott, who was perhaps ten years his senior, although Abbott, like Costello, was vague about his age. Abbott, born in Asbury Park on the New Jersey shore, had an exotic show business background – his mother and father both worked in the circus. By 1936, Abbott and Costello had paired up as a team in burlesque, vaudeville, or whatever bookings they could find. Costello, agile but short and stout with a well-shaven, pudgy baby face, played the comic, and Abbott, taller and thinner with sharp features and a moustache that made him seem slick in the manner of a carnival barker, performed as the straight man. In 1938, they were appearing in such venues as the Capitol Theater in Washington, doing bits they had developed about baseball and an army training camp. A few weeks later, they were at Loews State in New York, appearing on a bill that also included the MGM film star Judy Garland.[39]

At this point, they received what turned out to be their big break in the form of an invitation to be guests on Kate Smith's radio show. The popular singer hosted a variety show that aired on CBS on Thursday nights at 8:00 opposite the formidable competition of crooner Rudy Vallee on the NBC Red network. Abbott and Costello made their debut on February 3, 1938. Although their first performance was a little shaky – apparently the radio audience could not tell which performer was which as easily as the studio audience could – the pair was asked to return the next week, and they became regulars on the program for the next two years.[40]

The gig allowed them to perform in stage shows and nightclubs in the New York area while continuing to gain in popularity from their radio performances.[41] In this manner, Abbott and Costello used radio to audition for Hollywood, which was something relatively new on the entertainment scene. The first round of radio performers, such as Jack Benny, went straight from vaudeville to radio with little or no preparation. Jack Benny did one show for Ed Sullivan and then launched his own show. Abbott and Costello, like Bob Hope and the other comedians who emerged at the end of the 1930s, could apprentice as radio guest stars on established programs and use that experience as a springboard for greater fame. Many of these comedians who did radio guest shots before getting their own programs and going into the movies became bigger movie stars than did radio pioneers such as Benny or Fred Allen or Rudy Vallee. It was as if these older stars were mired in radio and could not get past it, while the others were rising stars who were just passing through.

The next step for Abbott and Costello was a Broadway revue. In June 1939, *The Streets of Paris*, opened on Broadway. The presence of the World's Fair helped to sustain the theater season through the summer, so that Abbott and Costello appeared on Broadway during the same, highly successful season that also featured Katharine Hepburn in *The Philadelphia Story*. Brooks Atkinson wrote that "Out of vaudeville and motion picture stage shows some one has had the wisdom to bring Lou Costello and Bud Abbott to town with some remarkably gusty stuff." Their radio appearances apparently did not register with the august critic.[42]

Abbott and Costello became New York celebrities. That September, they came to the World's Fair to appear with the cast of *The Streets of Paris* as part of what was billed as "Abbott and Costello Day" at the Fair (not quite the honor it seemed, since it was also the Police Athletic League Field Day, Lafayette Day, and the Boy Scout Day of Fun at the multi-faceted fair). Mayor Fiorello LaGuardia, who noticed his own resemblance to Costello, wrote Costello, "If you want to take over my job, it's yours."[43]

In the summer of 1940, Abbott and Costello moved up several rungs on the show business ladder by substituting for Fred Allen on the radio and getting a movie contract with Universal Studios. Louella Parsons could not wait for their arrival in Hollywood. She told her readers that she had appeared with them on the Kate Smith show and they had reduced her to stitches.[44]

RADIO NEWS AND DEBATE ON THE DRAFT

When Abbott and Costello did their summer stint on Wednesdays at 9:00 in the evening over the main NBC network, many of the old hits from the 1930s, such as *The Goldbergs* in the morning and *Amos 'n' Andy* in its customary spot at 7:00 in the evening, remained on the air. Baseball games and concerts also filled the airwaves. Unlike earlier in the decade, however, radio featured programs that in one way or another involved current events. Playing opposite Abbott and Costello on radio station WOR, for example, was a news commentary program hosted by Gabriel Heatter. This program complemented other news commentaries that appeared at various times during the day, such as Lowell Thomas at 6:45 and H.V. Kaltenborn at 7:45. These commentators, like Katharine Hepburn's movie character Tess Harding, debated how far the United States should go in aiding England and in preparing for its own entrance into the war.[45]

The presence of the news commentators in prominent spots during the broadcast day reflected a new focus on news and current events that had developed toward the end of the 1930s. In that decade, the networks discovered that the commentators had their own sort of star power and could attract sponsors. These commentators, many of whom had worked on newspapers, functioned somewhat like the columnists (again like Tess Harding) who provided their personal slants on the day's news and offered an inside look at politics.

At the same time, radio also became a source of basic information on breaking news and of live debate on public policy questions. The radio networks tended not to put on news programs in the newspaper sense of a daily digest of the news, at least during the 1930s. The news commentator served as an attractive alternative, as did the live broadcast of a breaking event. By the end of the 1930s, radio had become the nation's most important source for breaking news. In the summer of 1940, both NBC and CBS ran programs dedicated to bringing listeners the latest news from war-torn Europe.[46]

Americans wondered what their response to the European crisis should be, and the radio reflected the national debate. Just after Abbott and Costello signed off on August 14, 1940, for example, radio station WEVD in New York broadcast a fifteen-minute forum, *Should the Draft Be Decided by Congress or Referendum*. This question occupied a prominent place in people's minds because Congress was considering instituting the first peacetime military draft in the nation's history. To some, the peacetime draft seemed tantamount to preparing the nation for war.

ABBOTT AND COSTELLO AT THE MOVIES: THE RETURN OF SLAPSTICK

Abbott and Costello, who represented an escapist alternative to contemplating the nation's problems, who strived for an easily accessible form of humor, and who had none of Katharine Hepburn's earnest engagement

with President Roosevelt and the New Deal, ended up benefiting from all
of the talk over war preparedness. In the fall of 1940, while the team was
making its first picture for Universal, Congress passed the Selective Service
Act.[47] Although the subject did not appear to be inherently funny, the
studio put Abbott and Costello in a comedy about the draft with the
popular Andrews Sisters.[48] It was a mark of the prewar times (at least in
the United States) that the movies could contemplate forced conscription
and military training as humorous subjects. No fewer than six studios
announced plans for movies about newly inducted soldiers. Paramount
put its emerging star Bob Hope into *Caught in the Draft*. Universal sped
Buck Privates into production and managed to release its picture first.[49]

Despite the subject matter, Abbott and Costello did not do topical
humor. Their material often consisted of adaptations of older routines
from vaudeville and burlesque. Their most famous bit, "Who's on
First?" which they did on stage, the radio, and several times in the movies,
came from a familiar form of wordplay in burlesque – the confusion of a
common word or phrase with a proper noun, as in this exchange, "Who's
your boss?" "Yes." Who's the guy you're working for?" "That's exactly
correct." "Who's on First?" transplanted that situation to the field of
baseball, with the names of all the position players being common words
or phrases. Bringing off the routine depended on excellent timing, with
the two often speaking simultaneously, on Abbott's ability to project a
serious demeanor and not break character, and on Costello's skillful voice
modulations and physical gestures.[50]

In many respects, Abbott and Costello represented a throwback to the
earlier era of the Marx brothers, but the differences were also instructive.
Like the Marx brothers before them, and unlike the screwball actors of the
1930s, they performed their stage bits, which had already made them a big
hit on radio, on the screen. Abbott and Costello marked a return to a
physical style of comedy that the Marx brothers and legions of comedians
before them had popularized on the stage and screen (in contrast to the
much more gentle Jack Benny, who came in between them and the Marx
brothers, and enacted what might be described as a comedy of manners).
At the same time, Abbott and Costello were less cerebral than the Marx
brothers, who were influenced not only by vaudeville traditions but also by
the smart set comedy of the Algonquin Roundtable and the *New Yorker*
during the 1920s. No George Kaufman nor S. J. Perelman, with their
surrealistic turns of phrase, wrote for Abbott and Costello.

Groucho and his brothers always dressed up in outlandish and anach-
ronistic costumes. Abbott and Costello tended to wear regular business suits,

although Costello often dressed more flamboyantly than did those around them. Funny costumes had gone the way of blackface. The Marx brothers did dialect humor, and many of the puns depended on Chico's Italian accent, as in his mistaking "sanity clause" for Santa Claus. Chico's character always had an Italian name. Abbott and Costello always appeared as generic Americans, not easily identified by ethnicity, who spoke regular, unaccented English and had common last names, as in the Slicker Smith (Abbott) and Herbie Brown (Costello) characters they played in *Buck Privates*.

As the 1930s progressed, comedy seemed to beat a retreat from ethnicity, just as the world was heading toward a cataclysmic conflict in which ethnicity and nationality figured prominently. The Marx brothers made heavy use of ethnicity, which was integral to their act. A radio comedian, like Jack Benny, surrounded himself with ethnic characters but was not a distinctively ethnic character himself. The later 1930s' radio comedians, like Abbott and Costello, omitted ethnicity from their acts altogether. They engaged America more broadly, confident that America included them.

Buck Privates opened in the winter of 1941, after the beginning of the draft but nearly a year before Pearl Harbor. It played with reality, with a beginning newsreel sequence showing Washington officials selecting the first numbers in the draft lottery and file footage of military maneuvers of World War I vintage. Ultimately, the picture succumbed to fantasy and also offered a message of social uplift. The fantasy was that military training camps were somehow extensions of civilian life, like summer camps filled with the boys down the block and complete with female hostesses who looked after the creature comforts of the recruits. The message was that the camps were places that brought people of all social classes together and forged a new American identity in which the traits that united the American people overshadowed ethnic, race, and class differences. In this regard, *Buck Privates* was not only the first picture about the draft but also the first World War II film to use the "we are all in this together" metaphor that would become a staple of such films.

The film features Abbott and Costello as two hustlers who sell ties on a street corner, with Costello acting as Abbott's shill. When the police bust their operation, they fold up their table and run down the street, hoping to hide in a movie theater. The trouble is that the movie theater is being used that day as the location for Army induction physicals, and Abbott and Costello unwittingly get signed up to join the army. A rich man also breezes into the makeshift recruiting office, thinking that there has been some sort of mistake about his being called into the army and expecting his rich, connected father to get him out. They all march off from Grand Central

Station to the train waiting to take them to the army camp, and it is as if the 1940s are saying goodbye to the 1930s. The Andrew Sisters add to the festivities with their harmonic renditions of "Boogie Woogie Bugle Boy of Company C" and "I'll Be Waiting at Apple Blossom Time," doing jitter-bug steps in which they hunch up their square shoulders.

In the army camp, the rich man remains aloof and looks out only for himself. In the end, however, he joins the group and learns to appreciate his fellow soldiers – the army has acted as a force of social solidarity without one shot having been fired in anger. Americans from all walks of life are being molded into a fighting force, tough enough to make war but sensitive enough to appreciate the fundamental values of decency that the war will help preserve.

Buck Privates did not let its message weigh it down. It preserved a comic spirit from beginning to end, with Abbott and Costello doing their various routines involving gambling and other forms of hustling and cutting up during the military drills. The critics approached the film with minimal expectations and found themselves pleasantly surprised that it made them laugh and that it all held together. Louella Parsons reported that the movie was so funny that "you will hang onto your chair laughing at Lou Costello and Bud Abbott."[51]

ABBOTT AND COSTELLO IN HOLLYWOOD

Buck Privates turned into a sleeper hit that made major stars of Abbott and Costello. They became "the hottest thing in the comic line." Both built big homes with swimming pools; they bought large cars for themselves and smaller cars for their wives; they purchased the contract of a prizefighter, and they got lucrative radio contracts as well. The team had once felt lucky to get $100 a week. Now they commanded $7,500 for an eight-day stand at the Steel Pier in Atlantic City. In the summer of 1941, they expected to earn $200,000 for their next forty weeks in radio and pictures. Universal offered them a substantial bonus and an extended contract.[52]

The studio began to throw them into picture after picture in the established manner of exploiting a hot property.[53] By the time of Pearl Harbor, Abbott and Costello had found a comfortable niche for themselves in Hollywood. They would be among the comedians whom the nation had met on radio, gotten infatuated with during the tense developments of 1941, and would find funny and reliable enough to spend time with during the war. In the fall of 1942, Abbott and Costello launched their own highly successful radio program. In November 1944, their radio show ranked sixth in popularity.[54]

Personal disasters slowed down the team's momentum. In March 1943, Costello came down with a crippling case of rheumatic fever that left him barely able to walk. He had to leave the radio program and stop making pictures, and Abbott found he could not carry the radio program alone. Costello did not return to work until November 1943, and during rehearsals for his first radio show back, he received a phone call in which he learned that his infant son had drowned in the family swimming pool. As word spread, other stars offered to step in and help with the broadcast, but Costello decided to go on with the program, making it nearly all the way through before breaking down at the end.[55]

Even before Costello took his forced leave, the critics, the advance scouts for audiences, had begun to tire of Abbott and Costello. The team would never gain the cult following of the Marx brothers, whose material was more sophisticated and whose pictures came out infrequently enough that they were considered events. A movie buff could name each of the Marx brothers' pictures in the order they appeared. No one could do that with Abbott and Costello – there were simply too many pictures, most hastily produced by a studio that did not have the high production values of Paramount and MGM. By 1944, *Times* critic Bosley Crowther wondered how long "even the sturdiest comedy team can stand up under plotless pictures in which rehashes of well-worn pieces of business furnish the only relief."[56]

In a way, such sentiments formed self-fulfilling prophecies just as they did with Katharine Hepburn. Abbott and Costello found that after their fabulous success between 1941 and 1943, they tended to fall back into the pack. Inevitably, Costello, like Fred Astaire and Groucho Marx, slowed down as he approached his forties. Abbott began to drink more heavily, and antipathy developed between the two partners in the middle of the decade, in much the same way Chico's gambling proved a problem for Groucho and the rest of the Marx brothers. Both Abbott and Costello ran into income tax problems that created financial difficulties.

They continued to work through their differences, and eventually they patched them up. Although they appeared steadily in radio, movies, and finally television and enjoyed something of a revival in pictures at the end of the 1940s, they never made their way back to the very top.[57]

CONCLUSION

Abbott and Costello's success in movies came just before the war broke out and continued throughout the war. Katharine Hepburn, whose career also took off in this period, had to reinvent herself on Broadway and at the movies to reach her second wave of success. Unlike Hepburn and the first generation of sound actors to come from New York to Hollywood, Abbott and Costello used radio to audition for later movie stardom. In both cases, a pivotal year was 1939, when Hepburn and Abbott and Costello all appeared on Broadway. That experience allowed them to negotiate the space between the Depression and the war. So did the fortunate circumstance of receiving material that meshed with the nation's growing interest in military preparedness and international affairs at a time when those weighty matters still contained a lighter side.

5

Bogie, Bob, and the Boys at War

At the beginning of 1943, as the second long year of World War II began, Rita Hayworth's handlers released a publicity photo that was intended to demonstrate her understanding of the new Hollywood etiquette. In the picture, glamour girl Rita, dressed in sensible slacks and sandals with the sleeves of her blouse rolled up, hunched down in front of a stove. She wanted everyone to see her, so she looked back toward the camera rather than down at the stove, and apparently found it necessary to wear makeup while cooking. The caption explained that Rita had decided to get along without a servant and cook her own meals. That would allow her to save money and to invest the savings in war bonds.[1] The idea of Rita Hayworth's needing to save money was preposterous, but the instinct among publicists was to emphasize that Miss Hayworth wanted to do her part for the war effort.

As the publicists understood, the war had changed the nature of economic citizenship in America. During the 1930s, it had been patriotic to spend and consume in an effort to jumpstart the stalled economy. During the 1940s, it became patriotic to save and invest, in an effort to conserve suddenly precious resources and mobilize the American economy for the war. In the 1930s, policy makers looked for ways to spread work around among as many people as possible. Putting in overtime was officially discouraged through laws that required employers to pay higher wages to workers after they had put in forty hours a week. In the 1940s, policy makers exhorted employees to work as long and hard as possible, so as to maximize production for the war effort. As a result, even movie star Rita Hayworth could show her solidarity by cutting down on her luxury lifestyle and pitching in on the housework so that her servants were free to take jobs in wartime industries.

The war put Hollywood in a potentially precarious position. Movies cost a great deal of money to produce and distribute. They represented a possible indulgence that might be dispensed with for the duration. Alternatively, movies might become an item similar to cars. Just as car manufacturers turned to military production and stopped producing new cars, so the film industry might recycle its old movies, rather than producing new ones, for the duration. Resources once spent on making movies could instead be put to uses more directly related to the war.

That vision of the place of Hollywood in the wartime economy never materialized. Instead, the government accepted the movies as a partner in war mobilization and promoted the movies as a force for reducing stress and boosting morale. As FDR noted, "the American motion picture is one of the most effective media in informing and entertaining our citizens."[2] The same industry that provided an escape from the economic woes of the Depression would now take on the tasks of helping stressed workers stay motivated, content, and productive.

War proved a help, rather than a hindrance, to the movie industry. For one thing, the government's priorities shifted from protecting the interests of small-time distributors and exhibitors to making sure that as many movies got produced as possible. As a result, the anti-trust initiatives of the late 1930s aimed at the large studios were shelved during the war, and the studios thrived. Movie attendance reached new heights, fueled by wartime prosperity that created a high demand for a leisurely means of escape from pressured jobs and crowded homes. By 1940, after the start of the war in Europe but before America's entrance, weekly movie attendance approached 80 million, and it climbed to 100 million by the end of the war. Increased attendance had a favorable effect on the balance sheets of the major studios. Warner Brothers showed an after-tax profit of $5.4 million in fiscal 1941 and $8.5 million in 1942.[3]

Exhausted workers coming out of factories at odd times of the day and night provided a ready movie audience. So did military personnel in the field. Five hundred movie theaters sprang up in military camps around the world, with an estimated attendance of a quarter of a million people a day. One soldier commented that the movies were "the sole remaining contact we have with civilization." A journalist reported that to the soldier in the field the voice of a big star on a record was like listening to the voice of God.[4]

The fact that a number of big-time stars and important Hollywood executives and technicians left their jobs to go to war did create some serious problems. Four hundred members of the Screen Actors Guild had entered military service by September 1942, including Ronald Reagan, Jimmy Stewart, Henry Fonda, and Clark Gable. Some, like Reagan, stayed in Los Angeles and made movies for the military. Others, like Stewart and Robert Montgomery, got involved in real action. The studios, which recognized the obvious threat to their productions, responded by trying to stockpile as many pictures as they could so that they could release an actor's movies while he was away at war. Before Ronald Reagan went into active service on April 18, 1942, for example, he made two pictures without taking a vacation. That enabled him to retain his active status as a film star into 1943. Jimmy Stewart had two pictures released after his induction in March 1941. No one knew, of course, how long the war would last.[5]

Stockpiled pictures meant more of the same, but the war nonetheless influenced the context and content of movies between 1941 and 1945. Directors, such as Alfred Hitchcock, used the war as a subject of their films. New stars, such as Humphrey Bogart and Bob Hope, replaced the ones away at war. A perceived need to stress unity among the American people put a new slant on old movie situations.

In this regard, the war created new ethnic and racial sensitivities on the part of both the movie industry and the government. It became a matter of some concern, for example, when the *Chicago Defender* cheered the presence of a Washington rally that helped to sell $250,000 in war bonds but complained that black stars, such as Eddie (Rochester) Anderson of the Jack Benny radio show, were not invited to join the likes of Bing Crosby and James Cagney. The paper noted that such a gesture would have added thousands of dollars to the take. It did not comment on what it might do to Washington's segregated social structure or segregated public facilities.[6] The federal Office of War Information (OWI), staffed by enthusiastic New Dealers who wanted to send a positive message about the war and at the same time use the war to advance liberal goals, made suggestions to the film companies about observing racial sensitivities. MGM, at the urging of the OWI, spent four weeks re-shooting its picture about President Andrew Johnson so as to make the character of Thaddeus Stevens more sympathetic. American Negroes regarded Stevens as a hero, and the OWI did not want to send out a picture that offended such groups as the NAACP.[7]

THE WARTIME MUSICAL

In the build-up to the war, Hollywood seemed determined not to take the tense international situation too seriously. Fred Astaire's *You'll Never Get Rich*, released in September 1941, resembled the Astaire vehicles of the 1930s, with emerging star Rita Hayworth in the place of Ginger Rogers. The plot contains the usual misunderstandings concerning just who loves whom, and the basic set-up, about a beautiful female dancer and a male choreographer/dancer who gets drafted into the army, provides lots of opportunities for Fred and Rita to dance. Military life does not seem to be very separate from civilian life. Rita gains access to Fred's military base with ease – it appears to be just down the road from New York and to contain more than adequate accommodations for Rita and her traveling party. Fred violates army policy at every turn and ends up in the guardhouse, which is, among other things, racially integrated and spacious enough to permit elaborate dance routines. It appears to be a far more comfortable place than the regular barracks, and getting in and out of it is relatively easy when it comes time for Fred to put on a camp show. The elaborate camp show features lots of beautiful chorus girls, who apparently have also made the trip from New York, as well as a large pit orchestra assembled seemingly from nowhere. The soldiers are a lovable bunch of guys, who do various comic bits such as double-talking, and they drill with a notable lack of urgency. Their uniforms come from World War I and look nothing like the uniforms that Americans will wear in the Pacific and North Africa only a few months later. No blood gets shed on any of the uniforms.[8]

Pearl Harbor made it harder to release a picture with such a relaxed and zany view of military life, although the chaotic life on the home front continued to be a perfect target for ridicule. Fred Astaire turned to musicals that did not attempt to make a connection with the war, such as *You Were Never Lovelier*, in which he teamed once again with Rita Hayworth. The advertisement for this 1942 picture touted Hayworth's "glowing beauty," Astaire's dancing ability, and the melodic perfection of the Jerome Kern score. The project was not totally divorced from the war. It took place in Buenos Aires – part of a deliberate outreach on the part of Hollywood to Latin America – which the Allies hoped to neutralize and keep out of German hands. Still, the setting was incidental to the plot, and the point was that viewers could sit back in their seats and look at Fred and Rita, who had never been lovelier.[9] About eight out of ten 1942 movies made no mention of the war, reflecting what critic

Bosley Crowther described as a period of "confusion and uncertainty," one in which Hollywood dodged the war by submerging it in the old routines.[10]

THE WAR MOVIE

It took until late 1942 for straight dramatic movies about the war, rather than musicals or comedies, to appear. Of 1,313 feature films released in the three years after Pearl Harbor, 374, a significant number, concerned some aspect of the war. The first wave of films dramatized the action in the South Pacific, such as *Wake Island,* which appeared in September 1942, and *Air Force* in 1943. Subsequent waves of films touched on the campaign in North Africa (*Sahara,* 1943) and finally the war in Europe.[11]

Although many of these movies strove for a documentary feel, bringing the action back home to America, they observed certain proprieties related to the war effort. The buffoonish top brass and drill sergeants of the 1941 films gave way to officers who bonded with their men and often fought alongside them. All of the social classes were in it together. So were Americans of every possible background, who were melded together into a cohesive force that fought on America's behalf. The crew with a Jew or Italian from Brooklyn, a country Baptist from the South, and a Lutheran farm boy from the Midwest became a new movie cliché. In these pictures, the overriding priority of the war sapped old grievances. A discontented John Garfield holds old grudges at the beginning of *Air Force,* but these evaporate when he flies into a decimated Pearl Harbor and gets swept up in the war.

In the war movies, uplift always predominated over pessimism. Defeats were temporary setbacks on the way to victory, an important message for Americans to hear in the first discouraging days of the war when it seemed as if the Japanese were capturing one Pacific Island after another. The movies, even those that strove for realism, portrayed the Japanese enemy as an immoral fighting force that refused to play by the rules and took advantage of America's generous and trusting nature. American soldiers pinned down on Pacific Islands held out beyond the limits of human endurance. The implication was that America would regroup, rearm, and defeat the Japanese on the new level playing field.

CASABLANCA

It took until the end of 1942 and the beginning of 1943 for Hollywood to produce *Casablanca,* the ideal war picture that both entertained the audience and interpreted the war to the American people. The picture starred Humphrey Bogart, a new leading man who would show up as a top box office star during the war and remain an audience favorite until his death in 1957. The emergence of Bogart showed how Hollywood coped with the most critical wartime shortage – the absence of leading men. It simply recruited new ones, in the case of Bogart, from its own ranks.

In *Casablanca* the chance elements of writing, casting, and filming came together with current events in an appealing way.[12] With the picture ready for release, the city of Casablanca became a focal point of World War II when the Allies invaded North Africa in November 1942. This battle brought new attention to the relatively obscure Moroccan port city that increased exponentially in January 1943, when Roosevelt and Churchill met there to discuss the progress of the war and to declare their goal of unconditional surrender on the part of the Germans.

Warner Brothers used all of the attention to boost the picture. It held the world premiere of the picture in Casablanca itself before a military audience. Hedda Hopper wrote approvingly that it was "not only dramatic but highly appropriate" to open the movie "in the city where its story is being fulfilled."[13] At the end of November, the company gave the picture its domestic release in New York as a film for the holiday season. Then the story of the Casablanca conference broke, and a Washington journalist declared Casablanca to be the "hottest word in the English or any other language." Warner Brothers decided to move *Casablanca* ahead of its other pictures and put it on its main screens across the country. In little more than a week after the Casablanca conference, the movie opened in Washington, DC, and elsewhere. In the capital city, one could see the picture on a bill with a newsreel devoted to the Casablanca conference, along with a Walt Disney cartoon in which Donald Duck exhorted Americans to pay their income tax.[14]

The picture probably did not need the box office bonanza brought by the fortunate timing of its release to succeed, but it helped. Hollywood, which had seemed to be out of sync with the war and overtaken by the urgency of current events, showed it was limber enough to deliver relevant entertainment in a timely manner. The picture itself contained a highly stylized version of recent history. The story, in which Humphrey Bogart and Ingrid Bergman fall in love in Paris and then meet again in Casablanca, has become familiar to generations of Americans – particularly the parents of the baby boomers and the baby boomers themselves – who can recite the movie's catch phrases, such as "we'll always have

Paris" or "this could be the start of a beautiful friendship." One's first viewing of *Casablanca* continues to be a generational rite of passage. The picture endures as one of the screen's great romances; it is often shown on television on Valentine's Day.

Contemporary audiences appreciated the movie's romance but also were stirred by the film's patriotism. Humphrey Bogart plays a hard-edged, pragmatic American who runs a saloon/café and gambling casino in Casablanca but who personally takes no precipitous actions without evaluating the odds. He has had an idealistic past, having dabbled in the Spanish civil war, run guns to the Ethiopians in their battle with the Italians, lived in Paris, and fallen in love with Ingrid Bergman. The affair with Ingrid remains a tarnished memory in his mind, one that the Germans have spoiled because their occupation of Paris has sent Bogart into flight, and he and Ingrid have somehow missed connections. Bogart resettles in the remote location of Casablanca, hoping to escape from his previous passions and take money from both sides in the world conflict. In this regard, he is not unlike the American people of the 1930s, who had their European fling during World War I, and it ended badly, with no world peace or prosperity. With the approach of World War II, they have decided to hunker down, remain neutral, and try to stay on good terms with both sides. Other countries can gamble. Americans will take the house odds.

Bogart learns that it is difficult to escape from moral responsibility. Morocco is under the nominal control of the French, but France is under German occupation, and the Vichy government in charge of Morocco is a puppet of Germany's. People come to Casablanca hoping to flee from the conflict, as Bogart has done. While Bogart remains in his Moroccan limbo, others with political or personal reasons for wanting to get out of German-occupied territory seek papers that will allow them to leave Casablanca, travel to Lisbon, and from there go on to a safe haven – such as the still neutral America. Bogart does what he can for people in desperate need but does not stick his neck out and attract the attention and animosity of the German or Vichy authorities. He resembles President Roosevelt in his second term, observing the terms of the 1935 Neutrality Act but making occasional sidewise gestures to the English and their allies.

Soon, however, the conflict comes to Bogart. People who face torture and death in custody get arrested in his casino, and the tensions between the Germans and the French break out within his saloon. As the visiting German officer sings one of his country's patriotic songs, the crowd at

Rick's café starts to sing "La Marseillaise," timidly at first and then in a rising wave of emotion. They make it clear that their sympathies lie with Free France, not Vichy France. The incident proves disturbing enough to the authorities that they shut down Bogart's business, showing just how hard it is for him to remain neutral and ignore the political situation. The incidents in Rick's café bear some resemblance to the way in which the United States, while trying to maintain its neutrality, nonetheless got into shooting matches with the Germans, even before Pearl Harbor.

Bogart's past catches up with him when Ingrid Bergman and her husband, a leader of the Czech resistance to Nazi occupation, show up in his establishment, to the bittersweet strains of "As Time Goes By" on the piano. Ingrid and her husband need papers to get out of the country, which Bogart just happens to have. At first, he holds to his old caution and nurses his old resentments, but Bergman has a way of unleashing his old idealism and passion. In the end, he does the right thing by taking a stand opposing the Germans, coming to the aid of Bergman and her husband, who are doing battle on behalf of the free world, and leaving his limbo in Casablanca to join the Free French.

In this way, Bogart, like the United States, has abandoned his neutrality, not for self-serving gain, because his change of heart will mean a financial sacrifice, and not for selfish love, because he has let Ingrid Bergman go off with her husband. Rather he has learned that one cannot escape the specter of evil in the world, that there is no place to hide. Try as one might to flee, trouble will always catch up, just as it soon will with America at Pearl Harbor. As the hero of an Alfred Hitchcock picture had said the year before, the world is choosing up sides, and there is no question that America belongs on the side of the Allies. Having made that commitment, the Americans, in the manner of Humphrey Bogart, will bring their sensible outlook and pragmatic skills to the conflict, cleaning up the situation and leaving behind a better world.

The action in *Casablanca* takes place within a compressed time frame from the fall of Paris in June 1940 to just before Pearl Harbor in December 1941. How Humphrey Bogart manages to set up such a thriving business in such a short time remains something of a mystery, but of course everyone comes to Rick's. In a symbolic sense, the movie interprets the actions of the United States in its debate over neutrality from 1935 to 1941 and, more broadly, from the battle over the League of Nations in 1919 through the Depression. The picture accomplishes its mission, without allowing the propaganda to intrude for a minute on the romance or suspense, nicely demonstrating the capabilities of the Hollywood studio system at a time of war.

As with nearly every movie, the elements that went into the making of *Casablanca* were near things, beginning with the star. The studio, in this case Warner Brothers, constantly moved directors, actors, and other creative talent from one project to another according to the contingencies of the moment. In April 1942, for example, the studio announced that because Ronald Reagan was scheduled to go into the army on the nineteenth of the month, Humphrey Bogart would take his place on the *Casablanca* project, playing opposite Michele Morgan, in a cast that would also include Ann Sheridan and Dennis Morgan. As things turned out, only Bogart made it into the final production, and Ingrid Bergman took over from Michele Morgan.[15] As in all artistic products, the movie reflected the creative choices of its creators. Only in retrospect did these choices seem inevitable.

THE LONG RISE OF HUMPHREY BOGART

Humphrey Bogart was no sure thing to play a romantic lead. At the time of *Casablanca*'s release, Bogart was forty-three years old, a little long in the tooth for a screen lover at that time. His career reflected a unique path through Broadway and Hollywood, with his final success assured by the disruption of the war.[16]

Bogart came from an upper-class New York background, of Dutch stock, with a society doctor father and a talented artist mother. In an indication of his genteel upbringing, his parents sent him off first to the Trinity School and then to Andover for high school. His bad behavior and poor grades led to his dismissal from Andover. He decided to join the navy, just at the time of World War I, serving on mine sweepers in the Atlantic. The move turned out to be important for his career, since it established his military credentials and made it easier for him to pass up active duty in World War II. Returning home, Bogart drifted into a life in the theater during the 1920s.

Working fairly steadily, he left a small mark in the annals of Broadway. Theatrical notes from the *New York Times* declared in January 1923 that he had been engaged to join the cast of a comedy called *Mary the 3rd*. The following year he received some notoriety for his performance in a play called *Nerves* – his sixth professional appearance on the stage – about a group of Long Island socialites (shades of *The Great Gatsby*), who go off to fly wartime missions in France.

Bogart played one of the preppie young men about to be sobered by the realities of war, in a performance that the *Times* called "dry and fresh." The next season found him in another comedy called *The Cradle Snatchers*, earning him the accolade of "pleasing."[17]

While in this show, he married an actress he had met in one of his first stage appearances. Although the couple first got a marriage license in 1922, they waited until 1926 to be married. Bogart's father, said to be traveling in Peru, failed to attend the ceremony. Most of the guests came from the world of the theater. The marriage lasted little more than a year, since Bogart's wife felt that he put the demands of his career above those of his marriage. This initial failure did not stop him from marrying another actress less than a year later.[18]

Humphrey Bogart, a reliable Broadway player at the time of the movies' transition to sound, became a logical target of the talent raids that the movies were making on Broadway. In April 1930, word came that several studios were bidding for his services, with Fox eventually winning the competition. Others snared by the studio included reliable character actor Nat Pendleton, who would appear with Abbott and Costello in *Buck Privates*.[19]

Bogart went to Hollywood and began to grind out pictures for Fox. Movies with Bogart in the cast, always in a minor role, came out on March 14, March 30, and May 30, 1931. In none of these pictures, one of which was a western, did Bogart make much of an impression. Unlike Katharine Hepburn or Groucho Marx, Humphrey Bogart failed to achieve instant success in the movies, nor did he find a comfortable place within the studio, as Fred Astaire did with RKO. Bogart came and went. By the end of the year, Bogart was back on Broadway, appearing in a play with Helen Hayes.[20]

Bogart went from part to part from 1932 until he had a breakout performance at the beginning of 1935 in Robert Sherwood's *The Petrified Forest*. In the same year that the Marx brothers made *Night at the Opera* and Fred Astaire released *Top Hat*, Bogart scored a triumph on Broadway with his portrayal of a gangster named Duke Mantee. Leslie Howard played the lead, a failed writer tramping through the Southwestern desert who stops at an Arizona café and filling station, only to encounter the fierce Duke Mantee, who is running away from the cops. Mantee, a criminal with a sense of fair play and honor, holds Leslie Howard and the family that runs the filling station hostage. Howard gets the idea that he can perform a noble act for the daughter of the family, who wants to get away from Arizona and see her mother in

Paris, by having Mantee shoot him, leaving the money from an insurance policy to the daughter.[21]

The play led to a turn-about in Bogart's career and a second chance at Hollywood. Warner Brothers bought the film rights to *The Petrified Forest* and decided to keep Leslie Howard in the lead. Howard already had a track record in Hollywood, and he had already appeared with Bette Davis, who played the female lead in the picture. Apparently at Howard's urging, the studio also agreed to have Bogart, rather than someone already under contract such as Edward G. Robinson, reprise his role in the picture. Howard made a great show of public support for Bogart, telling one Hollywood columnist that in the play he often had his back to Bogart and could not watch him act. When he saw a preview of the movie, Howard said, he realized "what great acting [Bogart] does."[22]

Released at the beginning of 1936, *The Petrified Forest* earned good notices from the critics. Howard and Davis came in for particular praise, but the critics did not neglect Bogart. The *Times* critic voted him "a large measure of praise" for his portrayal "of a psychopathic gangster more like Dillinger than the outlaw himself." Warner Brothers put Bogart under contract.[23]

For the next four years, Bogart appeared in one film after another, often in the role of the villain, since his performance in *The Petrified Forest* typecast him as a menacing figure. He became a member of the Warner Brothers stock company, along with such players as Edward G. Robinson, James Cagney, Paul Muni, Ann Sheridan, and Bette Davis. Unlike in his sojourn at Fox, he managed to stick with Warner Brothers, but he was not yet a star, someone who could carry the lead in an important picture. The studio saw no reason to change the way it handled Bogart, who naturally hoped for bigger and better roles, yet who remained gainfully employed making movies in Hollywood. He was not handsome, like the dashing Errol Flynn, nor quite as distinctive looking or sounding as the short, squat Edward G. Robinson, with his rat-a-tat verbal delivery, nor as energetic or talented as song and dance man James Cagney.

Bogart's studio had enough leading men. With his slight lisp and imperfect features, Bogart had to make his mark as a supporting player and hope that someone would notice him. But even rave notices, such as one for the 1937 *The Great O'Malley* that called him "one of the finest actors on the screen or off," who "cuts to the heart of a characterization with the art of a great surgeon," failed to stir the studio. It looked as though Bogart had found his niche as "the screen's most rational bad man" in the era of Bette Davis, Pat O'Brien, and others. He settled into the Hollywood community, buying a house with a swimming pool in November 1937 and reporting for duty in picture after picture.[24]

More of the same followed. Bogart supported Edward G. Robinson in *The Amazing Dr. Clitterhouse* (1938) and James Cagney in *Angels with Dirty Faces* (1938). He starred in some B movies along with second-string Warner Brothers actors such as George Brent, with whom he made *Racket Busters* (1938), a picture based in part on the exploits of New York district attorney and future presidential candidate Thomas Dewey. In the role as the boss of the rackets, Bogart earned good notices. The *Times* called him "tops, as usual." Another critic described Bogart "as a dish of pure poison in criminal parts" who "does his role to order, although it is not an especially fat one."[25]

BOGART BECOMES A STAR

Bogart finally caught a break. In July 1940, Louella Parsons told her readers that the distinguished actor Paul Muni, who had made *I Am a Fugitive from a Chain Gang* and a number of prestigous biography pictures, was leaving Warner Brothers. Muni, who thought of himself as an actor in the grand tradition, objected to being assigned to a gangster movie rather than to *The Life of Beethoven*, which the studio believed would not make money. With Muni on the way out, the studio "discovered Humphrey Bogart," according to Louella, "and from now on he is going to be one of their top men."[26]

If that were true, Bogart came with considerable baggage. He did not possess a fresh face, having been in and around Hollywood for a decade, and he carried an automatic association with criminal types. He also had a number of completed pictures awaiting distribution, and these were the usual gangster and criminal films. In the summer of 1940, a further complication arose, when a supposed chief functionary of the Communist Party in Los Angeles testified before a Los Angeles grand jury that Humphrey Bogart was a Communist sympathizer who contributed $150 a month to Communist causes. The matter was cleared up quickly when Martin Dies, the chairman of the House Un-American Activities Committee, made a public statement that Bogart, along with James Cagney and Frederic March, was a patriotic American, not a Communist.[27] Despite the strong way in which the Hollywood studios rallied around their stars, the incident marked Bogart as a member of the Hollywood left, acceptable in 1940 with Roosevelt running for a third term, but less acceptable later.

In *High Sierra*, released at the beginning of 1941, Bogart's character Roy Earle, just released from the penitentiary, contemplates retirement, but his criminal associates have lined up one more job for him. At some level, Bogart knows that despite his desires for an ordinary life, he cannot escape from the rush toward death that is the fate of someone with his past. On a hillside in the high sierras, he makes his final stand against the police, an isolated gunman from an era that has already passed, faced with impossible odds and the inevitability of failure but clinging to an instinct for survival and a doomed sense of hope. The picture works because of Bogart's ability to convey complex and contrary emotions and also because of the relationship he has established with the movie audience as a hard-working gangster. The picture signals his possible retirement as a gangster and the beginning of something else that will make use of his past resume.[28]

With two strong performances to his credit, Bogart earned a promotion within the studio hierarchy, at just the moment World War II was starting. Just as Paul Muni's departure made it possible for Bogart to get the part of Roy Earle, the disruption in the studio caused by the war also worked in his favor. Unlike younger actors such as Ronald Reagan, Bogart, in his forties and with previous service in World War I, was not likely to get drafted, nor did he have a desire to enlist. This situation meant the studio could depend on him being around for the duration.

Humphrey Bogart got star billing in *The Maltese Falcon* (1941), and he got to kiss Mary Astor. In the picture, he played more of a cop than a robber in the role of private detective Sam Spade. As a private investigator, he occupied a space in between the police and the criminals, not always following the letter of the law but observing his own code of good conduct. Sam Spade, like all of Bogart's characters, possessed flaws, such as greed and a susceptibility to pretty women. Not above sleeping with his partner's wife, he nonetheless felt honor-bound to avenge his partner's death.[29]

Although the picture did not receive a very big build-up, the tightly made movie came as a pleasant surprise for those expecting the usual Warner Brothers feature. Bosley Crowther pronounced it the "best mystery thriller of the year," and he advised moviegoers not to miss it, "Far from being just a routine cops-and-robbers or a normal Warner Brothers 'muscle film,' it is a distinguished excursion into a world of mystifying criminal intrigue." Bogart received strong notices, and the public appeared willing to accept him as a romantic lead. He was on his way toward establishing the hard-bitten, cynical, yet idealistic character that would become his new trademark. When George Raft, another veteran of the Warner Brothers Company who had turned down the leads in both *High Sierra* and *The Maltese Falcon* went to see *The Maltese Falcon*, he realized that Bogart had overtaken him in the Warner hierarchy.[30]

With *The Maltese Falcon*, Bogart got more than a good role. He also began to gather a company of talented writers, directors, and actors around him. The picture helped to cement his relationship with first-time director John Huston, the son of talented actor Walter Huston, who would go on to direct many of Bogart's important pictures. Huston's wartime absence made it possible for Bogart also to forge a relationship with Howard Hawks, another director who would be important in his career. *The Maltese Falcon* featured Peter Lorre and Sydney Greenstreet, two foreigners who found themselves in Hollywood at the outbreak of war and who would make many movies together, several with Bogart.

At the start of World War II, Bogart stood on the threshold of super-stardom, and *Casablanca*, the quintessential war film, put him over the top. In May 1942, just before filming of *Casablanca* was set to begin, John L. Warner saw a preview of *Across the Pacific*, another John Huston–Humphrey Bogart collaboration, with Lorre and Greenstreet in the cast. He cabled back to the Warner publicity department that the "reaction of audience ... convinces me beyond a shadow of a doubt that Humphrey Bogart is one of our biggest stars." Warner saw Bogart as his studio's Clark Gable.[31]

The publicity department worked overtime to concentrate attention on Bogart. Even his flaws, such as his embittered, alcohol-fueled marriage to actress Mayo Methot, his third wife, were portrayed as virtues. An article about the "Battling Bogarts" detailed the constant fights that marked the marriage, but implied that these fights were somehow good for the relationship.[32]

HUMPHREY BOGART AS HOLLYWOOD CITIZEN

Humphrey Bogart had a good war. He captured the nation's attention at just the right time to become the movie industry's face of World War II. When President Roosevelt traveled to Casablanca, people joked that "he flew over to Africa to see a Warner Brothers picture." When Humphrey Bogart fired his gun, he generally hit his target – a new symbol of his potency. He also gained marginal advantage in his relationship with the studio. In the usual manner, Warner Brothers wanted to capitalize on

Bogart's popularity and put him in as many pictures as possible. Bogart held out for a vacation between projects and got further in his protests than he had before. When the *Motion Picture Herald* released its survey of the top moneymaking stars of 1943, it placed Bogart seventh on the list. The previous year he had been twenty-fifth. A few weeks later, *Casablanca* won the Academy Award as the best movie of 1943 in a ceremony that, in the spirit of the times, replaced the usual fancy dinner party with a formal presentation at Grauman's Chinese Theatre, with the public invited to attend at $10 a head.[33]

With fame came responsibility. Bogart, already a high-profile political figure in Hollywood with his support for the Democrats and President Roosevelt, accepted his obligation to appear as a spokesman for the war effort and the various charities associated with it. He filmed a pitch for the Red Cross 1944 War Fund that was shown in theaters to motivate patrons to give money to ushers who circulated through the audience with Red Cross coin boxes. Paul Muni, Paul Robeson, and Bogart – a perfectly ecumenical trio of a Jew, a black, and a WASP – made a short movie that was screened in 500 theaters as part of the seventh annual drive of the Manhattan Committee of the Greater New York Fund. Bogart contributed time to short motivational films intended to inspire people to buy war bonds, appearing always in a prominent position among the other Hollywood stars. In November 1943, he and his wife went on a ten-week trip to visit the troops in Africa and Italy, giving shows and touring hospitals. On his return, he made a short subject called "Report from the Front" at the request of the Office of War Information.[34]

In using his celebrity in this manner, Bogart showed his solidarity with the war effort and also conformed to the accepted behavior: Hollywood stars were expected to use their celebrity to raise money for the war.[35] Hyped as altruism, such appearances were part of the business.[36]

BOB HOPE

Bob Hope, who was ranked second in the 1943 poll of stars, became the model of the wartime Hollywood performer who put his talent in the government's service and reaped personal rewards. Born in England in 1903 and raised in Cleveland, Hope followed the vaudeville-Broadway-radio road to stardom.[37] He could sing and dance and tell jokes, perfecting a rapid-fire delivery and a quick recovery that made him a master of stand-up comedy. Like Jack Benny, he specialized in the master of ceremonies role in variety shows, using his comic skills to smooth the transition from one act to another.

After success on Broadway in the mid-1930s, notably in the Jerome Kern musical *Roberta* that later became a vehicle for Fred Astaire and Ginger Rogers, Hope turned his attention to the movies. He had already made short subjects but had not developed the momentum for a full-fledged movie career. In August 1937, Paramount Studios announced that it had bought a Damon Runyon story to serve as a vehicle to introduce Bob Hope. Before this film was made, however, Hope gave a breakout appearance in *The Big Broadcast of 1938*, singing his future theme song, "Thanks for the Memories," in a duet with Shirley Ross. W. C. Fields had the lead in the movie, but Hope got considerable notice.

In the fall of 1938, Hope was given his own half-hour radio program (he had been a guest star on a number of shows), and in November of that year, Hedda Hopper wrote, "I believe that in less than six months Bob will be the biggest personality on the air." His radio show, sponsored by Pepsodent toothpaste, became a Tuesday night institution, challenging and occasionally surpassing Jack Benny in the ratings.[38]

By 1938, Hope had established a hard-working routine in which he made movies for Paramount, appeared on the radio for Pepsodent and NBC, gave personal appearances, and wrote books. What distinguished him from others was that he was successful in every one of these endeavors. Unlike Jack Benny, who made movies for Warner Brothers and Paramount and enjoyed a certain amount of film stardom in the war years, Bob Hope became a top-flight movie star. He developed a screen persona as a character whose blustery self-confidence and bravery, advancing and retreating from situations with a rapidly delivered comic patter, evaporated at the first sign of real danger. Like Lou Costello, he used his facial expressions and expressive body language – he had the athleticism of many great comedians – to sell his jokes. Where Jack Benny was good looking in a bland sort of way, Hope was also handsome in the manner of a Broadway leading man, but with a prominent ski-slope nose that marked him as a comic player rather than as a romantic lead.

As with Humphrey Bogart and Abbott and Costello, the war played a prominent part in Bob Hope's career from its very beginnings. In August 1939, Hope decided to take a European cruise, taking along the script for what eventually became *The Road to Singapore*, the first of his famous Road pictures with Bing Crosby. It was a glamorous crossing on the French liner *Normandie*, with Hope in the company of movie stars

Norma Shearer, Charles Boyer, and George Raft and Treasury Secretary
Henry Morgenthau. The return crossing on the British ship *Queen Mary*
at the beginning of September coincided with the outbreak of the war,
and the ship sailed with business tycoons J.P. Morgan and Leonard
Firestone and an overload of passengers anxious to flee Europe. Ten
men slept on cots in the ship's library, and forty women crowded into
the tea dance room. Hope gave up the space he had reserved, except for
his bedroom, in order to accommodate the crowd.[39]

The *Road to Singapore* opened on March 14, 1940.[40] A breezy comedy,
it teamed up Hope and Crosby, who became one of the great screen
couples. Although Hope was the comedian of the pair, Crosby got his
share of laugh lines, with Hope playing the straight man. They were
Groucho and Chico, topping one another, rather than Abbott and
Costello, with a straight man and a comic. Like Groucho and Chico,
they were both con men, but with Hope as the more trusting of the
two (the Costello and not the Abbott in this regard). Although Crosby
was the singer of the pair, Hope sang his share of the songs and showed
a particular talent for harmonizing with Crosby. In each of the pictures,
they took turns chasing Dorothy Lamour, the sexy female lead, who also
got to sing the occasional song. More often than not, Bing won the
girl. Often cast as touring performers, Hope and Crosby did dance routines, with Hope displaying his considerable talent as a dancer and often
taking the lead in physical comedy stunts such as being shot out of a
cannon or walking a tightrope.

In the accepted manner of the 1940s, neither Hope nor Crosby played
ethnic. Like Abbott and Costello, they were cast as generic Americans
who, like America itself, found themselves exploring the world. They
had none of Bogart's alienation. Their stints abroad were simply performing gigs in out-of-the-way places, and they had every hope of getting back
home.

The places they visited, such as Morocco and Singapore, figured in
the war, but as in the Fred Astaire musicals of the time, the war was off
in the distance. In the *Road to Utopia*, released at the end of the war,
the setting was Alaska, where many troops were stationed, but the time
was the turn of the century. The settings for the pictures, such as
Zanzibar or the South Seas, reflected places on the movie map, not the
political map.

The humor played on Hope and Crosby's contemporary identities as
movie and radio stars, with, for example, people crossing the screen and
announcing that they were simply making their way from one sound

stage to another, or with Hope describing Crosby as a cheese salesman (as he was on the Kraft Music Hall). In *The Road to Utopia*, humorist Robert Benchley interrupted the action to explain the rough edges of the plot, although he admitted that the studio had added material to the picture that he had not seen.

Like the Abbott and Costello pictures, the Road pictures became popular just before the war and retained their popularity in the war and immediate postwar years. *The Road to Zanzibar*, the African safari picture, opened in New York in April 1941. Some 68,000 people crowded into theaters that Easter weekend.[41]

Such success naturally fed the demand for a sequel, but there were fewer Road pictures than, say, Marx brothers or Abbott and Costello pictures. Abbott and Costello always appeared together – they were a single performing entity. The remarkable thing about Hope and Crosby was that they each had their own radio programs and their own thriving independent film careers – they were both huge individual stars during the war. They were a flexible team in the manner of Hepburn and Tracy, each free to pursue his separate career but forever linked in the public mind so that, in their independent appearances, they made jokes about one another.

If anything, Crosby was a bigger wartime star than Hope. On the strength of his comedies with Bob Hope and sentimental films like *Going My Way* (1944) in which he played a priest in an urban setting far removed from the war and for which he won a best actor Oscar, Crosby rose to the top of the exhibitors' poll of movie stars in 1944 and 1945.[42]

Crosby projected a relaxed, casual, and unruffled image that the audience found soothing and reassuring in a period of international conflict. He played to this image by recording songs such as Irving Berlin's "White Christmas," which was featured in a 1942 movie (*Holiday Inn*) with Fred Astaire. The song provided a powerful nostalgic image of what was right with America and supplied a subliminal rationale for fighting to preserve the American way of life. It was, as composer Irving Berlin noted, "a peace song in war time." People found it very moving, with its reminder that, even as the war was bogged down in the South Pacific, it would assure a future in which Americans would celebrate white Christmases, just as they had done in the past. Christmas, a religious holiday whose modern origins lay in Germany, had become part of a secular celebration of America.[43]

Hope and Crosby, like Bogart, recognized the necessity of making public appearances to support the war and entertain the troops. Outside

of those actors on active duty, Bob Hope, whose age and family responsibilities kept him out of the draft, became the American entertainer most
closely associated with the war effort. On May 6, 1941, during the preparedness period, he decided to broadcast his radio program from a
military base. After one week back in the studio, before a sluggish civilian
crowd, he opted to take his show on the road on a permanent basis,
beginning a stint that lasted throughout the war.[44]

Hope became a headliner on what might be described as the wartime
vaudeville circuit. By the fall of 1941, 186 army and navy theaters existed
in bases across the country, and the circuit soon expanded to cover the
Americans stationed abroad in places like Bermuda, Newfoundland,
the Caribbean, and England. By the spring of 1943, there were some
119 overseas units entertaining troops, most of them small ensembles
that could be shipped easily from one location to another. Hope toured
with his sidekick Jerry Colonna and singer Frances Langford. He made
a trip to the Aleutian Islands in October 1942, although during the trip
the company returned to Seattle so that Hope could do his broadcast.
Eventually he traveled throughout the theaters of war in North Africa,
Europe, and the South Pacific. Often, as in Sicily, he performed very
close to the front lines, and always visited the men in the hospital. By the
fall of 1943, *Time Magazine* called Hope the one "legend" to emerge
during the war.[45]

Hope proved indefatigable. In a typical gesture, he joined the
Hollywood Victory Caravan that left Los Angeles for Washington, DC,
in April 1942. The large entourage, including Crosby, Cagney, Cary
Grant, and many others, had tea at the White House. On this American
tour, Hope not only performed as the master of ceremonies for the show
and encouraged people to buy war bonds, but he also did his weekly
radio show wherever he happened to be. Hedda Hopper announced in
August 1942 that Bob Hope was cutting down on his motion picture
schedule so that he could appear in more army camps. He still managed
to make his share of pictures, do his broadcast, and play benefit
golf matches with Bing Crosby for the benefit of the Red Cross and war
relief.[46]

BOGART AND BACALL

The war had personal consequences in Hollywood that went beyond
who played the lead in a particular picture. Humphrey Bogart was an
important case in point. When Humphrey Bogart came home from his

troop tour in Italy, he began work on a movie, *To Have and Have Not*, directed by Howard Hawks, that was an unofficial sequel to *Casablanca*. Once again Bogart plays the cynical American, this time working as a fishing boat captain, who lives in a French colony, this time in the Caribbean. To underscore the basic decency of Bogart's Captain Harry Morgan, the picture focuses on his relationship with Eddie, his friend and second mate played by character actor Walter Brennan doing his best to steal the picture from Bogart. Eddie, overly fond of drink and past his prime, is, in the modern idiom, high maintenance, yet Morgan stands by him, to the point of endangering himself out of a sense of loyalty. *To Have and Have Not* was based on a book by Hemingway – hence the emphasis on loyalty and on performing one's duty without complaint – and was shot from a script by William Faulkner, an unlikely sort of collaboration between two Nobel Prize–winning authors.[47]

Director Howard Hawks decided to put one of his new discoveries, a fashion model billed on the screen as Lauren Bacall, in the part of the girl who finds herself on the Caribbean island and meets and falls in love with Bogart.[48] Unlike in *Casablanca*, Bogart gets to keep the girl, after *he* does the honorable thing by buying her a plane ticket out of the French colony and *she* demonstrates her love for him by not using the plane ticket and remaining by his side instead.

Earlier in his career, Bogart had failed to land the romantic lead in a picture with Bette Davis because another actor was having an affair with her. At this point in his career, as the most important actor on the lot, Bogart got to make love to Lauren Bacall in *To Have and Have Not*. Bogart, still one of the Battling Bogarts and married to Mayo Methot, fell in love with his new co-star. As the world war entered its final phases, Bogart and Bacall became a hot couple who captivated the nation's attention. It was a sign that the nation was beginning to look past the war and turn its attention to more frivolous pastimes.

Would Bogey divorce his wife and marry Bacall? The nation's gossip columnists and Hollywood reporters speculated endlessly on this question. Hedda Hopper reported on October 26, 1944, that "Now that the Humphrey Bogarts have admitted my tip on the air was true and they've separated you can expect Laurena Ball [sic] to be the next Mrs. B. Pals are saying she got her man both on the screen and off." The romance coincided with the 1944 presidential election in which Bogart had a speaking part as an articulator of liberal wisdom – "skin color doesn't matter a thing." He moderated a radio show in support of FDR right before the election. Hedda speculated that his temporary reconciliation

with Mayo was "an armistice till the campaign was over." She kept the
item alive through the New Year, reminding her readers that "if Lauren
Bacall eventually becomes Mrs. Bogart, there'll only be a little matter of
26 years between them." That spring, the season of the victory in
Europe, came word that Mayo Methot had obtained a divorce from
Bogart, and the next day Bogart announced that he would marry
Bacall. On May 22, 1945, Humphrey Bogart and Lauren Bacall were
married in a three-minute ceremony held in the Mansfield, Ohio, home of
novelist Louis Bromfield.[49]

It was the most famous wartime marriage. Lauren Bacall became
Humphrey Bogart's ultimate wartime trophy, and since they were both
in the movie business, they became a screen couple before they settled
down and contributed to the postwar baby boom by having children. If
the war proved that Americans had a common identity that superseded
their ethnic, racial, and generational differences, then Bogart and Bacall
embodied the wartime lessons. He was of old Dutch stock; she was a
Jewish girl from Brooklyn. He had been married three times; she had
never been married. More than a generation separated them. He had
served in World War I, and she had been born six years after the
Armistice. He looked every one of his forty-five years; she had the
flawless look of youth. Yet the nation tolerated this mixed marriage
because it regarded Hollywood as a fantasy world, and few people
begrudged Humphrey Bogart, who had done so much for the country
during the war, anything.

CONCLUSION

The Bogart and Bacall marriage, like the movie *Casablanca*, illustrated
how Hollywood served as a means of escape for the American people
during the war and also inspired the American people to fight in a
common cause. Abbott and Costello and Bob Hope provided comedies,
and Humphrey Bogart supplied uplifting melodramas. Each of these
show business figures positioned themselves in the 1930s to be the
major stars of the 1940s. The comedians used the radio as a means of
making a connection with the American people. Humphrey Bogart used
the studio system. In the case of Hope and Bogart, it was the war that
put them over the top. Bogart, for example, changed his screen identity
to fit wartime responsibilities while building on a relationship with
the audience that the studio and the serendipity of available roles had
already established.

Each of the new stars recognized that the boundaries between one's public and private lives were thinner than ever. To act the star meant making public appearances for wartime charities and on behalf of the United States government, the most important charitable cause of all. The stars conveyed the message that public sacrifice would translate into private gain. For the general public, that transformation would occur in the postwar era. For Hollywood and its wartime stars, the gains were immediate.

6

The Postwar Movie Scene

In a 1960 movie, Jack Lemmon comes home to an empty apartment, defrosts a TV dinner, and, using a device that enables him to flip from channel to channel, turns on the television. Westerns are playing on station after station, but Lemmon is delighted to find that the movie *Grand Hotel* (1932) with Greta Garbo is being shown. As he settles down to relax and enjoy himself, commercials for things like dentures twice interrupt the presentation, even before it begins. He turns off the television in disgust. The moral: television makes movies unwatchable.

POSTWAR PROBLEMS

In the postwar era, motion picture executives worried that television made movies unwatched, not just unwatchable. In what for many businesses was a prosperous postwar era, the movies experienced reduced profits and a declining box office. Three interrelated factors contributed to the decline. Television provided a cheaper and more convenient alternative to movies (after purchasing the set, it was essentially free), particularly in families that were largely housebound because of the presence of young children. Judicial rulings required the studios to divest themselves of their theaters, and that made businesses such as MGM less lucrative operations. Finally, the growth of suburbs put the movie industry, with its downtown movie palaces, at a disadvantage.

Public policy, long a factor in the industry's growth, no longer worked to the movies' advantage. The regulatory impulse in the executive branch, and the publicity-seeking investigative impulse in the legislative branch, became reinvigorated after the war. The Justice Department geared up its anti-trust actions against the movie industry, reviving old complaints that the studios engaged in restraint of trade in their dealings with exhibitors. In May 1948, the Supreme Court ended a long period of uncertainty and handed down three decisions that weakened the studio system. As a result, the major studios had to divest themselves of their theater holdings and function only as production and distribution companies. Simply put, movies were less profitable businesses to be in after these decisions than they were in an earlier era when studios had guaranteed outlets for their products. For example, the studios could no longer require exhibitors to take a whole slate of their pictures. Instead, exhibitors bid for each picture on its commercial merits. Rather than being well-oiled machines that produced a picture each week, the studios eventually became companies that made deals with independent directors, producers, actors, and exhibitors to create and distribute movies.

Congressional investigation of movies, on hold during the war, also acquired a new life after V-J Day. Control over such vital matters as what constituted decency in motion pictures lay in state, local, or judicial hands. Congress got involved at a more global level, holding hearings on whether the movies compromised national security because studios put creative decisions in the hands of Communists or Communist sympathizers. The postwar era marked a reconsideration of the wartime alliance with the Soviets and the beginnings of a cold war between the United States and Russia. It therefore appeared natural for the House Un-American Activities Committee, on the alert to links between the movie industry and Soviet communism, to resume its prewar investigation of Hollywood in the summer of 1947.[1] Pictures made to support the war effort, such as *Mission to Moscow* and *The North Star* (both 1943), looked in retrospect to be forms of Communist propaganda.

The Red Scare and the Supreme Court decisions may have had only an indirect effect on the box office in the 1940s, but by any measure, box office receipts fell. In 1946, with the economy facing many bottlenecks and uncertainties, the movie-going habits of the war years persisted. The next year, however, profits dropped from $122 million in 1946 to $89 million in 1947. In the longer run, the total number of moviegoers declined 73.4 percent between 1946 and 1962.[2]

Looked at another way, television or some other feature of postwar life had robbed the movies of close to half their audience by 1953. Declining box office meant that many theaters – perhaps a quarter of all theaters – closed. Cutbacks in the number of pictures and in the budget for the typical picture became the norm in the once opulent and recession-resistant movie business.[3]

THE INDUSTRY RESPONDS

As it became clearer in the 1950s that television was the main competition, the movies tried to differentiate their products from the typical television program. That suggested a new strategy: the studios might produce fewer movies than they did when they were feeding the weekly viewing habit, but among those movies would be must-see spectaculars. Technicolor pictures made with new wide-screen processes such as Cinemascope and recorded in stereophonic sound found a prominent place on the industry's postwar agenda. In March 1953, for example, studio chief Darryl Zanuck ordered all films at Twentieth Century Fox to be made in Cinemascope. He reached that decision mindful of the fact that not all movies were amenable to this treatment. It worked well for big epic films such as *The Robe* (1953), but less well for "intimate comedies or small-scale domestic stories."[4] The character-driven screwball comedies of the 1930s were less likely to be made in the 1950s.

The studios could charge more for a big picture like *The Robe*, but the increased ticket prices could not compensate for the other factors that were softening the demand for movies. As a result, studios cut back on their overhead by, among other things, restricting long-term contracts and reducing the number of actors they employed on a permanent basis. In 1947, an estimated 742 actors were under contract to the studios. By 1956, that number had fallen to 220. In April 1951, as part of the prevailing trend, Warner Brothers fired 6 percent of its employees.[5] The great Louis B. Mayer, the personification of the studio system, left Metro Goldwyn Mayer in June 1951.[6]

Even with the fall-off in business, movies continued to exercise an important influence over American culture. In the 1950s, Clark Gable, Cary Grant, Spencer Tracy, and Humphrey Bogart were still national celebrities, and none ever did a television series. (Of course, James Stewart, a big star of the 1930s and early 1940s who became an even bigger star in the 1950s and topped the box office poll in 1955, lasted longer than these other stars, and eventually did do a TV series.)[7] The biggest entertainment icons of the period, such as James Dean, Marlon Brando, Tony Curtis, and rock-and-roll sensation Elvis Presley worked in the movies, not television. That still left room for other new movie stars, such as William Holden, Kirk Douglas, Jack Lemmon, and Burt Lancaster. New female stars also emerged in the 1950s, among them Grace Kelly, Kim Novak, Marilyn Monroe, and Eva Marie Saint. All were beautiful women, with hair most often colored blonde, who photographed well in the big Technicolor productions of the postwar era. None regarded television as the pinnacle of their careers, and all passed beyond it as quickly as possible, restricting their appearances after the early 1950s to the occasional guest appearance.

IN CONGRESS AND *ON THE WATERFRONT*

These new stars made movies that engaged the nation's attention. Marlon Brando and Eva Marie Saint, for example, played the leads in the 1954 production of *On the Waterfront* by the celebrated director Elia Kazan. It was a rare instance in which current politics merged with Hollywood expertise to produce a blockbuster hit. Director Kazan, whose career already included celebrated collaborations with Arthur Miller and Tennessee Williams on the screen and stage, testified before the House Un-American Affairs Committee in 1952, recanting his earlier brief involvement with the Communist party and naming eight of his former colleagues as Communist infiltrators. Some of his fellow artists, in particular his friend and creative partner Arthur Miller, regarded this testimony as an act of betrayal. Kazan saw it differently, and the dialogue between him and Arthur Miller was played out in movies and plays of the early 1950s, notably in *On the Waterfront*.[8]

On the Waterfront dealt with political themes of the sort that animated dramas of the Depression decade but did so using the contemporary idiom of the individual facing psychological and existential dilemmas. The source of the movie lay in a series of articles by journalist Malcolm Johnson about corruption on the New York waterfront. Corrupt union bosses, with direct ties to the mob, exploited the longshoremen for personal gain. Union officials took illegal kickbacks from the ship owners to keep order on the waterfront and assure a steady supply of labor to load and unload the ships. The hard-earned dues of workers went into the pockets of union leaders who used them to purchase personal luxuries. The system depended on physical intimidation to keep the workers in line. Kazan employed this realistic setting to make a personal statement about the moral hazards of the time – the need in extraordinary circumstances to stand up to evil and expose it.

MUSICALS

To be sure, *On the Waterfront* was something of an anomaly on the postwar movie scene. Other directors turned out big-budget efforts such as *Quo Vadis* (1951) and *The Greatest Show on Earth* (1952). Still others experimented with three-dimensional effects that television could not duplicate, such as Alfred Hitchcock's *Dial M for Murder* (1954), or concentrated on pictures for newly popular drive-in theaters. In the midst of all of these efforts to blunt the effects of the downturn in the movie industry, some studios, notably MGM, had success with one of the oldest genres of the sound era: the musical.

Musicals enjoyed a second Golden Age (or was it the third or fourth?) in the early 1950s. MGM and producer Arthur Freed led the way with big-budget films starring Gene Kelly, the 1950s' musical performer of choice with his masculine, athletic style. The best of these films, such as *An American in Paris* (1951) and *Singin' in the Rain* (1952), took advantage of the features that made movie viewing superior to watching television, such as better sound reproduction, exotic settings filmed in color, and a screen large enough to show off the full range of a dancer's motions.

Although the movies broke new ground in the integration of dance and film, they featured old music, settings, and themes. The Academy Award–winning *An American in Paris* used a score of old songs by George and Ira Gershwin to tell the story of an American artist in Paris – something more closely associated with Ernest Hemingway and the 1920s than J. D. Salinger and the 1950s. *Singin' in the Rain*, which became a perennial audience favorite and another of the films that each generation of moviegoers had to see, contained recycled songs from the first Golden Age of musicals in the late 1920s and early 1930s. Its plot centered on the transition from silent films to talkies at a time of transition from the movies to television.[9]

MARILYN MONROE

In the early 1950s, musicals represented one profitable path for the movies at least some of the time. Sophisticated comedies, aimed at the adults in the house rather than their young children, constituted another area in which movies exploited their advantages over television. Movies, presented in a more segregated environment than television, which occupied a place of honor in the family living room, could make more knowing references to sex and other taboo subjects.

The Seven Year Itch became a celebrated movie of the 1950s, for example, not so much because of the movie itself – a rather ordinary comedy about a married man who finds himself alone in town and having to resist sexual temptation at a time in the marriage when many men stray – but because of the circumstances surrounding its production. It featured Marilyn Monroe, the big star of the 1950s who was nearing the zenith of her fame. In her personal life, she became the center of a well-publicized psychodrama as the sexy and often dumb blonde who went through violent mood shifts and yearned to be a well-respected, thoughtful actress. Like Judy Garland, another troubled actress trying to make her way through the 1950s, Monroe acquired a reputation as being notoriously difficult to work with, frequently blowing or forgetting her lines, or showing up late because of a debilitating bout of insecurity.

The public perception of Marilyn Monroe reflected in part the popularization of psychology as a means of explaining people's actions. Jean Arthur, the star of the 1930s and early 1940s, suffered from similar bouts of insecurity and stage fright, but even though they caused her to retire from the movies and drop out of Broadway plays, people seldom tried to psychoanalyze her. With Marilyn Monroe, the star of the 1950s and early 1960s, it was different. Words like neurotic, fantasy, and insecure became attached to her. Asked about working with her, director Billy Wilder said, "It was Monroe who had problems with Monroe. She had trouble concentrating – there was always something bothering her. Directing her was like pulling teeth. But when you finished with her, when you had made it through forty or fifty takes and put up with her delays, you found yourself with something unique and inimitable. When the film was finished, you forgot your troubles with her."[10] Reading this description, amateur psychiatrists might be tempted to diagnose her as having an attention deficit disorder.

Monroe's troubled life and death became one of the great tabloid stories of the twentieth century. Born in 1926, she endured a childhood that included stints with foster parents, the nervous breakdown of her mother (the identity of her father remained a mystery), and a period of residence in the Los Angeles Orphans Home. Her first marriage, a hastily arranged affair to prevent her from having to go back to an orphanage, took place when she was only sixteen. During the war, she worked in a munitions plant and came to the attention of a photographer who suggested that she might try modeling. Like Lauren Bacall, Marilyn Monroe became a successful model who was noticed by a film producer and signed to a contract with Fox in 1946. In this initial phase, she failed to catch on at the studio. It took her until 1950 to secure a seven-year deal with Fox. Only then did the studio begin to promote her and give her starring roles in films such as *Niagara* (1953) with Joseph Cotton, filmed in opulent Technicolor and promoted heavily. In *Gentlemen Prefer Blondes* (1953), Monroe turned her hand toward the musical. Veteran director Howard Hawks, who had done so much to start Lauren Bacall's career, showcased Monroe's beauty and her ability to sell a song in a breathy, sexy manner.[11]

Now a major star, Marilyn Monroe filmed *The Seven Year Itch* in the fall of 1954. In one scene, initially filmed on location in New York and later reshot in Hollywood, Monroe was to walk over a subway grating outside of a movie theater and have her skirt blow up in the breeze and expose her legs. Director Billy Wilder remembered that "there were a good 5,000 people there waiting to see Marilyn's legs and under the grating the electricians who were working the ventilator were accepting jugs of wine from gawkers who wanted to see Marilyn from below." As the crowd shouted "higher, higher," Wilder did fifteen takes.[12] It was the sort of scene, with its suggestion of nudity, that could never have been done on television. Sex comedies of this sort fell squarely in the domain of the movies, eager to carve out an exclusive niche in the entertainment industry, thus beginning a long drive to undo the restrictions of the production code that had been in place since 1934.

SOME LIKE IT HOT

Some Like It Hot, a good example of a 1950s' sex comedy, previewed at the end of 1958 and became the third biggest grossing picture of 1959.[13] Jack Lemmon and Tony Curtis play two musicians in the wide-open Prohibition world of 1929 Chicago who happen to witness the St. Valentine Day's massacre and find themselves being pursued by the mob. Desperate to escape, they accept a job in an all-women's band that has been hired to perform at a stylish Florida beach resort. Their new gig requires them to cross-dress and pass themselves off as women. The picture chronicles the complications that arise when Lemmon and Curtis, alternating between the roles of male suitors and female confidantes, pursue ukulele player and vocalist Marilyn Monroe.

The basic setup of the picture has a European feel, and the original source for the movie is a German movie script. At the same time, director Billy Wilder, himself a German immigrant, takes pains to ground the picture in an American setting and give it an American sensibility. He fills the picture with references to the gangster movies that were being made at just the time that *Some Like It Hot* was supposed to take place. Reprising their roles from the 1930s, George Raft, a product of the old Warner Brothers Studio, plays the main gangster, and Pat O'Brien, another Warner veteran, plays the main cop. When the gangsters appear on screen, they engage in actions meant to remind the audience of the earlier movies. George Raft tossed a coin in *Scarface* (1932), and a character in *Some Like It Hot* tosses a coin. James Cagney squashed a grapefruit in Mae Clark's face in *Public Enemy* (1931), and *Some Like It Hot* contains a similar action. The movie treats the risqué subject of cross-dressing, a staple of European comedy, in a very American manner. There is little or no sense of cross-dressing as a decadent form of sexual pleasure. The creators of the movie assumed that American audiences could more readily accept cross-dressing if they perceived that the characters had no alternative and if they were reassured that the characters retained their basic heterosexuality.

If the old gangsters from Warner Brothers were in the background of the picture, a new American company of movie actors occupied the foreground. The emergence of the three *Some Like It Hot* leads as stars demonstrated the vitality of the 1950s' movie scene. Lemmon, Curtis, and Monroe were all born between February 1925 and June 1926. Each became a breakout star at about the same time in the 1950s, after serving brief apprenticeships with Hollywood studios. Curtis, born as Bernard Schwartz, came from a poor Jewish family. His immigrant father, like Groucho's father, worked as a tailor, and his mother, like Monroe's mother, suffered from mental illness. He entered the navy at the earliest opportunity. He used the GI bill to get acting lessons, and in 1948 came to the attention of a Hollywood agent while performing in an off-Broadway play. That led to a contract with Universal Studios, and by 1952 starring roles in movies.

In some ways, Curtis was the male Marilyn Monroe. He came from a similarly troubled background and suffered from the same sorts of insecurities. Like Monroe, he made high-profile marriages to entertainment figures, like Janet Leigh, and ended up getting married six times (twice the number of Monroe's marriages, but he lived more than twice as long). Like Monroe, he craved recognition as more than a sex symbol. More importantly, he was handsome to the point of being beautiful; people could not help but notice his looks.[14]

Jack Lemmon, the third member of the company, grew up in comfortable circumstances near Boston, attended Andover, and graduated from

Harvard in 1947. Like Curtis, he was a naval veteran who made his way to New York to try to break into show business. He managed to get a succession of jobs in radio, in the new medium of television drama, and on the stage before coming to Hollywood as a contract player for Columbia Studios. He made his official movie debut in 1954 and had a breakout performance in 1955 in the movie version of the Broadway play *Mister Roberts*. If Curtis was a romantic lead, Lemmon more often played comic leads in his movies.[15]

Although *Some Like It Hot* features red-blooded American movie stars chasing the sexiest woman in America, like all of the great pictures of the 1950s it contains its share of subtleties. Tony Curtis not only dresses up as a woman to escape the mob but also poses as a Cary Grant–like playboy to pursue Marilyn Monroe. In seducing Marilyn, he takes advantage of the information he has gained from their earlier girl-to-girl conversations (as fellow members of the all-women band). From these chats, he knows that Marilyn wants to marry a millionaire but has had a bad time with men who paw her and take advantage of her trustworthiness. She confides to her girlfriend Curtis that she prefers a man with weak eyesight and mild manners.

Curtis becomes that man. He steals the clothes of the band manager and passes himself off as the heir to the Shell Oil fortune. In romancing Marilyn while trespassing on the yacht of a real millionaire, he wins her over by feigning frigidity and acting passively. His behavior encourages her to become more aggressive in an effort to awaken his sexual appetites. In this manner, Curtis, the sexy male movie star, feminizes his character, and Marilyn Monroe, the sexy female movie star, makes her character more masculine.

Jack Lemmon, as the comic lead, is not about to get the girl, but in a concession to European sensibility that can be made because it does not affect the key Curtis–Monroe story, he does get the guy. Like Monroe, Lemmon is a fortune hunter, and he sees in aging millionaire Joe E. Brown a chance to get married, divorced, and then claim a large settlement. Brown falls in love with Lemmon when Lemmon is dressed as a woman, and they dance a torrid tango. In the end, Lemmon reveals himself as a man, making it clear that he cannot marry Joe E. Brown, who appears unfazed by the revelation. Of course the audience does not take Brown seriously. He simply adds froth to the production, and the audience somehow understands that it need not fear for Lemmon's virtue.

THE APARTMENT

Some Like It Hot showed that movies in the television age filled entertainment niches that the tube, by virtue of its need to uphold community moral standards for its mass audience and its economic imperatives to produce shows on the quick and cheap, could not occupy. Much the same could be said of *The Apartment*, a 1960 Jack Lemmon vehicle that topped his performance in *Some Like It Hot*.[16]

The Apartment, like *Some Like It Hot*, uses a relatively artificial setup to launch its plot. In this case, Jack Lemmon plays a junior white-collar employee of a large insurance company in New York. He also happens to have an apartment in Manhattan. His bosses, who are married and live in the suburbs, find out about this apartment and use it as a trysting place for them and their mistresses, who are unmarried and usually live in one of the outer boroughs with their mother or roommates. Just as the previous movie, *The Apartment* takes place at a very specific time – November 1, 1959, through the holiday season – and place – the Manhattan of tall glass office buildings that house corporate headquarters on Park Avenue. Lemmon plays the part of a very small cog in a large machine that lubricates the financial transactions fueling the postwar economic boom. He works at a desk in a large room filled with countless other employees who total up sums on adding machines, start and stop work at the sound of a bell, and exercise little autonomy over their lives.

As we get deeper into Jack Lemmon's world, the scale of the movie becomes more intimate. The period details are perfect. Lemmon's apartment has an air conditioner in one of the windows, a stove with a pilot light, and a record player that plays long-playing records. In his disposable bachelor life, he drinks instant coffee and eats pizza that comes from the freezer. Starved for companionship, he seldom gets a chance to eat a sociable meal at Longchamps or Childs, middle-class restaurants of the era.

Despite a loneliness that casts a sense of melancholy over his life, Lemmon plays the corporate game with an earnest intensity. The object of the game is to move through the executive ranks and rise to a higher floor in the office building. To play the game, he has given up his hearth and home to accommodate the sordid wishes of his superiors, even to the point of standing out in a driving rain and sacrificing his health. He does his share of work on his bulky calculator, but his most important tool is his Rolodex, which contains the names and numbers of his bosses who use his apartment.

Everyone in this arrangement breaks the formal rules. Jack Lemmon misuses his apartment and earns the enmity of his neighbors. These include a Jewish doctor of the old school who makes house calls and treats his patients with warmth and concern; the doctor's wife, who faces crises with bowls of chicken soup; and his landlady. Because of all the commotion in his apartment, the neighbors regard Lemmon as some sort of unfeeling playboy who entertains different women night after night. By way of contrast, his bosses reward him by breaking the rules of executive conduct and giving him good performance ratings that help him to make his way up the corporate ladder.

Within this setting, *The Apartment* functions as a love triangle. Jack Lemmon loves elevator operator Shirley MacLaine, who works in a sort of purgatory ferrying employees from one floor to another, but she loves Fred MacMurray, a senior executive on the 27th floor. Adding to the complications, MacMurray uses Lemmon's apartment to sleep with Shirley MacLaine before catching the train back to his wife and family in White Plains. In return for this favor, MacMurray rewards Lemmon by promoting him all the way up to the 27th floor.

When Jack Lemmon accidentally finds out at the office Christmas party that MacMurray and MacLaine are lovers, he begins to feel less sanguine about the arrangement. Even with his new knowledge, he continues to defer to MacMurray, who in turn strings along MacLaine with promises of marriage. In the end, though, Lemmon decides, in the language of the doctor next door, to be a mensch. He returns the key to the executive washroom to MacMurray and gives his junior executive hat to a janitor. Lemmon wins over MacLaine, not because of what he can buy but rather because he is a caring human being.

What distinguishes *The Apartment* (which won the Oscar for best picture in 1960) from other movies about corporate life, such as the movies Doris Day made with Rock Hudson at just about the same time, is its dark tone. Filmed in black and white, rather than the bright Technicolor of the era, the movie alternates between the harsh fluorescent light of the office and the dimmer light of the New York streets and the apartment. For a comedy in which things more or less turn out all right in the end, the movie takes excursions into some very dark territory. It shows people who use alcohol as a means of solving their problems by obliterating them. In clinical detail, the movie chronicles Fred MacMurray's callous indifference, to the point of cruelty, to the fate of MacLaine and Lemmon and gives MacMurray's character little or no redemption. The pain that MacLaine suffers is not handled in a comic or sugar-coated way; she does not have the plasticity of a cartoon character. Instead, the audience sees MacLaine attempt suicide and learns that Jack Lemmon, too, once tried to kill himself.

CONCLUSION

Movies in the 1950s could go to dark places in bittersweet comedies in ways that television could not. If the industry did not do as much business in the 1950s as it did in the 1930s and 1940s, it remained a vibrant cultural influence over American life and the center of innovation in wide-screen presentation and stereophonic sound. Such improved modes of presentation increased the pleasure of watching Biblical epics or large-scale musicals on the big screen. Those who starred in more intimate films of a sort meant to appeal to adults, rather than to the mixed audience that watched television, saw a movie career as the pinnacle of show business success. Stars of the magnitude of Marlon Brando, Jack Lemmon, Tony Curtis, Marilyn Monroe, and Eva Marie Saint regarded starring in movies such as *On the Waterfront, Some Like it Hot,* and *The Apartment* as opportunities to participate in artistic presentations of the very highest order.

7

Make Room for TV

On October 20, 1952, Frank P. Walsh, who ground out a living as an industrial plant guard and worked the night shift, shot and killed his television set with a .38 caliber revolver. He complained that the noise from the set, in constant use by his wife, mother-in-law, and five children, disturbed his sleep in his small West Hempstead, Long Island, house. His wife reacted to the assault on the family entertainment center with shock and dismay. She called the police, who investigated the matter and determined that there was no law against shooting one's own television set.[1]

It took a surprisingly long time for the diffusion of television to occur, but when it did, television predominated over the movies and the radio in the Walsh household and in other American homes. This reordering of entertainment priorities posed little problem for the radio networks because they simply transformed themselves into the dominant television networks. As for the movie industry, worries that television would take away its audience produced both the high art described in the previous chapter and the ultimate realization that the movie companies could make TV shows in the same way they had once churned out feature films, short subjects, and other products. Breakout hits, in particular *I Love Lucy*, showed television executives that telefilms could be as profitable as the live broadcasts that had characterized radio and the early years of television.

THE DIFFUSION OF TELEVISION

Television did not sneak up on the Walsh family or any other American family. Americans who lived in the 1930s were thoroughly familiar with the invention – they knew it was coming into their lives, and it was only a question of when. In this regard, people heard more about television in the 1930s than, say, baby boomers did about personal computers in the 1960s. During the Depression, people followed well-publicized accounts of trials of the new television technology. In November 1936, for example, 250 spectators went to Radio City to see a television demonstration. Most had never seen any images projected on a television set. They discovered that a television was something like "a miniature motion picture tinted green" and were encouraged to think of television as "radio movies."²

In the economic backwater of the 1930s and the national emergencies of the 1940s, television failed to reach the general public. RCA installed the first television station in the Empire State Building when Herbert Hoover was president of the United States. Regular telecasting began in New York during the World's Fair summer of 1939 – television was itself a much publicized exhibit at the Fair – but only about 500 sets were receiving television signals at the end of the summer, not nearly enough people to support the new enterprise. NBC, in particular, persisted with the new medium, continuing to operate an experimental station that broadcast signals from the top of the Empire State Building in 1940. But the station went on and off the air before the start of World War II shut it down for good. In 1942, the first war year, the United States government curtailed the manufacture of television sets.³

Even though television had not begun to pay off, corporate officials at RCA, owners of NBC, and others continued to believe that it would be a good investment in the long run. They supported experiments that led to the innovations that were necessary for network television. In 1937, for example, scientists and engineers succeeded in creating and demonstrating the use of a cable that could take television signals from one city to another. The laborious business of connecting the nation by cable and microwave relay lay ahead. Still, as early as 1937, wires carrying television signals connected New York and Philadelphia, and three years later, just before the war shifted technological priorities, the wires reached the GE manufacturing city of Schenectady as well.

In 1944, as the war neared its end, radio executives and others returned their attention to television and resumed at least a rudimentary television service. In the fall of 1944, the first real television season began, although the schedule contained many holes and the reach of the new medium was still limited. Television remained a curiosity limited to a very few cities. Still, NBC and CBS started doing live telecasts from

New York, broadcasting visual spectacles that took place within relatively confined spaces, such as boxing matches. The Friday night fights and programs such as the *Gillette Cavalcade of Sports* became early staples.[4]

Efforts to get television out of New York and into the rest of the nation proceeded slowly. CBS did not make serious efforts to extend its New York base until the end of 1947. By that time, the World Series had been televised, and interest in television appeared to be growing, with as many as 17,000 sets in operation. It was still a curiosity, a loss leader for the networks.[5]

The reach of television expanded at the end of the 1940s and into the 1950s, so an invention that had been around for a long time finally achieved the critical mass needed to make it an accepted part of American life. The number of stations on the air increased from 37 in 1948 to 108 in 1951. In the fall of 1951, the coaxial cable, as the national cable was called, connected 52 cites, located all across the country, into a wide-reaching network. A critical point had been reached in January 1949, at the start of President Truman's first full term in office, when webs of stations in the Midwest were connected to the web of stations in the East, with the result that about a quarter of the nation was within the reach of live broadcasts from the national networks.[6]

Even in 1951, only about a quarter of the nation's homes had television sets, although the percentage was on the rise. Some places, usually smaller communities not located near large cities, had only one television station. People in these secondary markets experienced television in a different way from people in the big cities, because not all programs were available to them on the one station their sets could receive. Even as late as 1958, with some 500 television stations operating across the nation, about a third of the nation's households received only one station. In the early 1950s, other places, including important urban centers such as Austin, Texas, and Portland, Maine, had no television stations at all.[7]

One reason for the slow expansion of television stations in the face of enormous consumer demand was the temporary freeze on issuing new television licenses promulgated by the Federal Communications Commission (FCC) in 1948. Television, like radio, remained a quasi-public enterprise, with stations regulated by a federal agency. This agency required networks to further the public interest, however that vague concept might be defined, and assigned individual stations to particular frequencies so that the signal of one station did not interfere with the signal of another.[8]

The licensing process involved the FCC in mediating conflicts not only among competing corporate entities bidding to get a station in a given city, but also among different cities and regions. New York, New Jersey, and Connecticut – three important and populous states – were crowded right next to one another, so that a television license for Newark, New Jersey, had an impact on television reception in Manhattan, and a license for Bridgeport, Connecticut, had implications for television reception in the Bronx. Similarly, southern New Jersey and northern Delaware had to be meshed with the important Philadelphia market, raising the question of whether there would be a station on the most accessible frequency for the city of Wilmington. These problems remained even after the licensing freeze was lifted in 1952.

Eastern cities (and Pacific coast cities such as Los Angeles) had the most developed television markets in the 1950s. The pattern of Washington, DC, was typical. Only about 150 sets in the entire DC metropolitan area received television signals at the dawn of the television age in 1946. Over the course of the next decade, however, the Washington television market grew rapidly. By 1954, nearly 200,000 homes in the Washington area had television sets, and only four years later, a whopping 90 percent of all the houses in the Washington, DC, area contained television sets. That meant that, although very few people had television sets in rural Montana, nearly everyone in the nation's capital and its surrounding Maryland and Virginia suburbs lived in a house with one. It was not surprising that each of the major networks – NBC, CBS, ABC, and the short-lived DuMont network – either owned (NBC) or had affiliations (CBS) with stations in Washington.[9]

The *Washington Star* owned a television station in the DC market in part because it already owned a radio station.[10] Despite the limitations of early television technology, many companies that owned radio stations expanded their operations to include television stations at the end of the 1940s. In Cincinnati, the 50,000-watt NBC radio affiliate became the nation's first NBC television affiliate. In Kansas City, the charter NBC radio affiliate started a television station in the fall of 1949 and remained the only station in Kansas City until 1953. In both Midwestern cities, the stations could only show films or kinescopes – films shot from a television set – of the network programs being broadcast from New York. This situation lasted until the fall of 1949 in the case of Cincinnati, when the station was connected by coaxial cable to the network. Kansas City had to wait until 1950 for live network shows from New York, as did less important Ohio stations, such as those in Dayton and Columbus.[11]

FROM RADIO TO TELEVISION WITH JACK BENNY

In this period, the networks still made money on radio and lost money on television.[12] It mattered, though, that the networks were betting on television and hence were able to use one medium to prop up the other. In particular, the networks allowed their top talent to move from radio to television. As always, the most successful stars of one medium, such as Jack Benny and Bob Hope, hesitated to leave the well-established radio networks for the more tenuous television networks. They waited until it became clear that television would become a truly national phenomenon before making the leap, and they eventually abandoned their radio programs in favor of at least occasional television appearances. Edgar Bergen kept his radio program on the air until 1956; Jack Benny ended his in 1955.

The earliest television stars – the ones who gained popularity during the transition from radio to television – generally came from the second ranks of radio performers. In the fall of 1948, the *New York Times* reported that "Vaudeville via television is upon us with a rush."[13] The most successful of the new TV shows followed a variety or vaudeville format in an effort to interest a wide range of viewers. The old vaudeville master of ceremonies – the role in which Bob Hope and Jack Benny among others had distinguished themselves – became the new host of the television variety program.[14]

During this early period, CBS, the perennial number two radio network, lured away some of NBC's top stars, and in so doing laid the foundation for CBS to become the leading television network by the middle of the 1950s. During the 1948–49 season, William Paley and his CBS network won over *Amos 'n' Andy*, still a valuable prize, from NBC. At the end of 1948, CBS pulled off its biggest coup by securing the services of Jack Benny. CBS got Benny by promising him tax advantages at a time when high tax rates on the upper income brackets made stars eager to seek shelters, and by promising his sponsor that the network would make good any loss in ratings. In time, other prominent radio performers, such as Edgar Bergen and Red Skelton, joined Benny in moving over to CBS.[15]

NBC did what it could to shore up its radio schedule, holding on to comedian Bob Hope and the talent that produced the popular *Fibber McGee and Molly* situation comedy. Those measures helped, but they were not enough to allow the network to maintain its dominance in the ratings. The fabled Sunday night lineup of Benny, Fred Allen, and Edgar

Bergen was no longer an NBC franchise. With Benny on radio and later variety show host Ed Sullivan on television, CBS would gain the upper hand on Sunday nights, and eventually on the other nights as well.

At the beginning of 1949, Jack Benny broadcast his first radio show on CBS and demonstrated his ability to hold on to his audience despite the change in network.[16] Although Benny continued to enjoy high radio ratings in 1949 and 1950, his audience, like the radio audience itself, began to drift over to television. Benny contemplated returning to a movie career that had stalled in the mid-1940s but realized that his strength lay in broadcasting.[17] Somewhat reluctantly, therefore, he decided to try television, and made his debut in October 1950, at a time when the coaxial cable ended in Missouri. That meant he had to go to New York to do the show, which he envisioned as similar to his traveling stage show.

Benny entered the new medium very cautiously, doing only occasional shows and continuing his weekly radio show.[18] It helped that he had developed routines on radio that could be transferred to television – sound effects could be expanded with visual gags. He had a persona both as a performing comedian and as the star of a situation comedy. His television program, like his old radio show, combined both formats. In some shows, he appeared in front of a curtain and did comedy turns with the guest stars; in other shows, the scene shifted to his Hollywood home and the familiar lives of characters developed on radio. To a large extent, therefore, he came pre-sold to the television audience.

Benny's slow delivery and gentle style aided him in the new medium. He was famous for his pauses, waiting for the audience's reaction to a situation to build into a laugh. His deliberate pace meant he used less material than, say, Milton Berle (probably the most successful of the performers who came to television in the late 1940s), conserving the creative strength of his writers and contributing to his longevity. As Benny put it, "Where I would use three jokes, Bob Hope or Milton Berle would use twelve."[19] Where Bob Hope needed to find new jokes all the time, Benny built on his established character, making it easier for his writers to create material for him.

In the 1951–52 television season, Benny had the added comfort of working in Hollywood, rather than broadcasting from New York. That allowed him to draw on the same guest stars who appeared regularly on his radio show, such as James Stewart and Ronald Colman. It also gave him a chance to retain interest in the program by including new Hollywood sensations as they came along, such as Marilyn Monroe, who made her television debut with him. Benny continued to resist the blandishments of network executives to do a weekly television show. Hence he did six shows in 1951–52 and eight shows in 1952–53. The appearance of Jack Benny on television became an occasional and much anticipated treat, rather than a mundane weekly offering. In 1953–54, utilizing the convenience of being able to film his program, he did a show every other week, the format in which he probably enjoyed his greatest television success.

Jack Benny made the transition to television relatively easily, preserving his status as one of Hollywood's top stars, even though his fame came primarily from broadcasting rather than the movies. His film career had stalled in the 1940s and never revived. Despite this situation, he was one of Hollywood's premier citizens, entrusted with things like emceeing the Academy Awards. He also played an important social role within the creative community, giving lavish parties at which Hollywood's biggest names assembled. As befit someone with high social status, he hosted a spring 1954 wedding for his daughter in the Crystal Room of the Beverly Hills Hotel. The fancy affair cost more than $50,000 and attracted some of Hollywood's brightest stars and executive talent.[20]

In the end, television swallowed Jack Benny, as it did nearly every other star (Bob Hope was the great exception). In 1960, lured by the money and the challenge, Benny agreed to do a weekly program. That year he placed tenth in the ratings but never again finished so high. During the 1962–63 season, he lost his Sunday evening time slot, and in 1964–65 he returned to NBC, where he lasted only one season. The situation comedy Gomer Pyle on CBS, about an endearing but dim-witted Marine recruit, ended his run. Jack Benny had become just another comedian, although, like Bob Hope, he continued to do television specials on a regular basis and to make many guest appearances on other programs. His run as a regular performer on radio or television lasted from 1932 to 1965, and his prominence as an entertainer lasted until his death in 1974.[21]

GROUCHO MARX REDUX

Jack Benny was a broadcasting natural; the emergence of Groucho Marx as a television star in the 1950s came as more of a surprise. Groucho's career had stalled with the demise of the Marx brothers in the 1940s, and he had struggled for years to establish himself as a radio star, with little or no success. None of his four radio series, even the one with his brother Chico as a co-star, had succeeded. Groucho's efforts at establishing himself as a solo star in movies also foundered, as the indifferent reaction to the movie *Copacabana* in 1947 showed. The critic from the *New York Times* noted that he struggled when he worked by himself because he was a performer "who is geared to companionship."[22]

He nonetheless persisted in radio, agreeing to appear as the host of a quiz program on the ABC radio network in the fall of 1947. Once again, his show was poorly received by critics and the general public. His admirers believed he had still not found the right radio format to capitalize on his talents. Although he worked on other projects, such as a co-authored play that opened on Broadway in the fall of 1948, and flopped, he managed to remain on the air beyond his first season, despite finishing 92nd in the Hooper ratings.[23]

A shift from live to recorded program proved crucial to the program's survival. By using the new tape-recording technology, Groucho could be freer in his interactions with the guests on the program, pushing the edges of his abrasive humor. Tape allowed dead or inappropriate spots in his interviews with the contestants on the program to be cut, and the entire program to be edited to highlight the best material.

Groucho Marx became an unlikely radio star and emerged as a hot property as the rivalry between CBS, which had begun to broadcast his radio program in its third season, and NBC heated up. By the spring of 1950, he had CBS "worshipping at his feet" and NBC "making overtures." At the end of the 1949–50 season, NBC announced that it had signed Groucho for an eight-year radio and television contract. "It was a tough fight but I won," he said. He called radio "the simplest racket I've been in yet." He could show up for work at a reasonable hour in casual clothes, with no need to paint a mustache on his face or wear a frock coat.[24]

With his new contract, which took effect in the 1950–51 season, the plan was to "simulcast" the radio show, with the show filmed for television and recorded for radio simultaneously. He made his television debut on October 6, 1950, at just about the same time as Jack Benny's first television show. On Wednesday night, listeners heard the recorded radio program, and the next night viewers saw the same filmed show on television – the first time, noted television beat writer Jack Gould, that "N.B.C. has conceded publicly that a televiewer is not apt to turn on his radio." According to Gould, the television program featured Groucho sitting in his shirtsleeves and smoking a cigar in a leisurely manner, "meanwhile lifting an eyebrow or puffing smoke to give added meaning to his quips." Gould believed that *You Bet Your Life* was one of the few programs that could be transferred successfully from radio to television.[25]

As Groucho Marx's film career continued to stall, his television career took off. Part of the appeal was the unscripted nature of the show (achieved by careful staff work in selecting contestants, skillful editing, and even a staff of writers to sweeten the occasional ad lib). It was comfortably predictable in format – with a succession of couples competing in a quiz – yet also spontaneous in its content. It wore well with the audience, in part because Groucho did not appear to be performing in the strenuous manner of many television stars so much as visiting with ordinary people and directing his caustic wit at them. Now in his sixties, he no longer played the confidence man and comic lothario he had portrayed in the movies. As an older man who looked like someone's New York uncle with his loose-fitting clothes and natural mustache, he became an object of affection, someone whose jests could be appreciated in good fun. As the program began its tenth season in 1956, it remained much as it had before. As the *Times* reported, "Groucho gives away some money and does most of the talking – and his admirers seem to like it that way," forgiving him for such old lines as reporting that the weather forecast from Mexico City was "chile today and hot tamale."[26]

Groucho's television career began to wind down at the end of the 1950s. At the end of 1958, the DeSoto division of the Chrysler Company sought to be released from its contract to sponsor the program. It took this action despite the fact that the program and the product had become identified with one another. Groucho did special programs for Chrysler dealers and pitched the product with reassuring conviction, urging viewers to visit the DeSoto showroom and "tell them Groucho sent you." After fourteen years first on radio, radio and television through the 1955–56 season, and then television, the show concluded its run at the end of the 1960–61 season. Groucho and his executive producer John Guedel tried a similar show on CBS that premiered in January 1962 but failed to achieve success. "By this time," wrote Jack Gould, "Mr. Marx's catalogue of wisecracks have become terribly worn."[27]

Despite losing his TV show, Groucho Marx enjoyed another resurgence in the years before he died in 1977. He remained in contact with the comedians of the succeeding generations. When Johnny Carson made his *Tonight Show* debut in the fall of 1962, Groucho Marx, who had guest hosted on the program that summer, introduced him. Bill Cosby and Woody Allen, among others, openly expressed their admiration of and debt to Groucho. Cosby did a new version of *You Bet Your Life*, and Allen featured snippets of the old Marx brothers pictures in his movies. In the 1970s, revivals of the Marx brothers films enjoyed considerable success, rediscovered by the baby boom generation on college campuses and art theaters. Groucho even gave a one-man show at Carnegie Hall to an appreciative audience.[28]

HERE'S LUCY

In terms of popularity, neither Jack Benny nor Groucho Marx was a match for Lucy. Lucille Ball, a Hollywood veteran with a much less stellar record than Groucho, achieved an unprecedented success on TV that has never been equaled. Her television program began in 1951 and lasted as a top-rated first-run situation comedy until 1974. She became the quintessential television star.[29]

Born in the southwestern part of New York State in 1911, some twelve years Groucho's junior, she migrated to New York City at age fifteen in search of show business success on Broadway.[30] Her acting lacked the necessary polish to assure her continuous roles, but she managed to work steadily as a model. That career provided the means for her to go to Hollywood, where she made fifty-four films over the course of the next twenty years. She worked as a Goldwyn girl, appearing in the chorus of an Eddie Cantor film (*Roman Scandals*, 1933). In 1935, she secured a contract at RKO and had a small part in the Astaire–Rogers movie *Top Hat* of that year. At RKO, she had a number of opportunities to break out as a star, such as *Stage Door* (1937), where she appeared with leading studio stars Ginger Rogers and Katharine Hepburn, and *Room Service* (1938), the movie the Marx brothers made on loan to RKO. She moved to MGM in 1943, where she acquired her trademark red hair in the lavish Technicolor musicals that studio produced, and then to Columbia, farther down in the Hollywood pecking order, in 1947. Although she worked steadily, she did not succeed in establishing a unique persona that allowed her to stand out from the other contract players and become a leading lady.

In 1940, she married Desiderio Albert Arnaz y De Acha III, better known as Desi Arnaz, who came from a prominent Cuban family forced into exile during one of the political uprisings in that nation. Arnaz gained fame as a musical performer of Latin specialty songs who helped launch the Conga craze in America. In 1940, he appeared in an RKO picture *Too Many Girls* in which he met Lucy.

In the postwar era, Lucille Ball decided to try her hand at radio, and she performed in a situation comedy *My Favorite Husband* between 1948 and 1951. During this time, she and her husband, in the hope of simplifying their lives and strengthening their marriage, looked for a vehicle on which they could work together. CBS saw *My Favorite Husband* as a successful radio program that could be spun into a television show. Ball insisted on a show in which she would keep her radio character as Liz Cooper, with mannerisms such as loud crying at times of distress, but in which Desi would also appear. Eventually her efforts led CBS to pick up a new show, *I Love Lucy*, with Ball and Arnaz, for the 1951–52 television season.[31]

Only a year after Groucho Marx and Jack Benny, Lucille Ball came to television in a situation comedy, set in a New York apartment, featuring her as a housewife named Lucy Ricardo married to Desi, as Ricky Ricardo, who worked in a nightclub as a bandleader and singer. Their neighbors, played by Vivian Vance and William Frawley, were constant companions. *I Love Lucy* was a breakout hit. After a few months, it secured the fourth spot in the ratings, and by the end of its first season it had become the top-rated show on television. Some 10 million homes tuned into the program each week, giving it some 40 million viewers.[32]

In its second season, *I Love Lucy* gained a greater hold over the American imagination, with its plot line about Lucy Ricardo's pregnancy. On December 8, 1952, the program revealed that the character Lucy Ricardo was pregnant, and program publicists also released word, first to the gossip columnists such as Walter Winchell and then to the general press, that Lucille Ball was in fact pregnant in real life. In the television series, it was to be the couple's first baby. In real life, it would be Lucy and Desi's second child, but the line between television and real life became blurred. Lucille Ball knew that she would deliver her second baby by caesarean section, which gave her a certain freedom to schedule the delivery. The producers decided to gamble on trying to have the real baby born on the same date as a television episode about the birth of Lucy Ricardo's baby. On January 19, 1953, this program aired, with its comic ballet of the Ricardos and the Mertzes stumbling over one another in their haste to get Lucy to the hospital, in the process losing track of Lucy herself. Lucy's real baby arrived on that day as well. The producers decided to make the television baby a boy, even though they had no advance knowledge of the real baby's sex. As it turned out,

Lucille Ball and Lucy Ricardo both gave birth to boys, who were named after their fathers. In a further conflation of the real and television worlds, Desi Arnaz Junior eventually appeared on the television program in the role of Little Ricky.[33]

Almost three out of four television sets tuned to the "Lucy Goes to the Hospital" episode, which gave it a higher rating than newly elected President Dwight D. Eisenhower received for his inaugural. The savvy Lucy and Desi used their newfound leverage with the network to sign a contract worth $8 million for the next two and a half years. The deal proved lucrative to both parties. At the end of the 1953–54 season, one out of every three Americans – some 50 million people – watched *I Love Lucy*.[34]

The show succeeded because of the sheer luck and serendipity that went into any popular success, its strong writing and production values, its comic take on ordinary experience, and because Lucille Ball was a superb performer. Television gave Lucille Ball a chance to do broad physical comedy, and she proved a master of it. Her best slapstick bits – stomping on grapes in a wine vat, stuffing candy in her mouth in a desperate effort to keep up with a conveyor belt – put her in the select company of such masters as Harpo Marx, Charlie Chaplin, and Buster Keaton.

The writing also helped to bolster the program's quality. A trio of talented writers, led by Jess Oppenheimer, worked on the scripts. Oppenheimer carefully coordinated a process that resulted in a script at the beginning of each week the show was in production. Lucy's writers developed great skill at creating material for the four central characters, knowing when it was appropriate for Lucy to go into her trademark crying bit, Desi Arnaz to speak in an excitable Latin manner, or Fred Mertz to make a sour remark directed at his wife Ethel.[35]

Because the program was so popular, it is tempting to see it as an essential text on the culture of the 1950s. To be sure, the program followed a trajectory that represented a fanciful version of many people's experiences. Lucy Ricardo started out in an apartment in New York City. She had a baby at a time when many other American families, slightly younger, were starting families. Her husband's success gave her the opportunity to take trips to Hollywood, giving her a chance to mix and mingle with great stars like William Holden and Bob Hope, and also to Europe. These escapes from the mundane were becoming possible for many middle-class Americans, in the era when the dollar enjoyed substantial purchasing power. The only difference between fact and fiction was that to keep up the comedy, Ricky and Lucy traveled with Fred and Ethel. In 1956, Lucy and Ricky, like many Americans, moved out to the suburbs of Connecticut. Three years later, in another imitation of ordinary American life, Lucille Ball and Desi Arnaz got divorced, ending their creative association and leading Lucy to continue her television series in the role of a divorced woman.

On the surface, then, *I Love Lucy* reflected the politics of the 1950s. Lucy remained at home with her pal Ethel, and Ricky went to the nightclub to work. Yet there was a subversive quality to Lucy's character. She, not Ricky, was the star of the show; he supported her not only within the conventional plot line but in the show business sense as well. The action centered on Lucy, not Ricky; she made it clear that she was not content being a passive housewife who waited for her husband to come home every night. On the contrary, she had ambitions to join Ricky in show business or to secure some other niche in the world of work. The fact that she seldom outwitted him, maintaining the usual division between the sensible male and the excitable female, was undercut by the fact that he was frequently excitable and childish in his Latin manner and by the way her skill at physical comedy dominated the show. She might have been something of a lost soul in the manner of Chaplin or Keaton, but the audience's sympathy lay with her, just as it did with the great silent film stars.

Because of the association between *I Love Lucy* and the 1950s, we tend to link the program and television itself with the baby boom. It was true that the baby boomers and the modern television industry, with its early shows like *I Love Lucy*, showed up at the same time. The baby boom did not peak, however, until 1957, when *I Love Lucy* was nearing the end of its first run. Someone born at the front end of the baby boom, say in 1950, would have been unable to follow the plots of the famous pregnancy and baby delivery shows of the winter of 1952–53. These baby boomers, like many others, came to love Lucy because of their subsequent attraction to the Lucy-without-Desi show and because they saw the original series in reruns. Like the presidency of Dwight D. Eisenhower, *I Love Lucy* became part of a nostalgia for the 1950s that many baby boomers experienced only at second hand – a good illustration of television's effect on historical memory.

HOLLYWOOD AND LUCY

Unlike other early television programs, *I Love Lucy* was filmed in Hollywood before a live audience, with three cameras capturing the action that took place on a sound stage with four sets, including the New York apartment and Ricky's nightclub. The performers memorized their lines and tried to run through the program as they would a play, without a break, and with only the most necessary interruptions. Cinematographer Karl Freund, an experienced Hollywood hand, supervised the camera work. The result was a program with the spontaneity and energy of a live performance and the polished look of an edited film.

Broadcasting had always had a bias toward live production. There was an immediacy and authenticity to radio and early television best expressed through live performance. A broadcast had a definite date and time, and one expected to tune into a program as it happened, in the same way that one assumed a newscast was being read at a particular moment in time. Once the broadcast was over, the same material was not repeated. Instead, performers gave different shows each week, and if they were powerful and secure enough, rested in the summer, while their advertising agencies produced another program to serve as a temporary replacement. Repeats, recordings of an earlier production, had little place among accepted radio or early television practices.

I Love Lucy, although not the first filmed program, helped change that custom. Television executives discovered that the viewing public did not mind seeing the filmed programs twice or even three times. That meant they could be repeated during the summer, saving the network money, or used to fill in the vast stretches of non–prime time. The episodes of *Lucy* looked about the same in rerun as they did in first run, unlike the live programs that were distributed beyond their first-run audience by means of kinescopes. And the commercials were not embedded in the program, as they were on *Jack Benny* and other popular radio and early television programs, which meant that the same program could be shown with different ads.

In the movies, a picture's distribution broadened from the first-run downtown theaters to the second-run neighborhood movie houses. Something similar happened in television in the early 1950s. Stations that had missed Lucy on the first round, perhaps because they were not yet in operation, could show the program in subsequent rounds. People too young to have seen the original episodes could catch the reruns.

By the middle of the 1950s, it was clear that Los Angeles would become the city where television programs were made. Short movies, produced in Hollywood, became the future of television.[36] This development helped to produce a rapprochement between the television and movie industries. During what might be described as the post-Lucy era from the mid-1950s into the 1960s, the television and movie industries, once bitter enemies, learned how to cooperate with one another to mutual advantage.

The new relationship reordered the American entertainment business. The movies reserved their "A" products – movies too long, sexy, violent, colorful, or laden with special effects to be properly shown on television – for the theaters. The studios had always made shorter, cheaper films that were destined for the second half of double bills or for the kids' matinees on Saturday mornings. Many of these "B" films took the form of serials in which the audience could follow the action from week to week or picture to picture. In the 1950s, the studios continued to turn out such films, but now they made them for television. In 1955, for example, Warner Brothers agreed to make thirty-nine hour-long films for the ABC television network. Columbia Pictures produced some 390 television films in 1955, including the situation comedy *Father Knows Best* with Robert Young. The movie studios realized that producing television series helped to bring them work at a time when they were no longer operating at full capacity.[37]

This transition toward television work created new film companies in Hollywood that eventually acquired some of the weaker, older studios. Lucy and her husband filmed their program through an entity known as Desilu Productions, which operated as an independent studio specializing in television. The main product was *I Love Lucy*, but the studio soon branched into filming commercials and television programs such as *Our Miss Brooks*, which starred Eve Arden, an old RKO colleague of Lucy's. In time, Desilu became a very lucrative business independent of *I Love Lucy*.[38] By 1957, it was producing more hours of television than Hollywood giant MGM was of movies, and it purchased RKO to give it more production facilities. Former Hollywood star-turned-producer Dick Powell, once featured in the great Busby Berkeley movies of the 1930s, ran a television production company named Four Star productions. It eventually acquired Republic Studios, which had specialized in westerns and B pictures.[39]

Thanks to the success of Lucille Ball and her Desilu studio, the difference in status between television and the movies was lessening, as the two mediums grew closer together. Movies shown in theaters now moved quickly to television as an accepted part of the entertainment life cycle. A key moment in the transition came in the fall of 1961 with the premiere of *Saturday Night at the Movies* on NBC. The new series debuted with the 1953 movie *How to Marry a Millionaire* that the network was able to broadcast in color. In 1964, the first so-called made for television movie aired, opening up another area of collaboration between television networks and movie studios.[40]

In a reversal of the process that applied to the pre-Lucy era, actors became famous on television and used that fame as a point of entry to the movies. In 1968, Clint Eastwood, only two years removed from his role on the television program *Rawhide*, ranked number five at the American movie box office, with his own production company and the ability to command a million dollars per picture.[41] Other major movie stars over the next twenty years, including James Garner, Steve McQueen, John Travolta, Denzel Washington, and Tom Hanks, gained their initial fame on television series. Veteran movie director and producer Alfred Hitchcock found he could use his weekly television program to promote his movies to the benefit of both products.[42]

THE MOVIE INDUSTRY AND TELEVISION – THE ADULT WESTERN

The western became one source of continuity between the B movie and television. In the early days of television, successful show business cowboys, who had already achieved fame through their records, their long-running radio shows, and their many movies, moved to television. Beginning in 1934, Gene Autry made pictures for Republic, some ninety films in all, establishing him as one of America's top box office stars. It seemed only natural to extend the Gene Autry franchise, already established on the radio, into television, leading to a CBS television program that aired from 1950 to 1956.[43]

Gene Autry and his colleague Roy Rogers, like Hopalong Cassidy and the Lone Ranger, appealed mainly to kids.[44] In September 1955, during the post-Lucy Hollywood era of television, the adult western – something a little different – appeared. Baby boomers and their parents could enjoy these programs together, a perfect solution to the problem of reconciling two generations with different tastes and only one television set. In the 1956–57 season, the networks aired sixteen different westerns. The following season the output of westerns nearly doubled, including the debuts of television classics *Have Gun, Will Travel* on CBS and *Wagon Train* on NBC. In 1958, the networks ran thirty westerns, and the genre dominated prime time.[45]

Gunsmoke, which ran for twenty years on CBS, dominated the ratings from 1957 until 1961. *Gunsmoke* began on radio in 1952 – one of the last network radio shows to achieve lasting fame – but the television series featured a different cast, led by 6-foot-7-inch James Arness in the role of Marshall Matt Dillon (William Conrad, star of the radio show and later the star of the television program *Cannon*, had a wonderful radio voice but was at first considered too fat for television). Marshall Dillon kept order in the town of Dodge City, Kansas, around the year 1873.[46]

PERRY MASON AND AMERICAN FREEDOM

Westerns, despite their success, were nonetheless guilty pleasures for the audience and a source of worry for television executives, who were vulnerable to the charge that they were replacing uplifting live drama with juvenile or violent westerns. Hence, television executives looked for some balance in their schedules in the form of cheap reality programs such as quiz shows that could still be broadcast live from New York or telefilms that were entertaining but also somewhat uplifting. Here again, the B movies provided a model in the form of shows about lawyers.

In the winter of 1956–57, CBS announced the launch of a new show based on the exploits of lawyer Perry Mason. The audience needed little introduction to this character, which derived from a highly popular series of books by former lawyer Erle Stanley Gardner. Gardner, a successful attorney in the area of California just north of Los Angeles, turned out his first novel in 1923. By 1959, Gardner, who dictated his books to a team of secretaries and who appeared immune to writer's block, prepared to release his ninety-ninth novel. More than half of his books sold more than a million copies each, and Perry Mason, first introduced in 1933, was his most popular character. Perry Mason became a highly saleable commodity, serving as the basis for a series of Warner Brothers movies in the 1930s and a popular radio drama between 1943 and 1955. CBS decided that the property would also make a good television show and purchased the rights to 272 of Gardner's stories. By this time, Gardner's novels had sold some 90 million copies, most in the popular Pocket Book paperback format.[47]

Perry Mason, which premiered in September 1957 with former movie actor Raymond Burr as the star, became a breakout hit on CBS.[48] People liked the show because it followed a rigid formula, with the case proceeding like clockwork through the commercial breaks until Perry Mason induced a confession from the guilty party, never his client, at the end of the hour. The show might be considered a legal procedural, following the progress of a criminal case from the murder, through the investigation, led by the often flustered Lieutenant Tragg played by veteran actor Ray Collins, to the trial.[49]

Unlike some of the western heroes, Perry Mason was an upstanding citizen, a fine representative of America in the Cold War era. Television cleaned up Mason's image from his earlier movie days. The movies, taking their cue from the earliest novels, portrayed Mason as a tough character who, in the manner of the characters in the hard-boiled Raymond Chandler detective stories, was not above bending the law to his advantage or possibly having a dalliance with his secretary. The television shows took the edge off Mason and made him, in the words of a 1962 *New York Times* profile, "genial, soft-spoken, polite, patient ... and dedicated to his clients in an ethical but not tricky way." His television relationship with his secretary remained platonic.[50] In other words, the 1930s' Mason showed some of the law's rough edges at a time when much about life appeared unfair; the 1950s' Mason was an advertisement for the best aspects of the legal system, a celebration of the constitutional right to a fair trial.

In November 1965, word came that *Perry Mason* would end its run at the end of the season. "CBS figures we are worn out," executive producer Gail Jackson said.[51] By this time in the history of television, however, few successful programs wore themselves out. *Perry Mason*, like *I Love Lucy*, lived on in reruns both at home and abroad. By 1960, Perry Mason had become the most popular program in such diverse countries as Sweden, Italy, El Salvador, Australia, and Japan, and by 1965, the program ran in some fifty foreign countries. At a time when President Dwight Eisenhower would receive international acclaim on his goodwill tour around the world, the program reflected pre-Vietnam Cold War America in a highly favorable light. As Raymond Burr put it during one of his many public appearances, "it gives the people something they need, a weekly affirmation that justice and law will prevail, that right comes out, and that there is no need to fear the courts."[52] The program helped to counteract the image that foreigners might have gained of American criminal justice in the movies of the 1940s, in which sadistic cops often indulged their penchant for violence at the expense of the unlucky suspects they brought in for questioning.

A SLIGHT CHANGE IN THE CLIMATE

By the start of the 1961 television season, the fad for westerns, although far from exhausted, had reached a peak. The networks began to introduce other sorts of programs, such as so-called rural comedies like *The Beverly Hillbillies* and programs about white-collar professionals such as doctors. One reason for the change in emphasis was the aging of the leading edge of the baby boom into the preteen and teen years, increasing the entire audience's level of maturity. Another reason was a change in the political climate, symbolized by the transition between Dwight Eisenhower, born in the nineteenth century and a lover of popular western novels, and John F. Kennedy, born in the twentieth century and a fan of spy novels and other racy fare.

The transition from Republican to Democratic president had consequences for the television industry, which never liked to make political waves. President Kennedy appointed Newton Minow, a law partner of two-time Democratic presidential candidate Adlai Stevenson, to the Federal Communications Commission, and Minow became a crusader against the television violence symbolized by the westerns. In 1961, Minow deployed an image from highbrow poet T. S. Elliott and called television "a wasteland" and threatened to hold up the renewal of broadcast licenses if changes were not made to raise the quality of television content.[53]

It was a sensitive time for the perception of American youth. People worried that the American education system lacked the rigor of its foreign counterparts and made urgent efforts to improve the quality of courses in the areas thought to be most relevant to the Soviet challenge, such as math and science. Social workers and other observers warned that the trend toward conformity among youth produced juvenile delinquency and other unproductive rebellions against societal authority. Bad influences on children, from comic books to television, came under Congressional review at a time when the major American project appeared to be raising children. Hence, Minow's criticism hit a sensitive nerve among opinion makers and others with influence over popular culture.[54]

Not surprisingly, then, a new set of shows appeared in the 1961 season. These included a new high-minded show about lawyers, a set of shows about doctors, a show about a teacher, and even a show about a social worker. Despite being part of the transform-the-wasteland campaign, none of these shows strayed too far from its roots in popular culture. Once again, the television industry put the old B movies to work.

CALLING DOCTOR KILDARE

In 1961, for example, both NBC and ABC announced the launch of doctor shows.[55] Doctors, still perceived as trusted, admirable figures in this pre-malpractice era, provided a healthy alternative to the private investigators, cowboys, gangsters, and other less-than-savory types who populated prime-time television. Where those malcontents wasted lives in rural and urban battle zones, doctors saved lives.[56]

As with most television ventures, the new doctor shows, *Dr. Kildare* on NBC on Thursday nights and *Ben Casey* on ABC on Monday nights, recycled old material from the movies. *Dr. Kildare* told the story of a young doctor who came to Blair General Hospital to do his internship, and there came under the stern tutelage of internist Leonard Gillespie. It had a long pedigree as a prized commercial property. It began as a series of short stories, magazine serials in publications such as *Argosy*, and cheap novels published in the late 1930s by popular author Frederick Schiller Faust, better known by his pseudonym Max Brand. Brand, like Erle Stanley Gardner, turned out pulp fiction by the ream, including a long series of western stories and novels.[57]

The stories attracted the attention of Hollywood and led to a 1937 Paramount movie and a series of MGM movies, with Lew Ayres in the role of Dr. Kildare and the avuncular Lionel Barrymore as Dr. Gillespie. The father–son bond between Ayres and Barrymore resembled that between Mickey Rooney (Andy) and Lewis Stone (Judge Hardy) in the popular *Andy Hardy* series that ran at about the same time. Although not as successful as *Andy Hardy*, *Dr. Kildare* enjoyed a long run at MGM. When Ayres became a controversial figure for his stand as a conscientious objector in World War II, the series shifted to Dr. Gillespie and continued its success. Ayres returned later to the role in a radio series that aired in the early 1950s. The television series therefore relied on established characters and the established locale of the urban general hospital.[58]

The doctors proved to be hits, paving the way for more doctor shows and such future television classics as *ER*, and *St. Elsewhere*. The success of Drs. Kildare and Casey led to one drama about a psychiatrist and another about nurses, who could be both inspiring and alluring, in the very next television season. Drs. Kildare and Casey remained fixtures on the television schedule until 1965, when more whimsical series, such as one about a talking car, came to television.[59]

CONCLUSION

In this way, television entered the American scene in the late 1940s with live programs produced in New York. Old radio broadcasters, such as Jack Benny, and old movie stars, such as Groucho Marx, became new television stars. Actors who had achieved only marginal success in the movies, such as Lucille Ball, also emerged as major stars on television and commanded the nation's attention. Lucille Ball helped to introduce a new production process that allowed television shows to be filmed and shown later in reruns. This process provided an opening for the hard-pressed movie industry to cash in on the television bonanza and to recycle some of its B movie plots and situations for television. Television's content changed with the seasons and with changes in the regulatory environment, but many programs, such as *Gunsmoke*, and many stars, such as Lucille Ball, enjoyed runs as long as any in show business.

8

Putting It Together

Walt Disney Introduces the Baby Boom to Television

The movie industry faced a difficult task in the postwar era. It had to keep people interested in what was playing at the local theater while forging a relationship with a growing television industry that was keeping people at home. In this touchy period, no one negotiated the relationship between the movies and television better than Walt Disney. The famous animator and film producer made television shows that promoted movies and movies that were taken directly from television shows. At the same time, he used television to introduce something new – the studio as amusement park – that featured characters from his movies and television shows.

In the 1950s, Disney enjoyed such a fine reputation that he made it onto a list of the "world's 100 most important living persons." Those who shared the honor with Disney in the arts and letters category included novelists Ernest Hemingway and William Faulkner, poet T. S. Eliot, composer Igor Stravinsky, and painter Pablo Picasso. Such honors came on top of the ones he had earned in the 1930s for creating the Mickey Mouse cartoons and producing the full-length animated feature *Snow White and the Seven Dwarfs*. Yale University confirmed the world's admiration for Disney by awarding him an honorary degree in 1938. At the time, Hollywood columnist Hedda Hopper called Disney an "authentic genius" who was nonetheless "the most down-to-earth guy I know."[1]

WALT DISNEY'S RISE TO FAME

Walt Disney's initial foray into the celebrity scene came in the late 1920s and the 1930s.[2] His fame coincided almost exactly with the sound era.

Born in December 1901, the fourth of five children, Disney spent his earliest years in Chicago, before moving at the age of four to the town of Marceline, Missouri. As someone who had spent nearly all of his life in urban and suburban settings, Disney remembered Marceline as a place of wonder not unlike the Iowa town portrayed in *The Music Man*. The good images of rural life predominated over the bad – the blue skies and fresh air blotted out memories of the primitive plumbing and the claustrophobic small-town existence of the sort portrayed by the smart writers of the 1920s, such as Sinclair Lewis.

Just as Ronald Reagan celebrated his childhood in Dixon, Illinois, conveniently shutting out the terrors of living in a house with an alcoholic father, so Disney would eulogize Marceline as the sort of place where one fished and swam in the local stream and watched the circus make its way into town.[3] The very fact that Disney only lived in Marceline for a few years, before heading back first to Kansas City, where he helped his father's newspaper delivery business by taking on a grueling paper route, and then to Chicago for high school, made the memories of his Marceline life all the more poignant.

Disney pursued a career in commercial art, and in a sense he grew up to become America's most successful commercial artist. After rudimentary training in Kansas City and Chicago and a stint as an ambulance driver in World War I, he obtained work with such companies as the Kansas City Slide Company and became interested in the primitive art of movie animation. His company Laugh-O-Gram films went bankrupt in 1923, but he decided to go to Hollywood in August of that year. There he made short subjects that mixed animation and live action, known as the *Alice Comedies*, and then he worked on shorts that starred an animated rabbit named Oswald.

In 1928, forced by necessity to create a new character, he came up with Mickey Mouse. That same year, he released *Steamboat Willie* starring Mickey Mouse and featuring synchronized sound. Mickey Mouse became one of the great movie stars of the 1930s.[4] In 1930, a Los Angeles journalist described Mickey as the hardest working star in Hollywood and "the most universally popular motion picture star in the world."[5]

Disney lost little time extending the character into new realms, such as newspaper comic strips, and into other commercial venues. From the beginning, he had a precocious talent for cross-marketing that would serve him well in the postwar era. He licensed the Mickey Mouse image to appear on toys and other products such as the famous Mickey Mouse watch. In England alone, twenty-three novelty companies put out such products as Mickey Mouse toys, dolls, and handkerchiefs. Since animation depended so much on action and so little on spoken dialogue, much like the American blockbuster films of the 1970s and 1980s, the Mickey character traveled well from one country to another, making Disney and his mouse an international success.

If one wanted to engage in some highbrow speculation, which the early Disney seemed to encourage in intellectuals, then the career of Mickey Mouse bore a resemblance to that of Charlie Chaplin.[6] Both Chaplin and Mickey Mouse were movie stars who appeared to come out of nowhere and were catapulted to the height of fame in an extraordinarily short time. Charlie, like Mickey, was the little guy who endured the outrages of the world with a comic sense of dignity. Chaplin had tremendous physical skill, demonstrated in such gags as the one in *Modern Times* in which he roller-skated blindfolded in a department store, coming precariously close to the balcony but never going over the edge. Mickey, as an animated character, was even freer of physical constraints – he could twist and turn and stop himself in mid-air. Mickey shared Chaplin's talents but had little of his temperament. Chaplin, as a living human being, could be finicky. He worked at his own pace, exhibited a cranky political sensibility, and sometimes had a lecherous manner. Mickey had none of that. He was a perfect gentleman (or mouse) toward Minnie. He was the mechanical man who could be made to do Walt Disney's exact bidding. If Walt Disney wanted him to endorse a product, he did so. As for Mickey's politics, they remained deliberately vague. In the 1930s, people just assumed that he was for FDR, who in fact loved to screen Mickey Mouse cartoons in the White House.

Over time, Chaplin took on the burdens of the great artist, and Mickey acquired a sense of dignity that limited the uses to which his character could be put. The more rough-and-tumble Donald Duck often took Mickey's place. Both Chaplin and Mickey Mouse have survived as recognizable images from the eras of their creation to the present day. But Chaplin eventually had to abandon his character of the tramp and step outside of his comfort zone to appear in sound movies. By the 1950s, his career had run out of steam. In a similar manner, Mickey had trouble making the transition from short subjects to feature films, despite a fabled appearance as the sorcerer's apprentice in the full-length feature *Fantasia*. He was largely retired by the 1950s.

Unlike Chaplin, however, Walt Disney kept on going, with spectacularly productive periods in the prewar period of the 1930s and 1940s and again during the 1950s. He deepened the sensual experience of watching cartoons by making them in color, beginning in 1932, and by experimenting with methods that created the illusion of depth in the picture. Making animated films was a detailed and laborious process that required 6,000 drawings to produce one reel of film. Although Disney hired a stable of artists and other technicians, he retained a stamp of control over his work, so that the association between him and his pictures was complete. He was an auteur, like Chaplin. "Disney has a force of people assisting him," wrote one Los Angeles movie critic, "but there is every evidence that he is the dominant inspirational force in the creation of his entertainment." He took animated short subjects from a relative afterthought, sometimes with "suggestively dirty" themes, to bring imagination, beauty, and whimsy to Mickey Mouse.[7]

In 1933, the *Silly Symphonies*, another line of Disney cartoons, paid off handsomely for the producer with the success of *The Three Little Pigs*. The short included an original song called "Who's Afraid of the Big Bad Wolf" that children everywhere could hum. The song became a major hit. This success seemed to close the gap between Disney's commercial entertainments and the world of high art. "You see what can be done with motion pictures when a great artist makes them," said a famous architect upon seeing a Disney short. It appeared only natural that the Art Institute of Chicago should put on an exhibition of Disney art in 1933. And somehow, the triumph was all Disney's. His supporting animators remained anonymous figures, apparently content to sit at the foot of the master, an unassuming figure they called Walt. "We all contribute something," said one Disney worker in 1933, "but when you see some unforgettable bit of these films, you can be pretty sure Walt put it there."[8]

Somehow the Mickey Mouse dolls and other products were not the same as Disney's art. Somehow Disney was not just a studio head, like Louis B. Mayer or Samuel Goldwyn. He was a creative genius. "Of course, Disney cartoons always have the elements of art, but the latest project promises to touch the highest art, which he has so well evolved in the past," wrote the film critic of the *Los Angeles Times* in 1937.[9]

SNOW WHITE AND THE FIRST FEATURE-LENGTH CARTOONS

The appearance of *Snow White*, a full-length animated feature film, on December 21, 1937, brought Disney even greater acclaim. The project, which had been in the works for more than three years, demonstrated Disney's willingness to take the cartoon to a higher level and his unwillingness simply to bask in the considerable acclaim for his work. Like the great silent comedians, he came to see the short subject as a confining art form. As always, there were commercial considerations involved. Feature-length movies might return more to the studio than did the short subjects. At some level, however, the challenge of mastering such a complicated task engaged Disney's attention. Neither the expense nor the time involved daunted him, even though the project did not fit into the assembly-line methods of the studio system.

Disney hedged his artistic bets by promoting the *Snow White* project with an unprecedented marketing blitz. As always, he was his own best salesman, describing the picture as an audacious and expensive experiment and inviting the public to come and see if the experiment was a success. Astute about cross-media promotion, another trait that would serve him in good stead in the future, Disney used radio to advance *Snow White*. A few days before the picture's gala Hollywood opening, ventriloquist Edgar Bergen, a particular Disney favorite, did a sketch based on *Snow White* on his top-rated radio program. The Hollywood premiere at the Cathay Circle Theatre included a live broadcast on the NBC Blue Network, hosted by Jack Benny's radio announcer and featuring appearances by the Disney cartoon characters. On the road outside the theater, Disney's employees unveiled "Dwarfland," a life-size replica of a scene from the picture. Most of the picture's publicity cost Disney nothing. Forty magazines put Snow White on the cover. Radio comedians mentioned "Snow White" on their broadcasts. One Hollywood publicist claimed that nothing since the Liberty Loan bond drives of World War I had received so much free publicity as did Disney's new picture.[10]

Disney won his gamble. The picture received rave reviews. "True poetry has been achieved in this first super production," gushed the *LA Times*, always eager to come to the aid of the motion picture industry. The picture set house records in its first run. When movie star Claudette Colbert saw the movie in January 1938, her reaction was typical. "Walt Disney had made 'Snow White and the Seven Dwarfs' so engrossing that its eighty minutes fly by as if they were eight and leave you begging for more."[11]

Snow White contained many of the attributes that people would come to associate with a Disney feature cartoon. It had luminous color, carefully detailed drawing, with every effort made to impart a sense of realism to the way the characters moved and talked, memorable tunes, and a plot that featured the antics of adorable characters who supported the main characters. "Those dwarfs gave me the chance to create some delightful personalities," Disney said.[12]

In this sense, all Disney feature cartoons were full-length spectaculars, usually with plenty of singing and dancing and always with plenty of opportunities for commercial exploitation. *Snow White* inspired dolls, dresses, umbrellas, children's jewelry, socks, puzzles, pencils, cut-out books, and coloring books, not to mention songs such as "Someday My Prince Will Come," "Whistle While You Work," and "Heigh-Ho," which had lucrative lives of their own. Although the movie, with its handcrafted drawings and color photography, was expensive to produce – *Snow White* cost some $2 million to make – Disney learned to amortize the return over time by re-releasing the picture at convenient intervals. Over its first twenty-five years, *Snow White* was re-released four different times and brought in some $15 million in film rentals alone.[13] That practice allowed new groups of children, as they reached an age suitable for movie going, to discover the picture.

As it was for anyone, Disney's career was not an inevitable triumph. He followed up *Snow White* with an ambitious slate of feature-length cartoons. Before the war put a shutter on the labor-intensive process, Disney released *Pinocchio* (1940), *Fantasia* (1940), *Dumbo* (1941), and *Bambi* (1942). These pictures continued to elicit wide interest in the movie and enthusiastic reviews from movie critics. When *Pinocchio* opened, for example, luminaries from all branches of show business attended, including Eddie Cantor, Amos and Andy, Bob Hope, Harpo and Groucho Marx, Lucille Ball, and Bing Crosby.[14] Gossip columnist Hedda Hopper was almost overcome with admiration when she saw *Fantasia* in 1941. She called Disney "the most important person we've ever had in motion pictures." She claimed that *Fantasia*, an effort to animate some of the great pieces of classical music, was "a great experience for every music lover." Disney, she believed, was a true artist who only wanted "to create beauty" at a time of extreme fragmentation in world affairs, and she thought he should be "hailed from the mountain tops."[15]

Despite this sort of praise and industry interest, the follow-up movies did not do as well as *Snow White*. Part of the problem was that the war in Europe – the fragmentation in world affairs to which Hedda Hopper had referred – cut off the adoring foreign market for Disney films. Cartoons traveled much better than most feature films because language presented no great barrier to enjoying them. The loss of revenues from

Europe therefore constituted a real financial threat for Disney. He tried to reach out to Latin America in partial compensation, but there was simply not as much money there. Another part of the problem was that, as more Disney full-length cartoons appeared, the wonder began to wear off, and audiences, although they remained appreciative, were more easily jaded and satiated. Still another part of the problem was that Disney ran into conflicts between his artistic and commercial visions.

Fantasia, in particular, confounded audiences with its mixture of elevated musical pieces illustrated by decidedly middle-brow cartoons in a full-length program that resembled a concert and did not tell a unified story in the same manner as *Snow White* or *Pinocchio*. Philadelphia Orchestra conductor Leopold Stokowski earned the condemnation of many music lovers for participating in a movie in which Disney illustrated Beethoven's Pastoral symphony with centaurs and centaurettes, and cute cartoon characters, including Mickey Mouse himself, appeared throughout. To some, it was an undignified way to handle a serious art form and not at all the best way to introduce Beethoven, Stravinsky, and other composers to a mass audience. The picture suffered further from Disney's continuing drive for technical innovation that he sometimes pursued at the expense of short-term profits. Each theater that showed the movie needed to be equipped with what Disney called "Fantasound," which required two weeks for installation and one week for removal, in addition to the $20,000 fee. As a result, *Fantasia* initially ran only in LA, Boston, and New York, making it difficult for Disney to recoup his investment quickly. Shirley Temple, Edgar Bergen, James Cagney, and Robert Montgomery enjoyed the movie when they attended the Hollywood premiere. One New York patron gushed, "I never thought I could appreciate classical music, but this is the best evening's entertainment I ever hope to have." Most people never got that chance.[16]

Disney stayed closer to his audience with *Bambi* and *Dumbo*. One journalist noted that *Pinocchio* and *Fantasia* were charming but had an "aura of artistic straining." *Dumbo*, a tale about an elephant who could fly, was "in the original Disney style – which is the style of the caricature and cartoon rather than of oil paintings, the influence that dictated the manner of *Fantasia*." Flights of artistic fancy remained under relative control, as in a widely acclaimed sequence featuring the dance of the pink elephants. A contemporary journalist noted that this sequence "out Dali's Dali [a reference to surrealistic artist Salvador Dali] and succeeds where *Fantasia* failed in creating an inner logic of its own."[17] Columnist Westbrook Pegler said that *Fantasia* disturbed him because it indicated that Disney had fallen into the hands of the "art artists and had become, like Chaplin … a man with a mission." *Dumbo* reassured him, and at a time just before America's entry into World War II, made him proud to be an American.[18]

Fantasia showed that Disney could occasionally overstep his artistic and budgetary boundaries at a time when World War II put economic stress on his company. The period just before Pearl Harbor went particularly badly for the company, and Disney became embroiled in a labor strike that tarnished his image among those who admired his artistic creations. Part of the problem was the simple one of an economic downturn that, unlike the Depression that had crushed the country like a tin can in a vise, affected the movie industry, and Disney in particular. The company claimed that the war reduced revenues by half, forcing many people to take salary cuts and the company to cut back on its benefits. Employees reacted with alarm, undermining the communal nature of the enterprise. Disney liked to think of his studio as an exciting place to work that inspired creativity among the artists and the loyalty of all the workers to the goal of making the best animated pictures possible. Economic pressure made Disney a less happy place to work and exacerbated other persistent problems.[19]

THE STRIKE

As the studio grew to house a workforce of 1,200 people, the informality of the early operation began to fade. Walt's workers began to question his paternalism, as in his habit of calling his staff "my boys." Although Disney paid generous bonuses, they were necessarily selective and arbitrary and gave rise to charges of favoritism. Then there was the fact that everyone in the growing studio needed to subvert his ego to the collective entity known as Walt Disney. The conceit of the place was that Mickey Mouse, Donald Duck, Snow White, and their colleagues were the stars of the studio. Those who created the cartoon characters, like the people who advised Clark Gable on his makeup at MGM, were supposed to stay behind the scenes, part of a collective process that was nonetheless headed by Walt Disney. Subverting one's ego at a time of financial insecurity made workers more amenable to the sorts of protections employed by the workers at other studios, and in particular to labor unions.

Disney thought he could get by with a company union – essentially an organization run by the company itself in the interests of the workers.

He remained adamant about the idea of a real union entering his studio and changing its routines, not to mention further straining the company's financial capacity. "You know how I am boys. If I can't have my own way ... if somebody tries to tell me to do something, I will do just the opposite...."[20] The National Labor Relations Board eventually ordered Disney's company union to disband, although it later reconstituted itself as the American Society of Screen Cartoonists. The American Federation of Labor's Screen Cartoon Guild, a division of the Painters and Paper Hangers Union, moved to represent the Disney workers. On May 28, 1941, the Walt Disney Studios underwent a strike that shattered the sense of community and had the effect of making Disney look less admirable in the eyes of left-leaning intellectuals and New Deal reformers. Perhaps he was concerned with making a profit and not concerned with art.

The other studios, with their bureaucratic structure and factory-like environment, accommodated unions relatively easily and regarded them as one of the costs of doing business in Hollywood. Disney, by way of contrast, vowed to fight the Cartoon Guild. He insisted on dealing with the tame American Society of Screen Cartoonists, and he promised to keep his studio open, even during a strike. "This studio will never make a bargain with anybody to bar employees because they do not join this or that organization," he said. He resented pressure from the American Federation of Labor craft unions who, according to Disney, threatened to turn his studio into "either a dust bowl or a hospital" if he did not give in to their demands. He realized that an outside union could stir up trouble, insisting, for example, that the studio obey the letter of the New Deal labor laws, such as the payment of overtime to artists who worked day and night during particularly harried periods.[21]

When the strike began, both sides accused the other of using intimidating tactics, such as the union's taking pictures of the workers who crossed the picket line. Soon, despite the company's claim that more people were remaining on the job than participating in the job action, the strike spread from the studio itself to some of the movie houses showing Disney pictures and to some of the newspapers that ran Disney comic strips. Meanwhile, the Screen Cartoon Guild hung an effigy of one of the company executives in front of the studio. The strike lasted two full months, and the studio did not resume full production until the early fall of 1941, which it did as a union shop.[22]

The strike angered Walt Disney and undercut the communal atmosphere at the studio at a time when the studio would have had to change anyway to accommodate the coming war. The experience revealed Disney as a conservative and a Republican. Such a political identity was perfectly okay for a big businessman like Louis B. Mayer, but it upset the progressive image that people had of Disney. Nonetheless, Disney joined such pillars of the Hollywood community as Lionel Barrymore, John Wayne, Robert Taylor, and Ginger Rogers as a reliable Republican, on hand for occasions such as presidential candidate Thomas Dewey's campaign stop in Los Angeles in 1948.[23]

In some respects, Disney resembled the great American car manufacturer Henry Ford. Like Disney, Ford lived in an increasingly urban world but craved the memories of his rural childhood. Like Disney, Ford became famous for his ability to tinker with machines and produce revolutionary products that he believed would change people's leisure habits. Henry Ford symbolized the modern technological age, but he maintained his identity as an individual rather than as a cog in a corporate machine. Ford unambiguously personified his company, which remained, for many years, privately held and under the control of his family.

Like Ford, Walt Disney did not hesitate to put himself forward as the face of his company, despite a reticent nature. Although he was a businessman who could make pitches to the banks when he needed money, and who knew how to merchandise his products, he concentrated his attention on the creative or production end of the business. His company did not even distribute his cartoons – he had to depend on other studios for that. His company did not produce a full slate of pictures in the manner of the other studios. Instead, Disney concentrated on a few feature films, just as Henry Ford lavished his attention on a few basic models of his cars. Ford, the great prophet of automation, helped to produce the future, but like Disney he held on to nostalgic memories of the past. Like Walt Disney, Henry Ford took the time to collect memorabilia from the past and put it on public display.

Again like that of Disney, Ford's reputation as a benign priest of high technology and a benevolent employer deteriorated in the 1930s. Ford had a nativist's intolerance toward those he felt controlled the financial markets, and toward Jews, whom he believed could not be assimilated into Western culture, in particular. A benevolent welfare capitalist, he railed against the entrance of the government, with its elections to certify unions, payroll deductions for social security, and minimum wage laws, into the workplace during the New Deal. Once in the vanguard of technology, Ford, his company, and his products all appeared to be a bit dated in the 1930s.

Disney's receptivity to innovation separated him from Henry Ford, and in any case the war tended to mute the discussion. Just as Ford settled down to making airplanes for a New Deal government that he claimed to despise, so Disney, like the other Hollywood studios, got a bounce from the war. To be sure, the conflict cut off the foreign markets for Disney cartoons and features. It made manpower and materials scarce. Still, it aided the bottom line. In 1940, reeling from the effects of the European war and the high costs of producing the full-length animated features, the company reported an operating loss of a quarter of a million dollars. After Pearl Harbor, the Disney studio essentially turned itself over to the military and the federal government for the duration – lucrative and steady work but an interruption to the studio's creative development and the end of the first great period of animation. In 1943, for example, more than 90 percent of the products Disney produced were for the government.[24]

Disney made all sorts of training films to instruct the soldiers going off to combat and propaganda films designed to raise morale, get people to buy war bonds, and even encourage people to pay their income tax. He sent his characters – particularly Donald Duck – off to war, never too close to the action, but as soldiers and concerned citizens nonetheless. In one Academy Award–winning short, Donald dreamed that he was enmeshed in the regimented horrors of Nazi Germany, only to wake up and realize, with a relieved sense of satisfaction, that he was an American citizen, free to do what he pleased, at least within the limits of the wartime state.[25]

DISNEY'S RETURN TO FULL-LENGTH FEATURES

After the war, Disney's company, like many businesses that had forged profitable relationships with the federal government in World War II, but unlike the rest of the movie industry, turned the corner toward profitability. If Walt was no longer the darling of the intellectuals, he still had his share of admirers. In 1957, for example, President Eisenhower took time off from the burdens of the Cold War to praise Walt Disney as a "genius as a creator of folklore" who helped children "develop a clean and cheerful view of humanity."[26]

At the time Eisenhower spoke, Disney was a conspicuous success. During the 1950s, Disney managed to expand his output, free himself of his dependence on other studios and distribute his own motion pictures, expand into television, and to move his company into new realms that capitalized on his motion picture and television work but opened up new revenue streams. For the big studios, the 1950s marked a time of decline and disintegration. For Walt Disney, the 1950s were the fulfillment of a great dream.

After a hiatus during the war, then features cobbled together from shorter pieces in the immediate postwar period, Disney's full-length cartoons began to appear with some regularity during the 1950s. So did a new line of Disney live-action features. They resembled other Hollywood movies, but they had the Disney touch. That meant they were wholesome offerings to which the family could take young children, or that older children could attend by themselves.

Treasure Island, the first of these new-styled Disney movies, opened in 1950. It was filmed in England because of government provisions that profits made in England had to be spent there, and it proved to be both a critical and a commercial success. The appearance of *Treasure Island* and the many feature films to follow meant that the baby boomers would have their own Disney memories that consisted not only of the recycled products from the first Golden Age, such as *Pinocchio* and *Snow White*, but also of new movies. Children's movies, at least those that came with the Disney imprimatur, appeared to be a safe niche in the precarious movie market. Hence the specialized nature of Disney's operation, and the fact that he was more of an independent producer than a major studio operator, worked to his advantage at a time when the studio system was coming apart.

In the same year as the release of *Treasure Island*, Disney also released *Cinderella*, a more traditional cartoon feature. This movie, with its endearing animal characters who helped the human characters reach their full potential, turned a big profit on its initial release that subsequent reissues in 1957, 1965, 1973, 1981, and 1987 (not to mention its release on videotape) only augmented. In some baby boom–generation households, *Cinderella* was the first full-length animated feature that both the baby boomers and their children had seen.

Even in this profitable era, not everything worked. *Alice in Wonderland*, next in line, did not do as well at the box office, in part because the public already had a firm idea of what that story looked like, having grown up with the illustrations of Sir John Tenniel. *Alice* came as close to being sacrosanct as any piece of literature in the English juvenile fiction canon. The status of the material gave Disney little room to improvise. Essentially he filmed an animated version of the book, adding a few songs that were hardly an improvement on the classic songs, poems, and other bits of doggerel in the original book.

The studio regained its stride with *Peter Pan* in 1953, which, among other things, contained breathtaking scenes of Peter, Wendy, Michael, and John's flight over London on the way to Neverland, as well as inspiring songs such as "You Can Fly." The property provided fertile ground in which to transform what had previously been a book and a stage play into an animated feature. As always, Disney accompanied the release of the picture with the release of new franchised products related to the film, such as Peter Pan toy television sets, an inflatable jingle ball that imitated the sound that announced Tinker Bell's appearance in the movie, and plastic drapes with pictures of the characters from the story.[27]

DISNEYLAND ON TV

The next year proved to be crucial for Walt Disney. He announced plans to create Disneyland, to produce a television series, and to distribute his own movies. In March 1954, word came that he was planning an amusement park near Los Angles that would sprawl over 152 acres of land and would include rides and exhibits derived from Disney properties such as *Pinocchio* and *Cinderella*, not to mention a simulated space ride on a forty-foot rocket.[28] In April, Disney revealed that he was entering into an agreement with ABC under which he would produce twenty-six hour-long television programs that would presumably include his classic characters such as Mickey Mouse and Donald Duck.[29]

As plans proceeded for the amusement park and the highly anticipated television series, Disney ended an eighteen-year-old agreement with RKO to distribute his pictures. He had already formed a special unit, called Buena Vista, to distribute another new line of pictures that he called True Life Adventures, but they were in fact nature documentaries such as *The Living Desert*. Beginning in the fall of 1954, Buena Vista would release all Disney pictures, including the feature-length cartoons and the live-action movies. A big new live-action movie, *Twenty Thousand Leagues Under the Sea*, based on the Jules Verne story, was in production. Like the amusement park, the new picture revealed the increased scope of Disney's ambitions. Not only would it be filmed using the big-screen Cinemascope process; it would also feature Kirk Douglas and James Mason, two of Hollywood's biggest stars.[30]

Disney already had had experience with television. As early as 1950, he produced a special Christmas program for Coca-Cola that aired on NBC and attracted an audience of some 28 million people. For Disney, the incentive to do the program, other than the $150,000 payment, was the opportunity to publicize his new full-length cartoon feature *Alice in Wonderland*. The conceit of the program centered on Disney's giving a Christmas party at his studio in the company of ventriloquist Edgar Bergen, Disney's own daughters, and many of his animated stars (who appeared in clips from their previous movies, cutting down on production costs). The program also included a short preview of the not-yet-released *Alice*, turning the neat trick of having NBC pay for Disney's movie trailer. Disney insisted that it all made sense. Television was only the "exploitation" of his latest movie. "I propose to use the medium only to enhance theatrical revenues," he said, a statement that would have been anathema to the heads of many other studios, who saw television as undermining the nation's movie habit.[31] Almost from the beginning, therefore, Disney realized that television could be used to boost his movies and other products.

The real star of Walt Disney's television shows was Walt Disney himself. "I'm not interested in acting," he said, "but TV is an intimate thing and I was persuaded to come into your living room personally to introduce these stories and characters."[32] In this manner, Disney created a personal bond with his audience. He projected a kindly image, with a slightly out-of-date mustache that made him look like a character from the MGM musical *Meet Me in St. Louis*, a genial smile, and an ability not to talk down to the cartoon characters who sometimes appeared with him on-screen. He spoke with a broad Midwestern accent, with none of the immigrant cadence of many of his fellow producers. Walt, in other words, was one of Hollywood's few regular guys. "Does Walt have the eccentricities of the usual creator?" Louella Parsons asked in 1955 on behalf of her readers. "He does not," she replied. He was happily married with two adoring daughters, loved baseball and model railroading, and liked nothing more than going into his tool shed and working with his hands. "Yes," said Louella, "this is a great man and a kind man and a good man."[33]

Disney's new series for ABC premiered on October 27, 1954, and began a run that lasted on various networks until 1990. The television program continued the Disney tradition of exploiting existing properties and promoting new ones. It also marked the beginning of a new partnership between Disney and the ABC television network. ABC, the weakest of the three major networks, would carry the Disney program on its stations and gained the right of first refusal to broadcast Disney's many films (which remained under his control). In return, the network gave Disney money to help finance the amusement park he was building.

It turned out to be a good deal for both parties. ABC gained a major hit that permitted it to compete against such big TV draws as Arthur Godfrey on CBS. The first program won a Nielsen rating of 41, which meant that some 30.8 million people watched it. For the two months following, the program never left the top ten, and it became the ABC television network's first solid hit. As for Disney's part of the bargain, the very title of the show, *Disneyland*, publicized the park that would open less than a year later. Indeed, the first program featured a preview of Disneyland.[34]

Disney devoted the television program's seventh show to a documentary on the making of the movie *Twenty Thousand Leagues Under the Sea*. Here was another movie preview for which he got paid several times over. "This was really just an hour-long commercial for his forthcoming movie," wrote critic John Crosby, "but brother, if you can make a commercial this interesting, I'll watch all of them." Disney claimed that he had recognized as early as 1948 that "television would be the greatest medium yet to exploit motion pictures."[35]

By the end of 1954, the Disney Company had racked up some big numbers. The company estimated that about a billion people had seen one of the 657 Disney films released over the course of the previous quarter-century. Every month, people in twenty-six countries bought 30 million copies of Disney comics. In December 1954, *Twenty Thousand Leagues Under the Sea* was playing at sixty movie houses across the country, and Disney's nature film *The Vanishing Prairie* was in the process of returning its $400,000 production costs to the studio ten times over. A Disney festival in Rio de Janeiro testified to the international dimensions of Disney's popularity. Department stores in that cosmopolitan city used Disney characters for their Christmas decorations. "Disney will soon be to us what Santa Claus is to the United States," said one excited Rio merchant. And all of these accomplishments came even before Disneyland opened.[36]

TRUE LIFE ADVENTURES

The Disney juggernaut made its way through the 1950s, and the large baby boom cohort bonded in highly personal ways with him and his products. Still, the great man had his critics, as the reaction to the True Life Adventure documentaries revealed. The project originated in the educational films that Disney had made for the government during the war. Encouraged by the experience, he wanted to produce more educational films aimed, he said, at school groups, churches, and clubs. So he sent a photographer off to Alaska to capture some of its natural beauty and to film its wildlife. As he thought about turning the footage into a usable project, however, he ran into conflicts with the educators with whom he was collaborating. Contrary to the desires of the educators, Disney insisted that any product released under his name would have to be entertaining, not just enlightening. The nature films would contain laughs, drama, and music, even if these forms did not necessarily appear in nature. The real animals in the nature documentaries, like their cartoon counterparts, were given human attributes that violated the sense of realism that some believed was an essential attribute of the nature documentary.[37]

Disney exerted his own sort of artistic integrity over the projects but still subjected them to what might be called the Disney treatment. If *Seal Island* needed to run for thirty minutes, for example, it would, regardless of the problems that a short of that length posed for motion picture exhibitors. The material for the *The Living Desert* proved to be so overwhelming and abundant that Disney released it as a feature film, without much advance knowledge that such a movie could be a viable commercial project. This true-life adventure featured a ground squirrel named Skinny, who, according to the *Times* critic, "could have jumped from a Disney drawing-board."[38] Disney brought nature to a nation that mostly stayed indoors but, like a Victorian starting a zoo, he also tamed it for entertainment purposes. In so doing, he painted a fanciful picture, just as he did with his cartoons.

Disney aimed the True Life Adventures and his other products at children who could only consume things with the approval of their parents. He made sure that his movies and television programs contained nothing to which a prudent parent might object, at a time when Hollywood was expanding the boundaries of adult content. Disney had good instincts for the baby boom generation, whose members learned to recognize Disney's distinctive signature on products even before they could read, and who would grow up with the Disney television programs and Disneyland.

THE *MICKEY MOUSE CLUB*, *DAVY CROCKETT*, AND DISNEYLAND

In 1955, the year that Disneyland opened, Disney signed a new agreement with ABC to create more television programming. He would produce a daily program, to be called the *Mickey Mouse Club*, which would combine information with entertainment and air in the 5 to 6 o'clock evening time slot.[39] It gave Disney new exposure and helped to start a block of daytime programs for ABC. It also provided families with a means of getting through the so-called arsenic hour, when the blood sugar of the children plummeted and many decomposed into crying fits, just as mom was busy getting dinner ready and preparing the house for dad's arrival from work.

When the *Mickey Mouse Club* premiered in the fall of 1955, it met with an indifferent critical reaction. Journalists complained that it differed little, if at all, from the kids' programs that were already on the air and, like all television programs, contained a plethora of commercials.[40] Kids did not seem to mind. They regarded it as their TV clubhouse, a private sanctuary just for them.

The new show operated on the premise of a children's club that the television audience was invited to join in the late afternoon. Jimmie Dodd, a veteran movie performer and an accomplished songwriter and singer, supervised a company of child performers. Jimmie and his charges sang and danced their way through the different days of the week. Thursday, for example, was Circus Day, and the Mouseketeers, as the company was called, did appropriate stunts. Typical programs also included a newsreel; a documentary; a filmed serial, such as the popular *Spin and Marty* series, set at the Triple R Ranch; and Disney cartoons.

In the Disney manner, the show also offered merchandising opportunities and strengthened Disney's hold over popular entertainment, without in any way detracting from his movies and other attractions. The company of Mouseketeers provided a new pool from which Disney drew future stars for his movies, such as Annette Funicello. Children, just learning to read, could subscribe to the *Mickey Mouse Club Magazine*, and the mouse ears and Mickey Mouse Club tee shirts worn by the members of the cast became popular novelty items. The familiar theme song that Jimmy Dodd wrote for the series, with its accompanying animation featuring Mickey and Donald and a host of Disney cartoon characters, became an early version of a music video that baby boomers would come to regard as a reassuring symbol of their childhoods.

Disneyland, the program already on the air when the *Mickey Mouse Club* debuted, created its own sort of cultural excitement. A three-part series of programs about frontier hero Davy Crockett led to a hit song, "The Ballad of Davy Crockett," which nearly every child learned to recognize, and then to the movie *Davy Crockett, King of the Wild*

Frontier, which took its title from a line in the song. The movie, released in the summer of 1955, was just a large-screen copy of the television show, proving that television, far from hurting the movie box office, could "pre-sell" successful movies. Disney, with typical foresight, shot the television programs in color, even though they were broadcast in black and white. That made it easy to turn the television programs into movies. Even if a movie betrayed its television origins by virtue of its frequent use of close-ups, it hardly mattered. "The unembarrassed closeness of the characters certainly permits you to get acquainted with them," reported the *New York Times*.[41] Another critic called the movie "the kind of juvenile adventure nobody wants to outgrow."[42]

The nation went wild over Davy Crockett in the mid-1950s. Fess Parker, one of the first non-cartoon stars created by Disney, gained tremendous fame from the title role, despite being an almost complete unknown when he was hired for the part in the summer of 1954. Less than a year later, Hedda Hopper reported that he had become "the idol of the nation." Buddy Ebsen, who had danced with Shirley Temple in the 1930s and would go on to star in such TV hits as *The Beverly Hillbillies* and *Barnaby Jones* in the 1960s, revived his career with the role of Crockett's sidekick George Russel.[43] Davy Crockett products such as coonskin caps helped to fuel the national Davy Crockett craze, the first of the baby boomers' great infatuations with particular products and activities, such as the Hula Hoop. San Antonio, Texas, out of the way for most tourists, suddenly became a hot destination, with parents dutifully taking their kids to see the place where Davy made his heroic last stand.

As if that were not enough, Disney followed up *Davy Crockett, King of the Wild Frontier* with the release a few weeks later of *Lady and the Tramp*, which was probably the best of the postwar cartoon features.[44] The color in the movie lacked the steady and vivid quality of *Pinocchio*, and the drawing had neither the whimsy nor the inventiveness of *Dumbo*. For all that, the picture had a warm, nostalgic look, another Disney celebration of small-town America at the turn of the century.

DISNEYLAND THE THEME PARK

Despite all of this activity, Walt Disney reserved most of his energy for the Disneyland theme park. Disneyland represented something new in the entertainment business – the movies as tourist destination. Disney bought a tract of land in Orange County, California, accessible only by car, and turned it into what he described as a "combination world's fair, playground, community center, and a museum of yesterday, tomorrow, and fantasy." From the beginning, Disney emphasized the park's compatibility with the automobile, as in the announcement that the facility would have 15,000 parking spaces. It would be one of the nation's first great suburban attractions, re-creating a downtown devoted to consumption rather than production in a setting removed from the center city.[45]

As Disneyland approached its July 1955 opening, Walt Disney orchestrated a sense of excitement. The *Los Angeles Times*, a major booster of the project, even produced a twenty-page color insert about the park right before it opened, noting in May that television viewers were already familiar with Tomorrowland, Fantasyland, Adventureland, and Frontierland from the popular Disney television program.[46] But Disneyland required something more, and Disney planned a ninety-minute television special on the day before the park's public opening. "So reserve Sunday July 17, from 4:30 to 6 p.m. for the kids around the television sets. I doubt whether you'll have any other choice," wrote one television critic.[47] The broadcast itself would include Hollywood stars such as Irene Dunne, who would christen the park's paddlewheel steamer, but most of the performers, such as Art Linkletter, Danny Thomas, Fess Parker, and Walt Disney himself, would come from the world of television. Disney used television, not the movies, as a way of publicizing his new attraction, even though the attractions themselves were largely based on his movies.[48] "We'll open on time, Monday, July 18," said Walt Disney. "I hope the public will remember that is our opening day, although the big television program and preview press party will take place the day before."[49] The ninety-minute television special created a "superb mélange of publicity and general excitement," confirming the fact that Disneyland was "undoubtedly destined to become one of Southern California's greatest attractions."[50]

The park's first day of regular operations did not go well, but that hardly seemed to matter. Some 15,000 people queued up in a mile-long line waiting to buy tickets. When they gained admittance, they discovered they had to wait for more than an hour for many of the rides and that some of the exhibits were not yet open. Hungry patrons suffered frustration when one of the main restaurants closed at noon because its dishwashing machine malfunctioned. And a gas leak shut down Fantasyland for an hour. Still, "the opening day crowds were tremendous and nearly everyone expressed awe, satisfaction, and enjoyment." That first year, more than 3.5 million people went to the park, including President Sukarno of Indonesia and Vice President Richard Nixon from nearby Whittier.[51]

The park celebrated everything Disney. One entered through Main Street, which marked Disney's nostalgic re-creation of the sort of street one might have found in Marceline, Missouri, when Disney lived there. It had all of the charm and none of the dirt and smell of the real thing. No alcoholics lurched their way over the sidewalks and picked fights. The smells of sewage from the outhouses or the many animals that fouled the streets did not permeate the air. In Disneyland, attendants picked up the manure almost as quickly as the horses could drop it. Main Street, like the rest of Disneyland, was a fantasy. It had the quality of a fully realized Hollywood set, using design features such as forced perspective, which made the buildings seem larger than they were. Picturesque fronts hid mundane interiors containing things like sprinkler systems and waste receptacles.

In Disneyland, visitors could connect with the Disney characters up close and personal, particularly in Fantasyland, which featured rides based on the characters from the animated films. The other "lands" all referred back to Disney ventures. Adventureland was a reminder of the true-life adventure films. Frontierland represented a place not unlike that inhabited by Davy Crockett. Tomorrowland expressed Disney's interest in the future. One went to Disneyland already familiar with the general setup and just waiting to be transported into comfortable, safe, but exciting realms of the imagination.

Visitors might have recognized the experience as something like a world's fair, which, beginning in the nineteenth century, mixed basic entertainments, games, and rides with exhibitions designed to show the scope of human progress. In the nineteenth and early twentieth centuries, a fair might exhibit aboriginal peoples, like animals in a zoo, to demonstrate just how far Western civilization had come. The latest inventions and products also had their place at a world's fair.[52] Disneyland contained the same mix of the old and the new, all displayed in a more coordinated fashion than in most world's fairs, with full attention to the visitors' comfort and safety. It allowed Disney to indulge his interest in the latest gadgets, such as the monorail, in close proximity to working models of a Mississippi steamboat or an old steam engine locomotive.

Disneyland's suburban setting and efforts at planning and crowd management pointed toward a hopeful vision of the future. At the same time, many of its rides and exhibits projected a nostalgic image of the past. It was a view of America's great past and better future – the perfect celebration of postwar America – that Disney shared with many of his guests if not with his intellectual critics, who found so much to object to in 1950s' culture.

EXPANDING THE EMPIRE AND CONSOLIDATING
SUCCESS

With the opening of Disneyland and the premiere of the *Mickey Mouse Club*, Walt Disney's influence over American life appeared to peak. In the remaining years until his death at the age of sixty-five, Disney expanded his empire. He started a new television series, *Zorro*, in 1957, under a new $9 million contract with ABC to deliver some 130 hours of programming.[53] Five years later, he agreed to stage a show at Radio City that would accompany one of his live-action films on the screen and be part of the Music Hall's Easter program.[54] He remained active as a movie producer, developing young Hayley Mills as a major star in such films as *Pollyanna* and *In Search of the Castaways* and giving new life to the career of Fred MacMurray by casting him in *The Shaggy Dog* in 1959. He also helped to launch Julie Andrews' highly successful movie career by awarding her the lead role in *Mary Poppins* (1964). This movie extravaganza blended animation and live action, grossed more than $30 million – or three times that of *Snow White* – within a year of its release, and introduced a number of hit songs.

At the same time, Disney's studios started a new line of three-dimensional animation or "audio-animatronics" that he used for exhibits at the 1964–65 New York World's Fair under contract to such corporate sponsors as Ford and General Electric. In his usual manner of making one project promote another, he said he did this new work to benefit Disneyland. "We won't lose money on the work," he said, "but we don't expect to make much either. We expect these exhibits ... to end up at the park, where they will add to our free exhibitions."[55]

With all of the activity, Walt Disney productions reported a net profit for fiscal year 1962 of $5.3 million. The gross income exceeded $74 million (it would be $86 million in fiscal 1964), with more than half resulting from motion pictures and some 27 percent deriving from the more than 5 million paid admissions to Disneyland. Then came the income from books, magazines, comic strips, phonograph records, and the licensing of Disney characters to manufacturers, followed closely by the money from television.[56]

The year before his death found Walt Disney caught up in a new cycle of activity. By now, he made no secret of his conservative political tendencies, having supported Barry Goldwater for president in 1964 and Ronald Reagan for governor of California in 1965. He reserved most of his energy, as he reached the traditional retirement age, for his new entertainment projects, including the new Disneyland East in Florida that would become Disney World and put Orlando firmly on the map of America, and a major expansion of Disneyland in California. At the same time, his studio, buoyed by the success of *Mary Poppins*, was preparing nine feature-length films for release.[57]

When Walt Disney died on December 16, 1966, he headed an entertainment empire that yielded some $100 million a year. He had won nearly thirty Oscars. *Mary Poppins* had grossed more than $50 million and Julie Andrews had won an Academy Award for her work in it. More than 50 million people had visited Disneyland, and when Soviet Premier Nikita Khrushchev was refused admission on security grounds, it created an international incident.[58]

A spectacular success in his own day, Walt Disney also pointed the way to a future of multi-media giants. His company would eventually buy the ABC television network, in a reversal of the 1954 deal in which ABC had provided some of the money to help build Disneyland. At the height of its influence in the 1980s, the Disney Company produced movies, television programs, Broadway shows, amusement parks, designs for urban renewal, and a host of other products.

Disney made this success possible by seeing the commercial possibilities in such things as full-length animated features, television shows made in Hollywood, and a studio specializing in movies that appealed to young people. He had the insight that forms of entertainment once thought to be antithetical to one another, such as television and the movies, could in fact be made to work together and produce greater profits than by working in one medium alone. More than any of his Hollywood colleagues, Walt Disney put it all together in the postwar era and proved to be the great exception to the truisms about Hollywood's decline. As much as anyone else, he aligned an old industry with modern trends.

9

The End of an Era?

Between the beginning of the 1950s and the end of the 1970s, the American entertainment industry functioned within a durable structure. In this period, what might be called the sound revolution that had begun in the 1920s with radio and talking movies reached its full maturity. Each medium had its specialty. Television supplied situation comedies, dramas, and variety shows to American homes during the evening hours on a daily basis. Radio filled the spaces of daily life that were not easily covered by television, such as the frenetic period in the morning when family members went off to work or school, or the quieter, more private time in the evening when a young teenager did her algebra homework with rock and roll playing in the background. The movies remained the major form of entertainment that people watched outside the home – one went to the movies for a night out or an afternoon's escape from the tedium of daily life, more of an occasional treat than a regular routine.

In the 1970s, new technology brought new entertainment formats that came into wide use in the 1980s and upset the existing structure. Satellites beamed radio signals down from space. Television, an industry once firmly anchored by the three networks, benefited from new satellite and cable applications that greatly expanded the choices available to viewers. Finally, the movies, the most enduring of all the elements of American entertainment between 1920 and 1970, became available first on videocassette and then on DVD, which made it possible to show almost any film on a home television set. Soon after all of these things happened, the Internet blossomed as an entirely new platform for entertainment.

RADIO IN THE POST-NETWORK AGE

By the middle of the 1950s, radio of the sort that had once nurtured comic talents Jack Benny, Bob Hope, and Abbott and Costello no longer existed. Radio, once home to variety shows and prime-time comedies and dramas that were broadcast across the nation on the major networks, now featured locally produced programs that often involved a disc jockey spinning records.

In the late 1950s and 1960s, radio benefited from the advent of transistor technology that made it possible to produce lightweight, battery-powered radios that were relatively cheap and portable. The technology came from the laboratories of the venerable communications giant American Telephone and Telegraph, but ATT agreed to license it at a relatively low price to the Sony Company in Japan. Sony led the way in the production of transistor radios, along with its Japanese competitors in the consumer electronics industry, and sold some 5 million transistor radios in the United States in 1959, and nearly twice that the next year.[1]

Transistor radios – taken to school on World Series days and to the beach on summer's days – became a common feature of American life. Radio moved from the living room, where the television set now held the place of honor, to the other rooms in the house. Despite the decline of primetime network radio, the number of radios in the United States increased, rather than decreased. Americans had more radios than bathtubs.

Transistors also made it easier to develop radios that could be installed in cars. Car radios were not new. Even in 1946, some 40 percent of cars had them. In the 1950s and 1960s, however, they became standard features on new cars. Since Americans spent so much of their time driving from place to place, listening to the radio in the car became a major American pastime. As early as 1957, about one radio listener in three tuned in from the car.[2] The expression "drive time radio" had entered the vocabulary of American entertainment.

In the post-network world of radio, drive time became prime time, and a new generation of stars broadcast during the morning and evening rush hours. Radio executives realized that the mornings were often stressful times in the typical American household, with all family members fighting sleep and facing deadlines to get out of the door. The great morning radio hosts fit into the routine, providing a soothing and reliable presence in the agitated atmosphere. They played the occasional record, and also broadcast important information. They gave frequent time checks, weather reports, and bulletins on traffic and transit. Their audience grew particularly large on days with inclement weather. It became an American ritual that was widely celebrated outside of the Sunbelt for kids to wake up early on a snowy morning, turn on the radio, and await the announcement that school was canceled for the day. In large metropolitan areas, with so many school systems and scheduled events, the morning host often had to lay aside the regular program features on snow days and devote himself to reading the list of cancellations.[3]

In 1966, the Federal Communications Commission ruled that stations could no longer simulcast their broadcasts over the AM and FM frequencies.[4] Before that time, listeners could tune into many programs on AM or FM. The FM signal was often clearer, with better fidelity and less static than its AM counterpart, which crackled during thunderstorms and picked up interference from other sources. Until 1966, FM remained an underdeveloped resource. After 1966, nearly all of the major stations on the AM dial were forced to develop new programming for their FM frequencies. That cleared the way for stations to experiment with new formats, such as progressive rock, in place of the older programming.

MOVIES AND MOVIE STARS IN THE POST-STUDIO ERA – THE CASE OF WOODY ALLEN

If radio changed a great deal in the half-century of the sound revolution, the experience of seeing a movie remained much the same. To be sure, technological improvements brought wider, clearer, sharper, deeper, more vivid pictures to the screen. Thanks to the development of stereo and other modern improvements, sound tracks more faithfully replicated what one heard in the street or concert hall. But going to the movies still meant leaving home. With the demise of neighborhood theaters in favor of multi-screen movies in suburban shopping centers, attending a movie usually meant getting into the car.

Although movie box office receipts bottomed out in 1962, people still went to movies. They went to the suburban multiplex for many of the same reasons they had traveled downtown to see a movie in the Golden Age of cinema. Movie houses remained safe havens in most places, cool in the summer, warm in the winter. They invited us to forget our troubles, away from the bills that were sitting on the kitchen table at home. Some people went to the movies out of habit or because their neighbor had told them that they must see a particular movie. Movie going became a much more discretionary activity in this period than it had been before, but it remained an important entertainment ritual.

The Hollywood big shots of the 1960s and 1970s did not get their start in the studio system. Instead, like Woody Allen, they found different paths to the movies. The big comedy stars of the early sound era such as Groucho Marx, who appeared on Broadway, in the movies, on radio, and on television, gained their initial training in vaudeville. When Woody Allen became famous at the beginning of the 1960s, vaudeville no longer existed, and he had to take advantage of opportunities created by the rise of television.

Allen makes an interesting case because he showed an appreciation for what had come before in comedy and in the movies. He borrowed his screen persona from Bob Hope, the style of his jokes from Groucho Marx and S. J. Perelman, and the subject matter of his many movies from earlier films by the Marx brothers, Hepburn and Tracy, Fred Astaire, and Charlie Chaplin. He also became a devoted fan of European directors such as Ingmar Bergman and Federico Fellini and took ideas from them as well.

Born in 1935, Allan Stewart Konigsberg grew up in the Brooklyn neighborhood of Midwood and came of age in the time of television.[5] Not a good student in a setting that placed a high value on academic achievement, Konigsberg remained aloof from the many strivers at Midwood High School who hoped to go to college and enter a respectable profession. Like many people whom a later generation would label gifted and talented, he tended to fixate on one activity to the exclusion of others. Although he showed the usual interest in girls, baseball, and other sports, he also devoted a great deal of time to mastering sleight-of-hand skills that were necessary to do magic tricks, and to learning how to play the clarinet, emulating the sounds of New Orleans jazz. As for more formal parts of his education, he showed precocious abilities in English composition and a related skill in composing jokes. "I could sit in a room by myself and come up with ideas. It's the one thing in life that I can do," he later said.[6]

As he recognized that he could do something unusual, he decided to capitalize on his talent by sending items to the Broadway columnists in the New York papers. These columns, such as the widely syndicated one by Walter Winchell, chronicled the comings and goings of New York celebrities. Each day's column was stuffed with many different items, some of which took the form of gags or jokes. In November 1952,

Earl Wilson, one of Winchell's competitors, ran a joke sent to him by high school student Konigsberg, his name now changed to Woody Allen. It played on OPS, a bureaucratic acronym of the Korean War era, which stood for Office of Price Stabilization, but Allen wrote that it really meant "Over People's Salaries."[7]

Allen's ability to write jokes led to his first jobs. He held these jobs while he was in high school and college, although he failed out of two different colleges and never finished. He worked first for a publicist named David Alber, whose job it was to get his clients mentioned in the Broadway columns. A witty line helped, and Allen and his colleagues supplied the funny remarks that were attributed to the clients. That experience led to jobs as a sketch writer for television and for a summer resort in the Poconos. In this early period of his career, Allen came into contact with many of the top writers, comics, and performers of the 1950s, such as Larry Gelbart, who later created the television series *M*A*S*H*; comedian Buddy Hackett; and singing star Pat Boone. Still, he found writing for television an insecure and unsatisfying way to make a living.

Despite a lack of experience as a performer and a nervous manner that was the antithesis of the brash persona of many comedians, Allen decided around 1960 to perform his own material. He received encouragement from the agents of Mike Nichols and Elaine May, a highly successful comedy act of the era. They booked Allen into a series of Greenwich Village clubs that often featured jazz and would soon feature a new generation of folk singers. At first, in common with many young Greenwich Village performers, Allen kept his day job as a writer for television star Gary Moore. Late in the evening, he would make his way downtown and do a twenty-five-minute comedy routine that was often met with indifference from a distracted, inebriated audience. Gradually, though, he learned to deliver his jokes with more force and to win the sympathy of the audience.

Allen's material made references to such topics as modern literature, modern marriage and divorce, and modern psychiatry. Not a college graduate himself, Allen nonetheless spoke the language of the educated, Americanized, second generation of Jewish immigrants, as in his line about listening to a record of the Welsh poet Dylan Thomas reading his work "We'd Fox Trot To It," or in his reference to a girl who liked to listen to "Marcel Marceau LP's." Such jokes were one-liners that rewarded the audience for being in the know.[8]

By the fall of 1962, the *New York Times* singled out Woody Allen as "the most refreshing comic to emerge in many months" and noted that he had moved on to more important venues, such as the Bitter End in Greenwich Village. The paper described Allen as a "Chaplinesque victim with an S. J. Perelman sense of the bizarre." Allen saw himself as "creating verbal cartoons," short narratives with frequent punch lines.[9]

At his best, Allen paired his hip jokes that identified him with the audience's social milieu with jokes that pointed out his differences with his parents' generation. In his act, for example, he said, "I went to NYU and got into the philosophy department and took all the abstract philosophy courses, like Truth and Beauty, Introduction to God, Death 101, and I was thrown out of college for cheating on my metaphysics exam." He then paid off this already comic premise with the line, "I looked within the soul of the boy sitting next to me," taking his humor from a slightly heightened description of a familiar situation into the realm of the absurd. Then he topped his own joke by coming back to his upbringing, "Whereupon my mother – she is a very high-strung type – tried to kill herself with an overdose of mah-jongg tiles."[10] It was a Jewish mother joke told in a highly original way. Allen contrasted his mother's pastime of playing mah-jongg with his activity of studying philosophy. He sharpened the joke by applying the psychiatric word "overdose" to the ethnic ritual of mah-jongg.

Between 1962 and 1967, as the New Frontier morphed into the Great Society and as Vietnam replaced Berlin as the leading edge of the Cold War, Woody Allen became a conspicuous success. He broadened his appearances to nightclubs outside of New York, and he played more important rooms in the city such as the Royal Box at the newly constructed Americana Hotel, a monument to postwar prosperity. In 1966, the *Times* "cabaret" critic wrote that Allen's "stories of his inadequacies and rejections have taken him in five years from the obscurity which inspired much of his material to stardom in films, television, and nightclubs."[11] By now he had already made many appearances on the NBC late night *Tonight Show* hosted by comedian Johnny Carson and broadcast from New York – *the* place for a hot comedian to make a favorable impression on the nation. In a sense, this show replaced the old Palace Theater at the pinnacle of the live performance chain.[12]

Allen had also already made his movie debut. In the summer of 1965, *What's New Pussycat*, opened to generally poor reviews. It was a big-budget production, starring Peter Sellers and Peter O'Toole and, despite the negative reviews, made a lot of money. Allen wrote the script (which the producers changed considerably) and also appeared in the film.[13]

At the end of 1965, Woody Allen announced plans to star in a movie that he had co-written and would end up directing. In the usual facetious manner he used to publicize his ventures, Allen described the movie as "fairly autobiographical," based on his "inclination toward crime."[14] *Take the Money and Run* opened in 1969. Allen had already written a play produced on Broadway and acted in another big-budget comedy with Peter Sellers, Orson Welles, and David Niven. He had also directed a novelty film in which he dubbed a Japanese monster film with a joke-filled English soundtrack. *Take the Money and Run* represented Allen's first directorial effort over which he had substantial control, and it introduced his enduring movie character to the audience.

The Woody character appeared in a series of six movie comedies issued between 1969 and 1975. That character, an extension of the persona that Allen had developed in his stand-up routines, was a slight, often downtrodden individual in the manner of Charlie Chaplin, who nonetheless possessed Bob Hope's blundering bravado and his misplaced romantic confidence. The Woody character tossed off a continuing series of self-deprecating jokes that often twisted conventional wisdom in the manner of Groucho Marx. The name of this character and the situation in which he found himself changed from picture to picture. Always, though, the picture consisted of a series of jokes and sight gags based loosely on a movie or literary category. As a result, the early Woody Allen movies had the loose and anarchic quality of the films the Marx Brothers made for Paramount at the beginning of their motion picture careers.

Sleeper, perhaps the best of Allen's early comedies, was filled with sight gags of the sort once associated with Buster Keaton, involving mechanical devices that failed to function properly. The Woody character falls asleep and, in the manner of Rip Van Winkle, wakes up in the future and discovers a dysfunctional world. At the climax of the movie, he is asked to perform an improbable operation on a repressive dictator, cloning him back to life working only with his nose. He approaches the task with Bob Hope's self-deluded bravado. "We're doctors, not imposters," he says. He and co-star Diane Keaton then blunder their way through the medical procedure in the broad manner of the Marx brothers' examination of Margaret Dumont in *A Days at the Races*.

After his series of early comedies, Woody Allen, like Charlie Chaplin before him, branched out into more ambitious pictures in which he tempered the comic gags and one-liners with real dramatic conflict. On occasion, he abandoned comedy all together.[15] His breakthrough in this format came with *Annie Hall*, a 1977 film that won the Academy Award for best picture of the year and earned Allen a best director Oscar. *Annie Hall* had a bittersweet quality. It alternated jokes and sight gags with more serious observations about the nature of contemporary relationships. It was Woody Allen struggling to be more of an artist and less of a comedian limited to telling jokes. He now wanted to experiment with movies that had poignant qualities or that dealt with serious philosophical questions, such as the existence of evil.

When Chaplin made the transition to being a self-conscious artist rather than someone with a special gift for gags, his output slowed considerably. Woody Allen did not have that problem. He poured out one movie after another. Like Chaplin, he assumed total control over his pictures, which made him a member in good standing of the group of post-studio directors who came to prominence in the 1970s. Woody Allen wrote, directed, acted in, edited, and even scored nearly all of his pictures.

JULIE ANDREWS, BARBRA STREISAND, AND THE RETURN OF THE HOLLYWOOD MUSICAL

Woody Allen came to the movies by way of television and standup comedy. Other emerging stars of the 1960s took the more traditional route and arrived in Hollywood after starring on Broadway. A mid-decade vogue for movie musicals helped to fuel the trend.

In March 1965, Twentieth Century Fox issued the movie version of Rodgers and Hammerstein's 1959 Broadway musical *The Sound of Music*. It won the 1965 Academy Award for best picture and earned so much money that in 1966 it passed *Gone with the Wind* to become the highest-grossing movie ever.[16] The movie featured Julie Andrews, the British actress who had taken Broadway by storm in the 1950s and who had became one of the movies' biggest stars in the 1960s. The career of Julie Andrews showed that even in the 1960s, Hollywood still recruited some of its most dependable talent from Broadway, just as it had done when Fred Astaire and Katharine Hepburn left the theater for the movies in the early 1930s.

Julie Andrews made her Broadway debut on September 30, 1954, at the age of nineteen. She appeared in the role of Polly Brown in the musical *The Boy Friend*, which spoofed romantic musicals of the sort the Gershwins had turned out in the 1920s. Although young, Andrews was already a theater veteran, the daughter of theatrical parents who gave her singing lessons at age seven and who toured with her on the English variety circuit. At age twelve, she sang an aria at London's Hippodrome to critical acclaim. Her already mature soprano voice had an amazing range, and she was said to have perfect pitch.[17]

During the run of *The Boy Friend*, Julie Andrews, still only nineteen, was cast in a new musical based on the George Bernard Shaw play *Pygmalion*.[18] *My Fair Lady*, as it came to be called, opened on Broadway on March 15, 1956, and became one of the decade's smash hits. On opening night, the cast took a dozen curtain calls before the house lights were finally turned on. The next morning, the line for tickets ran from the lobby and out into the street. Every one of the New York critics gave Andrews glowing notices, with the *New York Times* labeling her "one of Broadway's brightest stars."[19]

The Hollywood studios regarded *My Fair Lady* as an important property, and in February 1962, Warner Brothers paid $5 million for the film rights to the play.[20] With such a large investment, Jack Warner did not want to take a chance on the still relatively unknown Julie Andrews to play the lead. Instead, he decided on Oscar winner Audrey Hepburn for the Eliza Doolittle role, even though he felt it necessary to have her singing dubbed. In the end, the decision worked out well enough. The movie, released at Christmas time in 1964, set studio records at the box office and garnered eight Oscars at the 1964 Academy Awards, including best picture.

Turned down for *My Fair Lady*, Julie Andrews accepted an offer from Walt Disney to appear in his musical version of *Mary Poppins*. *Poppins* opened in August 1964, some four months before the premiere of *My Fair Lady*. It broke all box office records for a Disney production and won five Academy Awards. In what many regarded as poetic justice, Julie Andrews edged out Audrey Hepburn for the best actress award. The role of Maria in *The Sound of Music* followed for Andrews – another critical and financial triumph.[21]

Not every Hollywood musical worked out so well, as the case of the movie version of the Broadway musical *Hello, Dolly!* demonstrated. Twentieth Century Fox recruited Gene Kelly, the undisputed king of the early 1950s era of movie musicals, to direct rising star Barbra Streisand.

Born in the Williamsburg section of Brooklyn in 1942, Streisand suffered the loss of her schoolteacher father when she was still an infant. In stereotypical fashion, this trauma led to a rocky relationship with her stepfather. Nonetheless, she graduated third in her class from Brooklyn's Erasmus High School in 1959. Instead of going to college,

Streisand decided to try for a performing career, even though her mother discouraged her because, with her prominent nose and other features, she looked more like a Jewish girl from Brooklyn than a Broadway star. As with fellow Brooklyn resident Woody Allen, who came along about a decade before, Streisand did not have the opportunity to train in vaudeville or on the radio. Instead, she concentrated on the New York theatrical and nightclub scenes.[22]

Despite – and perhaps because of – her looks and blessed with a truly extraordinary voice, she made her way to Broadway in 1962 and played the lead in the 1964 musical *Funny Girl*. It concerned the life of Fanny Brice, a Jewish girl from the Lower East Side who became a star performer in vaudeville, Broadway, movies, and radio. Unlike Julie Andrews, who had paved the way, Streisand got to play the lead role in the movie based on the musical and won a 1968 best actress award for her efforts.

Funny Girl launched Streisand on a movie career that made her one of the top ten box office stars between 1969 and 1980. She did musicals, screwball comedies such as Peter Bogdanovich's 1972 remake of *Bringing Up Baby* called *What's Up, Doc?* and other popular movies such as *The Way We Were* (1973). Her movies often found her paired with a blonde, gentile leading man, such as Robert Redford or Ryan O'Neal, creating special chemistry through the conjunction of opposites. Streisand's obvious talent made her a Grammy-winning recording artist, an Emmy-winning television performer, and an Oscar winner for her singing, composing, and acting. Later in her career, she took up the additional roles of movie producer and director.

Gene Kelly's *Hello, Dolly!* opened in New York at the end of 1969, the year in which an American walked on the moon. It was a retro musical, set in Yonkers, New York, and New York City in 1890, with a lightweight plot about a widowed middle-aged matchmaker with her own matrimonial ambitions. A twenty-seven-year-old Barbra Streisand played the widow. Although the *New York Times* critic joked that he had an odd feeling that Streisand "must have been married ... at the age of eight and lost (her husband) at ten," he nonetheless acclaimed her as a "national treasure" ... "one of the few mysteriously natural performing talents of our time."[23]

In a year when Paul Newman and Robert Redford's *Butch Cassidy and the Sundance Kid* grossed more than $45 million at the domestic box office, *Hello, Dolly!* took in some $15 million, became the fifth highest grossing picture of the year, earned a best picture Oscar nomination, yet still lost money for its studio. At a cost of more than $20 million, it was rumored to have been the most costly movie musical ever made. Expensive sets, including a gigantic re-creation of New York's Fifth Avenue at the turn of the century, and fancy costumes, including a gold dress that weighed forty pounds, dragged the picture into debt.

That was the problem with the musicals. Some, like *Oliver Twist* and *My Fair Lady* won best picture Oscars and returned a handsome profit to their studios. Others, particularly those made at the end of the 1960s and early 1970s, represented expensive gambles that the studios lost more often than they won. By the end of the decade, as James Baughman reports, "The costly musicals had flopped, leaving their producers and studio partners awash in red ink and angry creditors banging on the door."[24]

THE GRADUATE

As always, reports of the demise of the movie industry proved premature. Instead, the 1970s turned out to be, in the words of one academic authority, "the last golden period of cinema in America."[25] Indeed, the revival began earlier than that, with two pictures released in 1967, *The Graduate* and *Bonnie and Clyde*, leading the way. *Bonnie and Clyde* was a gangster picture set in the 1930s, at the time in the early sound era when Warner Brothers was churning out gangster pictures by Humphrey Bogart and others. The genre may have been familiar, but *Bonnie and Clyde* represented a new generation's take on it and reflected the style of moviemaking at the end, rather than the beginning, of the sound revolution.

The Graduate, directed by former comedy performer Mike Nichols, was both a critical and financial success, and it came at the beginning of a long line of films that explored the relationship between the baby boomers and their parents. In Dustin Hoffman, it featured a lead with virtually no Hollywood and very little Broadway experience, who looked like the male counterpart of Barbra Streisand but who lacked her singing talent. Hoffman played Benjamin, a young college graduate returning to his home in Los Angeles for the summer before continuing his highly promising life.

Both pictures showed how movies differentiated themselves from television programs at the end of the 1960s. Both of the films contained an unusually high degree of sexual candor, both projected a hostile attitude toward established authority, both were the work of young directors who became prominent in the 1960s, and both appealed to an emerging audience of young adults.

Despite the success of *Bonnie and Clyde* and *The Graduate*, the nation never went back to the movie habit it had acquired in the early years, and the studio system was never reconstructed. Still, the movies enjoyed a double-digit leap in attendance in 1982 and 1989 and endured as a key legacy of the sound revolution.

TELEVISION IN THE MODERN AGE

For many years, television, as the dominant medium in America, had to make few adjustments to changing conditions. A remarkable continuity prevailed. In 1975, some 97 percent of American households had a television set, more than had a telephone.[26] The three major networks dominated the industry, accounting for some 90 percent of all programs watched. In the words of Fred Silverman, an executive who worked in prominent positions over the course of his career for CBS, NBC, and ABC, the networks were in such a favorable position that they had "a license to steal."[27]

Some performers, like comedians Lucille Ball and Red Skelton, and some programs, like the news show *60 Minutes* and Walt Disney's program, enjoyed remarkably long runs on television. To be sure, most programs failed, and even the most successful programs, such as those starring former radio comedians Jack Benny or Burns and Allen, eventually went off the air. Many big-name Hollywood performers failed to take hold on television, despite doing regular series. The list of top-notch movie stars who made television programs that were canceled after one season included Judy Garland and Ray Bolger, who couldn't repeat their success in *The Wizard of Oz* (1939) on television. James Stewart and Jean Arthur made movie history in Frank Capra's *Mr. Smith Goes to Washington* (1939), but neither was a hit on television. Debbie Reynolds enjoyed great success in *Singin' in the Rain*, but could not make a go of it on television. Nor could Shirley MacLaine, Ronald Colman, or Ray Milland.

For all of the volatility in any given season, the television industry made few real adjustments in the period of its dominance among the American media between 1955 and 1980. Americans treated their favorite television shows much as they did their cars. Dissatisfied owners returned their lemons to the dealer just as soon as they could afford to do so. But when they liked a car, they kept it for four or five years and then traded it in for a newer but similar model. Every fall, the car manufacturers offered a new line of cars, just as every fall the networks rolled out their new line-up of shows. Some of the line-ups needed little tinkering from year to year. On Sunday nights in 1970, for example, viewers could still watch *Lassie*, *Ed Sullivan* and the *Wonderful World of Disney* – all programs that had been on the air in 1954.

By the 1980s, however, even the television industry had to adapt to changing conditions. As a result of the considerable number of stations available on cable, the share of the audience controlled by the three major networks began to drop. In 1976, the three networks had some 90.3 percent of the television audience, but that percentage slipped to 82.3 percent in 1981.[28] Ratings for the networks went into a permanent decline, even though the television audience continued to grow. In the last quarter of 2008, for example, the broadcast networks (which now numbered four with the addition of the Fox Network) lost nearly 3 million of their viewers, or about 7 percent of the total audience. Cable networks, such as TNT and USA, continued to make gains.[29]

The Internet offered both a new platform for television programs and a challenge to the broadcast networks. When Barack Obama was inaugurated as president at the beginning of 2009, viewers could watch the ceremonies on the traditional networks – NBC, ABC, CBS, and Fox. Those with cable could also pull in the coverage of such entities as the Cable News Network, as well as the offerings of cable networks affiliated with the traditional networks such as CNBC and Fox News. For those people away from their television sets, news organizations such as the Associated Press and the Cable News Network offered live, streaming webcasts. These allowed Americans at work or in transit to watch the inauguration on their computers or other portable devices. The AP-TV streaming webcast featured cameras in several different locations and the same sort of expert commentary as could be found on the networks.

In March 2009, these new developments caused Jeff Zucker, head of the NBC network, to say, "Broadcast television is in a time of tremendous transition, and if we don't attempt to change the model now, we could be in danger of becoming the automobile industry or the newspaper industry." Robert A. Iger, the head of the Walt Disney Company, which now owned ABC, noted that there was more competition for people's time and attention and a new abundance of choices. "This clearly has had an impact on broadcast television," he said.[30]

CONCLUSION

If there were now more choices, there was also continuity. Nearly every American home had at least one television and one radio, and many of those television sets had the capacity to show movies, either through such features as the "On Demand" service that many cable companies offered to their subscribers, or through an attachment to a video or DVD player.

At the beginning of 2009, the movie box office at the theater was also experiencing one of its periodic upticks. People went to the movies to escape from the realities of a country in a financial recession. One mother felt that spending $60 at the movies was a cheap alternative to a day at Disneyland.[31] Even as media development entered a new phase, with the emergence of the computer as a new platform for movies, radio, and television programs, the older sound media continued to be important. But something had changed. In the days of the great studios, large companies such as MGM produced, distributed, and exhibited movies in theaters they owned. In more recent times, such forms of integration within an industry gave way to companies that operated across different parts of the entertainment industry. A cable company might, for example, own a television network, or an Internet company might have an affiliation with a movie studio. The process of cross-media promotion that Walt Disney had started accelerated as the number of platforms for showing movies and television shows increased.

As these changes in the industrial structure occurred, so did the routes people traveled to stardom. In the twenty-first century, performers no longer go from vaudeville to the movies, like Charlie Chaplin and Groucho Marx, although it is still possible to go from improvisational comedy to television and then to the movies.

Broadway continues to serve as a vehicle for upward mobility as it did for Fred Astaire and Katharine Hepburn, although in the modern age there are as many revivals as there are original productions on Broadway, and many Hollywood stars come back to Broadway for brief visits. Radio no longer provides a reliable platform for stardom as it did for Jack Benny and Bob Hope. Instead, performers struggle to get noticed on television – cable television is a particularly promising location – in the hope that they can go from there to the movies. Hope and Benny used vaudeville to get into radio, and radio to get into television. Lucille Ball prepped for stardom in the movies and the radio. Tom Hanks, John Travolta, and Clint Eastwood skipped the radio phase and did television shows before making it big in the movies. Changes in the media, therefore, altered the path to stardom, even as the radio, television, and movies, whose basic identities had been forged in the half-century between 1920 and 1970, endured under changing circumstances.

Notes

1. Sound Comes In, Vaudeville and Silent Pictures Go Out

1. Mordaunt Hall, "Amazing Invention Coupling Sound with Screen Images Stirs Audiences," *New York Times*, August 15, 1926, p. X2.
2. On the fabled lives of the Warner brothers, see Clive Hirschorn, *The Warner Brothers Story* (New York: Random House, 1987); Charles Higham, *Warner Brothers* (New York: Charles Scribner, 1975); Cass Warner Sperling and Cork Milner, *Hollywood Be Thy Name: The Warner Brothers Story* (Rocklin, CA: Prima Publishing, 1994).
3. Neil Gabler, *An Empire of Their Own: How the Jews Invented Hollywood* (New York: Anchor Books, 1988), pp. 120–50.
4. Tino Balio, *United Artists: The Company Built by the Stars* (Madison: University of Wisconsin Press, 1976), p. 95; Thomas B. Schatz, *The Genius of the System: Hollywood Filmmaking in the Studio Era* (New York: Henry Holt, 1986).
5. Douglas Gilbert, *American Vaudeville: Its Life and Times* (New York: Whittlesey House, 1940); Stan Singer, "Vaudeville in Los Angeles, 1910–1926: Theaters, Management and the Orpheum," *Pacific Historical Review* 61 (February 1992), p. 107; David Nasaw, *Going Out: The Rise and Fall of Public Amusements* (New York: Basic Books, 1993), pp. 23–29.
6. Richard Butsch, *The Making of American Audiences: From Stage to Television, 1750–1990* (New York: Cambridge University Press, 2000), pp. 108–20.
7. Robert Sklar, *Movie-Made America: A Cultural History of Movies in America* (New York: Vintage Edition, 1994), p. 42; Nasaw, *Going Out*, p. 155.
8. Nasaw, *Going Out*, p. 159; Sklar, *Movie-Making America*, p. 24.
9. Joseph Medill Patterson, "The Nickelodeons," *The Saturday Evening Post*, November 23, 1907, p. 82
10. Robert C. Allen, "Motion Picture Exhibition in Manhattan, 1906–1912: Beyond the Nickelodeon," *Cinema Journal* 18 (Spring, 1979), pp. 2–15; Schatz, *The Genius of the System*, p. 29.
11. Scott Eyman, *Lion of Hollywood: The Life and Legend of Louis B. Mayer* (New York: Simon and Schuster, 2005).
12. Neal Gabler, *An Empire of Their Own: How the Jews Invented Hollywood* (New York: Anchor Books, 1988.)
13. Eve Golden, *Vamp: The Rise and Fall of Theda Bara* (Lanham, MD: Vestal Press, 1997).

14. Robert C. Allen, "Motion Picture Exhibition in Manhattan 1906–1912: Beyond the Nickelodeon," *Cinema Journal* 18 (Spring 1979), pp. 4–9.
15. *Ibid.*, p. 12.
16. Michael G. Aronson, "The Wrong Kind of Nickel Madness: Pricing Problems for Pittsburgh's Nickelodeons," *Cinema Journal* 42 (Autumn, 2002), pp. 71–96.
17. Douglas Gomery, "Film and Business History: The Development of an American Mass Entertainment," *Journal of Contemporary History* 19 (January 1984), pp. 89–103.
18. Abel Green and Joe Laurie, Jr., *Show Biz from Vaude to Video* (New York: Henry Holt and Company, 1951), pp. 141, 245.
19. *Idem.*
20. *Ibid.*, pp. 270–72.
21. Sklar, *Movie-Made America*, pp. 34–38.
22. Gabler, *An Empire of their Own*, pp. 11–28; Terry Ramsaye, "The Rise and Place of the Motion Picture," *Annals of the American Academy of Political and Social Sciences* 254 (November, 1947), p. 6.
23. Balio, *United Artists*, pp. 5–8.
24. Jeanine Basinger, *Silent Stars* (Middletown, CT: Wesleyan University Press, 2000); Nasaw, *Going Out*, p. 191.
25. Richard Schickel, "Introduction," in Schickel, ed., *The Essential Chaplin: Perspectives on the Life and Art of the Great Comedian* (Chicago: Ivan R. Dee, 2006), p. 6.
26. *Ibid.*, pp. 13–21; Kenneth Schuyler Lynn, *Charlie Chaplin and His Times* (New York: Simon and Schuster, 1997).
27. Charles Chaplin, *My Autobiography* (New York: Simon and Schuster, 1964), p. 188.
28. Balio, *United Artists*, p. 17.
29. Chaplin, *My Autobiography*, p. 188.
30. *Ibid.*, p. 221; Schickel, "Introduction" to *The Essential Chaplin*, p. 6.
31. See Stark Young, "The Circus," in Schickel, ed., *The Essential Chaplin*, pp. 183–87.
32. Stuart Olderman, *Roscoe "Fatty" Arbuckle: A Biography of the Silent Film Comedian* (Jefferson, NC: McFarland, 2005).
33. David Robinson, *Chaplin: The Mirror of Public Opinion* (Bloomington: Indiana University Press, 1983), pp. 139–40; Otto Friedrich, *City of Nets: A Portrait of Hollywood in the 1940s* (New York: Harper and Row, 1986), p. 192.
34. John Sbardellati and Tony Shaw, "Booting a Tramp: Charlie Chaplin, the FBI, and the Construction of the Subversive Image in Red Scare America," *Pacific Historical Review* 72 (November 2003), pp. 495–530.
35. Buster Keaton in particular has become the darling of modern critics. See Judith Sanders and David Lieberfeld, "Dreaming in Pictures: The Childhood Origins of Buster Keaton's Creativity," *Film Quarterly* 47 (Summer 1994), pp. 14–28; Christopher Bishop, "The Great Stone Face," *Film Quarterly* 12 (Autumn, 1958), pp. 10–154.

36. "A Family that Makes Motion-Picture History," *New York Times*, February 17, 1929, p. 152.
37. "Gossip of the Rialto," *New York Times*, June 21, 1925, p. XI; George Jessel, *So Help Me: The Autobiography of George Jessel* (Cleveland: World Publishing Company, 1944); Jessel, with John Austin, *The World I Lived In* (Chicago: Henry Regnery, 1975).
38. Michael Rogin, "Making America Home: Racial Masquerade and Ethnic Assimilation in the Transition to Talking Pictures," *Journal of American History* 79 (December, 1992), pp. 1050–77.
39. "Jolson to Start on Film," *New York Times*, May 26, 1927, p. 23; Rachel Rubin and Jeffrey Paul Melnick, *Immigration and American Culture: An Introduction* (New York: New York University Press, 2006), pp. 28–29.
40. Mordaunt Hall, "The Screen: Al Jolson and the Vitaphone," *New York Times*, October 7, 1927, p. 24.
41. "How the Vitaphone Enters In," *New York Times*, August 28, 1927, p. X4.
42. James Fischer, *Al Jolson: A Bio-Bibliography* (Westport, CT: Greenwood Press, 1994); Michael Freedland, *Al Jolson* (New York: WH Allen, 1977); Herbert Goldman, *Jolson: The Legend Comes to Life* (New York: Oxford University Press, 1988); "Theatrical Notes," *New York Times*, January 4, 1910, p. 8; "Winter Garden's New Show: Al Jolson and Others in the New Extravaganza 'Sinbad,'" *New York Times*, February 15, 1918, p. 7; Alexander Wolcott, "The Play: Jolson," October 7, 1921, p. 28.
43. Wolcott, "The Play."
44. Mordaunt Hall, "Hollywood and Sound, Producers and Actors Talk of Little but The New Mode," *New York Times*, July 22, 1928, p. 93.
45. Mordaunt Hall, "Goldwyn Urges Caution," *New York Times*, August 5, 1928, p. 96; A. Scott Berg's, *Goldwyn: A Biography* (New York: Alfred Knopf, 1989) is one of the better biographies of an early Hollywood figure; Green and Laurie, *From Vaude to Video*, p. 266.
46. "Full Length Voice Film," *New York Times*, March 11, 1928, p. 111.
47. Herbert G. Goldman, *Banjo Eyes: Eddie Cantor and the Birth of Modern Stardom* (New York: Oxford University Press, 1997).
48. Henry Jenkins III, "'Shall We Make It for New York or for Distribution?': Eddie Cantor, 'Whoopee' and Regional Resistance to the Talkies," *Cinema Journal* 29 (Spring 1990), pp. 37–38.
49. I base much of this account of Cantor and his film career on the Goldwyn and Cantor biographies cited earlier and on Jenkins, "'Shall We Make It for New York or for Distribution?'"
50. Martin Rubin, *Showstoppers: Busby Berkeley and the Tradition of Spectacle* (New York: Columbia University Press, 1993); Betty Richardson, "Berkeley Busby," in Pat Brown, ed., *The Guide to US Popular Culture* (Madison, WI: Popular Press, 2001), p. 83; Brooks Atkinson, "The Play, Letting the Marines Tell It," *New York Times*, April 27, 1928, p. 16; "The Dance: New Musical Comedy Talent, Busby Berkeley's Direction Raises the Level of Our Stage Performances," *New York Times*, July 22, 1928, p. 96.
51. David Thomson, "Busby Berkeley," in Thomson, *The New Biographical Dictionary of Film* (New York: Alfred A. Knopf, 2002), pp. 77–78.

52. "Met at Show Rehearsals; Will Wed" *New York Times*, November 15, 1927, p. 31.
53. "Busby Berkeley Marries, Dance Director and Producer Weds Esther Muir, Actress," *New York Times*, November 27, 1929, p. 34.
54. "Myrna Kennedy Wins Divorce," *New York Times*, October 29, 1936, p. 31.
55. "Film Director Faces Murder Trial, Court Places Second-Degree Charges Against Busby Berkeley in Auto Deaths," *New York Times*, September 22, 1935, p. 13; "Berkeley Jury Splits, Los Angeles Dance Master to Be Tried Again in Auto Deaths," *New York Times*, December 25, 1935, p. 4; Berkeley Settles Auto Suits," *New York Times*, January 3, 1936, p. 13.
56. Jenkins, "'Shall We Make It for New York or for Distribution?'" p. 41.

2. From Broadway to Hollywood with Groucho, Fred, and Ginger

1. Thomas Schatz, *The Genius of the System: Hollywood Filmmaking in the Studio Era* (New York: Henry Holt, 1986), p. 159.
2. Abel Green and Joe Laurie, Jr., *Show Biz from Vaude to Video* (New York: Henry Holt and Company, 1951), pp. 368, 370.
3. *Ibid.*, pp. 399–400.
4. Ellis W. Hawley, "Herbert Hoover, the Commerce Secretariat and the Vision of an 'Associative State,' 1921–1928," *Journal of American History* 61 (June 1974), p. 117; Joan Hoff Wilson, *Herbert Hoover, Forgotten Progressive* (Boston: Little Brown, 1975).
5. Stephen Vaughn, "Morality and Entertainment: The Origins of the Motion Picture Production Code," *Journal of American History*, 77 (June 1990), p. 42.
6. Vaughn, "Morality and Entertainment," pp. 39–65.
7. Ellis W. Hawley, *The New Deal and the Problem of Monopoly: A Study in Economic Ambivalence* (Princeton: Princeton University Press, 1966); Bernard Bellush, *The Failure of the NRA* (New York: WW Norton, 1975).
8. Tino Balio, *United Artists: The Company Built by the Stars* (Madison: University of Wisconsin Press, 1976), p. 98.
9. A. Scott Berg, *Goldwyn: A Biography* (New York: Alfred Knopf, 1989), p. 331.
10. Schatz, *The Genius of the System*, pp. 140–47.
11. See Peter Roffman and Jim Purdy, *The Hollywood Social Problem Film: Madness, Despair and the Politics from the Depression to the Fifties* (Bloomington: Indiana University Press, 1982), p. 92.
12. I take much of this biographical account of Groucho and his brothers from Stefan Kanfer, *Groucho: The Life and Times of Julius Henry Marx* (New York: Alfred Knopf, 2000). It should be mentioned that Sam Marx came from the Alsace-Lorraine section of Germany, which was originally part of France. Other books that provide useful biographical information are Groucho Marx, *Groucho and Me* (New York: Bernard Geis, 1959); Wes D. Gehring, *The Marx Brothers: A Bio-Bibliography* (New York: Greenwood Press, 1987); Gehring, *Groucho and WC Fields: Huckster Comedians* (Jackson: University Press of Mississippi, 1994); Harpo Marx with Roland Barber, *Harpo Speaks* (New York: Bernard Geis Associates, 1962); Simon Louvish, *Monkey Business: The Lives and Legends of the Marx Brothers*

(New York: St. Martin's Press, 1999); Arthur Marx, *Son of Groucho* (New York: David McKay and Company, 1972); Arthur Marx, *Life with Groucho* (New York: Simon and Schuster, 1954).

13. A good source on Minnie is Louvish, *Monkey Business*. When she worked in Chicago, Minnie called herself Minnie Palmer, a possible effort to diminish the anti-Semitism that she and her performing family encountered; "Samuel Marx, Father of Four Marx Brothers of Stage and Screen Fame," *New York Times*, May 12, 1933, p. 17.

14. Kanfer, *Groucho*, p. 36.

15. Kanfer, *Groucho*, pp. 36–46; Charlotte Chandler, *Hello I Must Be Going: Groucho and His Friends* (New York: Doubleday, 1977), pp. 556–57.

16. "Comedy High and Low, From Sheridan to the Marx Brothers for Ample Variety," *New York Times*, December 13, 1925, p. X3.

17. Kanfer, *Groucho*, p. 83.

18. "Marx Brothers Caper at Palace, Stir Hilarity with Their Du Barry Scene," *New York Times*, April 15, 1929, p. 31; "Marx Brothers in Revue," August 21, 1931, *New York Times*, August 21, 1933, p. 23; "Four Marx Brothers Caper at the Palace, Zanies Resurrect Old Napoleon Sketch," *New York Times*, January 4, 1932, p. 27; "Marx Brothers Stir Hilarity at the Palace, Intensely Amusing in 'The Schweineries,'" *New York Times*, October 11, 1930, p. 33.

19. "Plucking a Few Notes from Harpo," *New York Times*, November 17, 1935, p. X4; "Groucho, Harpo and Chico, Three Insane Scientists, Test Their Gags," *New York Times*, July 26, 1936, p. X4; "Three Mad Marxes Test Gags for Movie, 'A Day at the Races' Given in Minneapolis by a Company of Forty-five," *New York Times*, July 19, 1936, p. N5.

20. Kanfer, *Groucho*, p. 95.

21. Scott Meredith, *George S. Kaufman and His Friends* (New York: Doubleday, 1974), pp. 149–75.

22. "The Play, Four Nuts in 'The Cocoanuts,'" *New York Times*, December 9, 1925, p. 30. Other first night reviews of the play can be found on the Internet at http://www.marx-brothers.org/whyaduck/info/broadway/coco-reviews.htm.

23. Groucho Marx, "The Return of the Four Mad Prodigals," *New York Times*, April 21, 1929, p. 113; S. J. Perelman to Ruth and Augustus Goetz, March 23, 1942, Perelman to Groucho Marx, April 7, 1943, Perelman to Groucho Marx, June 26, 1948, in *Don't Tread on Me: The Selected Letters of S. J. Perelman*, edited by Prudence Crowther (New York: Viking, 1987), pp. 46–47, 53–54, 76.

24. J. Brooks Atkinson, "The Play, Back Come the Marx Brothers," *New York Times*, October 24, 1928, p. 26; Meredith, *George S. Kaufman and His Friends*, pp. 379–86.

25. "Marx Brothers in Films," *New York Times*, May 19, 1929, p. X3; "Run of 'Animal Crackers' Ends," *New York Times*, April 7, 1929, p. 26.

26. Mordaunt Hall, "The Screen, Groucho and His Brothers," *New York Times*, May 25, 1929, p. 24.

27. "Those Marx Brothers," *New York Times*, May 4, 1930, p. X6.

28. Mordaunt Hall, "The Marx Brothers," August 29, 1930, p. 24.

29. Mordaunt Hall, "Groucho and His Brothers," *New York Times*, October 8, 1931, p. 29; S. J. Perelman to I. J. Kapstein, October 9, 1930, in *Don't Tread on Me*, p. 5; Mordaunt Hall, "Groucho Marx and His Brothers in a New Film Filled with Their Characteristic Clowning," *New York Times*, August 11, 1932, p. 12; S. J. Perelman to Betty White Johnston, October 17, 1931, *Don't Tread on Me*, p. 8.

30. Stefan Kanfer, *Groucho*, p. 162; Mordaunt Hall, "Those Boisterous Marx Brothers, 'Horse Feathers' Has the Necessary Quota of the Quartet's Twisted Wit," *New York Times*, August 21, 1932, p. X3.

31. Wes D. Gehring, *Groucho and W. C. Fields*, p. 121; Alan S. Dale, *Comedy Is a Man in Trouble: Slapstick in American Movies* (Minneapolis: University of Minnesota Press, 2000), p. 151.

32. "The Four Marx Brothers," *New York Times*, November 23, 1933, p. 24.

33. "What's New on the Rialto?" *New York Times*, January 24, 1932, p. XI.

34. "Rialto Gossip, The Marx Brothers Break Their Hollywood Chains," *New York Times*, December 31, 1933, p. X1.

35. Lawrence Jeffrey Epstein, *Mixed Nuts: America's Love Affairs with Comedy Teams: From Burns and Allen to Belushi and Aykroyd* (New York: Public Affairs Press, 2004), pp. 107–09; Wes D. Gehring, *The Marx Brothers: A Bio-Bibliography* (Westport, CT: Greenwood Press, 1987), p. 72.

36. Malcolm Goldstein, *George S. Kaufman: His Life, His Theatre* (New York: Oxford University Press, 1979), p. 246; Tino Balio, *Grand Design: Hollywood as a Modern Business Enterprise* (Berkeley: University of California Press, 1995), p. 267.

37. Andre Sennwald, "The Screen, Three of the Four Marx Brothers in 'A Night at the Opera' at the Capitol," *New York Times*, December 7, 1935, p. 22; Andre Sennwald, "On Second Thought," *New York Times*, December 15, 1935, p. X7.

38. Douglas W. Churchill, "A Script Survives the Marxes, in Unwonted Calm, 'Room Service' Proceeds at RKO," *New York Times*, July 24, 1938, p. 121; Frank S. Nugent, "The Screen, 'Room Service,' Which Was Daffy Enough Even Without the Marxes, Skips Lightly into the Rivoli," *New York Times*, September 22, 1938, p. 27.

39. "Marxmen Shoot to Kill," *New York Times*, November 19, 1939 p. X4; Frank S. Nugent, "The Screen, "Marxes Well Under Their Top in 'At the Circus' at the Capitol," *New York Times*, November 17, 1939, p. 17.

40. Groucho Marx to Arthur Sheekman (and Mrs. Sheekman), October 27, 1939, in *The Groucho Letters* (New York: Da Capo Press, 1994), p. 21.

41. Edward Buzzell, "Mocked and Marred by the Marxes," *New York Times*, December 15, 1941, p. 150; "At the Capitol," *New York Times*, February 21, 1941, p. 16.

42. Groucho Marx to Arthur Sheekman, July 25, 1941, in *The Groucho Letters*, p. 41; "Chico Marx to Head Dance Band," *New York Times*, November 27, 1940; Brooks Atkinson, "The Play in Interview, Groucho Marx Confirms the Rumor that His Knock-About Team of Foolish Brothers Has Broken Up for Good – To Act in His Show Smooth Shaven," *New York Times*, September 26, 1941, p. 27; "At the Capitol," *New York Times*, June 27, 1941, p. 14.

43. Biographical information about Fred Astaire can be found in Fred Astaire, *Steps in Time* (New York: Harper and Row, 1959); Joseph Epstein, *Fred Astaire* (New Haven: Yale University Press, 2008); Marshall Winslow Stearns, *Jazz Dance: The Story of American Vernacular Dance* (New York: Da Capo Press, 1994), pp, 223–24.
44. Alexander Woollcott, "The Play, Kreisler-Jacobi Operetta Presented," *New York Times*, October 8, 1919, p. 22.
45. Fred Astaire, *Steps in Time*, pp. 100–22.
46. See, for example, "'Funny Face' A London Hit, Patrons Wait 30 Hours in Line to See Gershwin Musical Comedy," *New York Times*, November 9, 1928, p. 19.
47. "Adele Astaire Fascinates, in Tuneful 'Lady Be Good' She Vividly Recalls Beatrice Lilly," *New York Times*, December 2, 1924, p. 23.
48. J. Brooks Atkinson, "Astaire and Others," *New York Times*, November 23, 1927, p. 28; "The Dance on Broadway, Musical Comedy's Contribution as Shown by the Astaires," *New York Times*, January 29, 1928, p. 110.
49. "Hearst Sails on Olympic. Fred Astaire, Dancer, Also on Board, Says Sister Is Recovering," *New York Times*, July 21, 1928, p. 29.
50. "Astaires, Dancers, Return, 'Talkies Are the Rage with Londoners,' Miss Adele Says," *New York Times*, August 5, 1929, p. 30.
51. "Star Role for Astaire, Engaged for 'The Gay Divorcé'" A Comedy with Music, *New York Times*, July 25, 1932, p. 11; Brooks Atkinson, "The Play, Fred Astaire in an Intimate Musical Farce Entitled 'Gay Divorcé,'" *New York Times,* November 30, 1932, p. 23.
52. "Astaire Marries Mrs. P. C. Potter, Ceremony for Actor and New York Society Woman by Justice Selah Strong, in Brooklyn Courthouse," *New York Times*, July 13, 1933, p. 17; Mordaunt Hall, "Fred Astaire, Ginger Rogers and Others in a Musical Film," *New York Times*, December 22, 1933, p. 25; "Fred Astaires Leave for Coast," July 15, 1933, *New York Times*, p. 14.
53. A good biographical source on Gingers Rogers is her autobiography, which emphasizes her attachment to her mother and her Christian Science faith. See Ginger Rogers, *Ginger: My Story* (New York: Harper Collins, 1991). She died in 1995.
54. "Gold-Diggers of 1933," in *Variety Movie Guide* (New York: Prentice Hall, 1992), p. 233.
55. Edward Gallafent, *Astaire and Rogers* (New York: Columbia University Press, 2002), pp. 16–24; Andre Sennwald, " The Screen,'The Gay Divorcee' with Fred Astaire and Gingers Rogers, at the Music Hall," *New York Times*, November 16, 1934, p. 27.
56. Gallafent, *Astaire and Rogers*, pp. 24–33; Andre Sennwald, "The Screen, The Music Hall Presents 'Roberta,' a Brilliant Musical Film," *New York Times*, March 8, 1935, p. 25.
57. Douglas W. Churchill, "Hollywood on the Wire," *New York Times*, April 21, 1935, p. X3; Edward Gallafent, *Astaire and Rogers*, pp. 33–43.
58. Andre Sennwald, "The Screen, Fred Astaire and Ginger Rogers in Their New Song and Dance Show, 'Top Hat,' at the Music Hall," *New York Times*, August 10, 1935, p. 12; "Top Hat," in *Variety Movie Guide*, p. 626.

59. A copy of this Christmas card is available at the John F. Kennedy Library, Boston.
60. Edward Gallafent, *Astaire and Rogers*, pp. 43–74; Frank S. Nugent, "The Screen, 'Follow the Fleet,' the Season's Best Musical Comedy Opens at the Radio City Music Hall," *New York Times*, February 23, 1936, p. 21; Frank S. Nugent, "The Screen, Another Astaire–Rogers Song and Dance Fest Comes Knock-Knocking at the Music Hall," *New York Times*, August 28, 1936, p. 21; Frank S. Nugent, "The Screen, 'Shall We Dance,' Astaire-Rogers Tunefest Opens at Music Hall," *New York Times*, May 14, 1937, p. 21.

3. Radio Nights

1. Mordaunt Hall, "The Screen, Bing Crosby, Leon Errol, Burns and Allen in a Musical Picture," *New York Times*, April 26, 1934, p. 27.
2. "Producing Company Finds Its Radio Stars a Ducky Problem," *Washington Post*, February 18, 1934, p. F1.
3. Gary Giddins, *Bing Crosby: A Pocketful of Dreams, The Early Years 1903–1940* (Boston: Little Brown, 2001).
4. "Projection Jottings," *New York Times*, May 1, 1932, p. X5; "Radio Invades Vaudeville," *New York Times*, May 8, 1932, p. X10; Mordaunt Hall, "The Screen," *New York Times*, October 15, 1932, p. 13.
5. For interesting comments on crooners, including radio star Rudy Vallee in particular, see Allison McCracken, "'God's Gift to Us Girls': Crooning, Gender, and the Re-Creation of American Popular Song, 1928–1933," *American Music* 17 (Winter 1999), pp. 365–95.
6. Alice L. Tildesley, "People of the Last Decade Just Thought It Smart to Appear Sophisticated and Kept Their Real Feelings Hidden Under a False Shell, Says Popular Screen Star," *Washington Post*, December 18, 1932, p. 46.
7. Richard B. Jewell, "Hollywood and Radio," *Historical Journal of Film, Radio, and Television* 4 (1984), pp. 125–41; "Movies Demand Stars Make Air Appearances," *Washington Post*, August 2, 1936, p. A6.
8. John Dunning, *On the Air: The Encyclopedia of Old-Time Radio* (New York: Oxford University Press, 1998), p. 323.
9. Samantha Barbas, *The First Lady of Hollywood: A Biography of Louella Parsons* (Berkeley: University of California Press, 2006), pp. 186–87; Michele Hilmes, *Hollywood and Broadcasting: From Radio to Cable* (Urbana: University of Illinois Press, 1999).
10. Among those who appeared in this movie was Ronald Reagan. See Stephen Vaughn, *Ronald Reagan in Hollywood: Movies and Politics* (New York: Cambridge University Press, 1994).
11. George Gascoigne Blake, *History of Radio Telegraphy and Telephony* (London: Chapman and Hall, 1928), reprinted by Arno Press (New York, 1974); Susan J. Douglas, *Listening In: Radio and the American Imagination* (New York: Times Books, 1999), pp. 46–51.
12. Leonard S. Reich, *The Making of Industrial Research: Science and Business at GE and Bell, 1876–1926* (New York: Cambridge University Press, 2002), p. 221; Christopher H. Sterling and John M. Kitross, *Stay Tuned: A Concise*

History of American Broadcasting (Belmont, CA: Wadsworth Publishing Company, 1978), pp. 52–54.

13. Douglas, *Listening In*, p. 51.
14. Detroit News, *WWJ – The Detroit News: The History of Radiophone Broadcasting by the Earliest and Foremost of the Newspaper Stations* (Detroit: Evening News Association, 1922).
15. Sterling and Kitross, *Stay Tuned*, p. 59.
16. Michele Hilmes, "NBC and the Network Idea: Defining the American System," in Michele Hilmes, ed., *NBC: America's Network* (Berkeley: University of California Press, 2007), pp. 12–13; Douglas B. Craig, *Fireside Politics: Radio and Political Culture in the United States, 1920–1940* (Baltimore: Johns Hopkins University Press, 2000), p. 19.
17. Hilmes, "NBC and the Network Idea," pp. 13–14.
18. Sterling and Kittross, *Stay Tuned*, p. 107; Eric Barnouw, *Tube of Plenty – The Evolution of American Television* (New York: Oxford University Press, 1975), p. 53; Arthur Frank Wertheim, *Radio Comedy* (New York: Oxford University Press, 1979), pp. 12–13.
19. "Announcing the National Broadcasting Company, Inc," 1926 advertisement reproduced in Sterling and Kittross, *Stay Tuned*, p. 106.
20. Craig, *Fireside Politics*, pp. 45–53.
21. Sterling and Kittross, *Stay Tuned*, p. 81.
22. Robert Staughton Lynd and Helen Merell Lynd, *Middletown: A Study in Contemporary American Culture* (New York: Harcourt Brace and Company, 1936), p. 119.
23. William C. Ackerman, "The Dimensions of American Broadcasting," *The Public Opinion Quarterly* 9 (Spring 1945), pp. 1–18.
24. *Ibid.*, p. 10; H. W. Heinsheimer, "Music and the American Radio," *Tempo* 3 (March 1947), pp. 10–14.
25. Ackerman, "The Dimensions of American Broadcasting," pp 5–11; Kenneth G. Bartlett, "Social Impact of the Radio," *Annals of the American Academy of Political and Social Science* 250 (March 1947), pp. 89–97.
26. Sterling and Kittross, *Stay Tuned*, p. 12; Craig, *Fireside Politics*, pp. 21–22
27. Ackerman, "The Dimensions of American Broadcasting," p. 9.
28. Alice Goldfarb Marquis, "Written on the Wind: The Impact of Radio During the 1930s," *Journal of Contemporary History* 19 (July 1984), p. 392.
29. LeRoy Ashby, *With Amusement for All* (Lexington: University Press of Kentucky, 2006), pp. 210–13; Orrin E. Dunlap, "In the Whirl Again: Phonograph, Disks, and Piano Tossed High on Flood Tide of Radio Music," *New York Times*, February 19, 1939, p. 134.
30. Barnouw, *Tube of Plenty*, p. 56; Sterling and Kittross, p. 112.
31. Dunning, *The Encyclopedia of Old-Time Radio*, p. 31.
32. Wortheim, *Radio Comedy*, p. 48.
33. Gerald Nachman, *Raised on Radio* (New York: Pantheon Books, 1998), pp. 278–79; Melvin Patrick Ely, *The Adventures of Amos 'n Andy: A Social History of an American Phenomenon* (New York: Free Press, 1991). I have relied heavily on Ely in this account of *Amos 'n' Andy*.

34. David Zurawik, *The Jews of Prime Time* [Brandeis University Press] (Hanover: University Press of New England, 2003).
35. For a full description of the development of *Amos 'n' Andy*, see Ely, *The Adventures of Amos 'n' Andy*, and Wertheim, *Radio Comedy*, pp. 18–48.
36. Dunning, *The Encyclopedia of Old-Time Radio*, p. 34.
37. Biographical sources on Jack Benny include Lawrence J. Epstein, *The Haunted Smile: The Story of Jewish Comedians in America* (New York: Public Affairs, 2002); Jack Benny and Joan Benny, *Sunday Nights at Seven: The Jack Benny Story* (New York: Warners, 1990); Irving Fein, *Jack Benny* (Boston: GK Hall, 1976); Mary Livingstone Benny and Hilliard Marx, *Jack Benny: A Biography* (New York: Doubleday and Company, 1978); Michael Leannah, ed., *Well! Reflections of the Life and Career of Jack Benny* (Albany, GA: Bear Manor Media, 2007).
38. "Who's Who," *New York Times*, August 29, 1926, p. X2.
39. "Coaxing the Elusive Laugh," *New York Times*, September 12, 1926, p. X2.
40. "Jack Benny Amuses at Palace Theatre," *New York Times*, November 12, 1928, p. 27.
41. "The Hollywood Revue," *New York Times*, August 11, 1929, p. X4; Nelson H. Hall, "Columbia, Hollywood Revue of 1929," *Washington Post*, October 7, 1929, p. 16.
42. "Those Quaint Musical Show Folk," *New York Times*, July 6, 1930, p. 89.
43. J. Brooks Atkinson, "The Play, for the Summertime, Earl Carroll's Vanities," *New York Times*, July 2, 1930, p. 32; "Year's First Girl Show at the National," *Washington Post*, October 11, 1934, p. A2; Nelson B. Bell, "The Theater Last Night," *Washington Post*, October 12, 1931, p. 10.
44. "Today on the Radio," *New York Times*, March 29, 1932, p. 22.
45. "Theatrical Notes," *New York Times*, April 13, 1932, p. 23; "The Play, Lou Holtz and Co.," *New York Times*, April 19, 1932, p. 25; "N.V.A. Show Gives Charities $26,000," *New York Times*, May 2, 1932, p. 13; Robert D. Hein, "Radio Dial Flashes," *Washington Post*, May 2, 1932, p. 5.
46. "Today on the Radio," *New York Times*, May 9, 1932, p. 18; "The Screen," *New York Times*, May 21, 1932, p. 9.
47. Arthur Wertheim, *Radio Comedy*, pp. 131–56.
48. I base these observations on listening to a sample of the shows from 1932 and 1933.
49. "Jack Goes into Training for a Fight with Fred," broadcast January 29, 1939.
50. "Masquerade Party," broadcast October 29, 1939.
51. "No Date for Jack," broadcast December 31, 1939; Margaret T. McFadden, "'America's Boy Friend Who Can't Get a Date'": Gender, Race and the Cultural Work of the Jack Benny Program, 1932–1946," *Journal of American History* 80 (June 1993), pp. 113–34.
52. "Behind the Studio Scenes," *New York Times*, June 3, 1934, p. X9; "Screen Notes," August 2, 1934, *New York Times*, p. 20; Douglas W. Churchill, "Notes from the Hollywood Piper," March 31, 1935, *New York Times*, p. X3; "On the Merry-Go-Round of the Air," April 7, 1935, *New York Times*, p. X11; "The Merry-Go-Round of Broadcasting," June 9, 1935, *New York Times*, p. X11; "The Screen, 'The Broadway Melody of 1936'

with Eleanor Powell at the Capitol Theatre," September 12, 1935, *New York Times*, p. 28.
53. "The Season Opens," September 13, 1936, *New York Times*, p. X10.
54. "Fabulous Funsters, Radio Pays Enormous Salaries to Comics Once the Stars of Vaudeville," May 14, 1937, *New York Times*, p. X12.

4. From the Thirties to the Forties with Kate, Bud, and Lou

1. "Bulletin for World's Fair Guests," *New York Times*, April 30, 1939, p. 175.
2. Books about Katharine Hepburn that describe her childhood are legion. Like many books about movie stars, they tend to be memoirs in which the authors engage in selective memory, adoring fan biographies, or sharply critical efforts that often try to match their subject with a particular thesis. In Hepburn's case, sexual orientation turns out to be a hot button that writers like to push. See, for example, Katharine Hepburn, *Me: Stories of Myself* (New York: Knopf, 1991); A. Scott Berg, *Kate Remembered* (New York: Simon and Schuster, 2003); Garson Kanin, *Tracy and Hepburn: An Intimate Memoir* (New York: Viking Press, 1970); Barbara Leaming, *Katharine Hepburn* (New York: Harper Collins, 1995); William J. Mann, *Kate: The Woman Who Was Hepburn* (New York: Macmillan, 2006).
3. "Display Ad 15," *New York Times*, October 3, 1932, p. 15.
4. George Cukor became an important personal friend of and professional influence on Katharine Hepburn. See Robert Emmet Long and George Cukor, *George Cukor: Interviews* (Jackson: University Press of Mississippi, 2001).
5. "The Screen Is Indebted to the Stage, 'Bill of Divorcement' Owes Its Success to Theatrical Brains," *New York Times*, October 9, 1932, p. X5.
6. Mordaunt Hall, "The Screen, John Barrymore, Billie Burke and Katharine Hepburn in a Film of a Clemence Dane Play," *New York Times*, October 1, 1932, p. 15.
7. "Pictures and Players in Hollywood, Studio Executive Welcome Returning Katharine Hepburn," *New York Times*, November 13, 1932, p. X5.
8. See, for example, Alexander Doty, *Making Things Perfectly Queer* (Minneapolis: University of Minnesota Press, 1993), pp. 17–38.
9. Mordaunt Hall, "When an Aviatrix Falls in Love," *New York Times*, March 19, 1933, p. X3; Hall, "The Screen, Katharine Hepburn and Colin Clive in a Film of a Gilbert Frankau Novel," *New York Times*, March 10, 1933, p. 19.
10. Mordaunt Hall, "The Screen, Katharine Hepburn, Douglas Fairbanks Jr. and Adolphe Menjou in 'Morning Glory,'" *New York Times*, August 18, 1933, p. 18; Hall, "Mr. Lasky's 'Narratage' Treatment," *New York Times*, August 27, 1933, p. X3.
11. Mordaunt Hall, "The Screen, Katharine Hepburn as Jo in the Film Version of 'Little Women' Now at the Radio City Music Hall," *New York Times*, November 17, 1933, p. 22.
12. "Ten 'Brainiest' Women of Screen Picked; Arnow Omits Four of Best Known Stars," *New York Times*, December 24, 1933, p. 15.
13. "Screen Honor Won by Miss Hepburn, She Is Voted Outstanding Film Actress of Year at Los Angeles," *New York Times*, March 17, 1934, p. 10.

14. "Katharine Hepburn Wins Ovation as Star, Her Debut in Leading Stage Role with 'The Lake,' Is Acclaimed in Capital," *New York Times*, December 19, 1933, p. 26.

15. Brooks Atkinson, "The Play, Katharine Hepburn in a Tragic British Drama Entitled 'The Lake,'" *New York Times*, December 27, 1933, p. 24; "No Tour for 'The Lake.'" Katharine Hepburn to Go Abroad After Play Closes February 10," *New York Times*, February 3, 1934, p. 8.

16. Mordaunt Hall, "The Screen, Katharine Hepburn as a Wild Girl of the Carolina Mountains in a Film Version of the Play 'Trigger,'" *New York Times*, March 9, 1934, p. 22.

17. Andre Sennwald, "The Screen, The Radio City Music Hall Presents a Tender Screen Edition of Barrie's 'The Little Minister,'" *New York Times*, December 28, 1934, p. 25; Sennwald, "The Screen, The Radio City Music Hall Presents Charles Boyer and Katharine Hepburn in 'Break of Hearts,'" *New York Times*, May 17, 1935, p. 24.

18. Andre Sennwald, "The Screen, Katharine Hepburn and Edmund Gwenn in 'Sylvia Scarlett,' at the Radio City Music Hall, *New York Times*, January 10, 1936, p. 16. This movie, because of its gender-bending nature, has received a great deal of attention from scholars and journalists who chronicle Hepburn's and Cukor's careers. See, for example, Amy Villarejo, *Lesbian Rule: Cultural Criticism and the Value of Desire* (Durham: Duke University Press, 2003), pp. 1–26; Mann, *Kate*, pp. 243–44; Charles Higham, *Kate: The Life of Katharine Hepburn* (New York: WW Norton, 2004), pp. 75–80.

19. "'Hades, The Ladies' a Hit at Harvard, Grandsons of Two Presidents Appear as Chorus Members at Hasty Pudding Show, Plot Based on 'New Deal,' R.H. Hepburn, Brother of Film Star, in Play That Finds Girls in University's Classes," *New York Times*, May 29, 1934, p. 25. At the same time, Katharine Hepburn's mother continued to attract attention for her advocacy of birth control and other causes: See "Forum Tomorrow on Birth Control, Mrs. Thomas N. Hepburn to Be Among Speakers at Meeting in Carnegie Hall," *New York Times*, December 1, 1935, p. N8.

20. Frank S. Nugent, "A Purely Personal Reaction," *New York Times*, April 8, 1937, p. 169.

21. "Stage Door," the first of the three pictures, put Hepburn in an adaptation of a George Kaufman and Edna Ferber play. See Scott Meredith, *George S. Kauman and His Friends* (New York: Doubleday, 1974), pp. 504–05; Andrew Briton, *Katharine Hepburn: Star as Feminist* (New York: Columbia University Press, 2004), pp. 66–70; Frank S. Nugent, "The Screen, 'Stage Door,' Hollywood Edition, Opens at the Music Hall," *New York Times*, October 8, 1937, p. 27; Douglas W. Churchill, "Hollywood's Footlights Club," *New York Times*, June 20, 1937, p. 139.

22. Todd McCarthy, *Howard Hawks: The Grey Fox of Hollywood* (New York: Grove Press, 1997), p. 255.

23. Robert Sklar, *Movie-Made America: A Cultural History of American Movies* (New York: Vintage Books, revised edition 1994), pp. 187–88.

24. Wes D. Gehring, *Screwball Comedy: A Genre of Madcap Romance* (Westport, CT: Greenwood, 1986).

25. Graham McCann, *Cary Grant: A Class Apart* (New York: Columbia University Press, 1996), pp. 93–96, contains a nice summary of the movie's plot. See also Peter Bogdanovich, *Who the Devil Made It* (New York: Ballantine Books, 1997), p. 306.

26. *Holiday*, the third in the series of pictures that RKO had lined up for her, fit a similar pattern. See Nelson B. Bell, "Katharine Hepburn and Cary Grant Score a Hit in Columbia's New Screen Version of 'Holiday,'" *Washington Post*, June 2, 1938, p. X18; Frank S. Nugent, "The Screen, a New Version of 'Holiday' Comes to the Music Hall," *New York Times*, June 24, 1938, p. 15.

27. "Film Exhibitors Propose Stars Take Pay Slash," *Washington Post*, May 5, 1938, p. X10; Douglas W. Churchill, "Shooting Stars in Hollywood," *New York Times*, May 8, 1938, p. 159.

28. Douglas W. Churchill, "Hollywood and Its Little Women," *New York Times*, May 15, 1938, p. 151; "News of the Screen, Katharine Hepburn's Contract with RKO Canceled," *New York Times*, May 4, 1938, p. 27; Alexander Kahn, "Hepburn Seems Enigma to All But Her Friends," *Washington Post*, May 15, 1938, p. TT1; "In Hollywood with Hedda Hopper," *Washington Post*, March 21, 1938, p. X9; "Actress Enters New Field," *Washington Post*, March 27, 1938, p. TT2.

29. Dudley Harmon, "Star in Seclusion," *Washington Post*, August 21, 1938, p. B8.

30. "Mrs. Reid Would Cast Hepburn in O'Hara Role," *New York Times*, October 26, 1938, p. 10; "Surveying Scarlett O'Hara," *New York Times*, February 19, 1939, p. 126.

31. "Hepburn Opens in New Comedy," *New York Times*, February 17, 1939, p. 14; Alice Hughes, "A Woman's New York, Katharine Hepburn Planning Comeback in Stage Play; Has No Bitterness Toward Critics," *Washington Post*, February 20, 1939, p. 11; Nelson B. Hall, "Katharine Hepburn Finally Hits Upon a Barry Hit!" *Washington Post*, p. T3; Hall, "Miss Hepburn Perplexed by Capital Audiences," *Washington Post*, March 9, 1939, p. 10.

32. Nelson B. Bell, "Packed House Hails Hepburn in Barry Play," *Washington Post*, March 17, 1939, p. 8; Richard Watts Jr., "Echoes Washington's View of a Play and Its Star," *Washington Post*, April 9, 1939, p. A3.

33. Brooks Atkinson, "The Play, Katharine Hepburn Appearing in Philip Barry's 'The Philadelphia Story' for the Theatre Guild," *New York Times*, March 29, 1939, p. 21.

34. Alice Hughes, "A Woman's New York, Stage Crew Likes Katharine Hepburn – Sure Sign of Theatrical Success," *Washington Post*, April 9, 1939, p. 58; "News of the Stage," *New York Times*, February 26, 1940, p. 11; "News of the Stage," *New York Times*, May 15, 1940, p. 35.

35. Bosley Crowther, "The Screen: A Splendid Cast Adorns the Screen Version of 'The Philadelphia Story' at the Music Hall," *New York Times*, December 27, 1940, p. 22; "Hepburn Picture Sets New Marks," *New York Times*, June 28, 1941, p. 23; Douglas W. Churchill, "Screen News Here and in Hollywood," *New York Times*, December 31, 1940, p. 19.

36. Charles Hurd, "Group of Writers Back Roosevelt," *New York Times*, September 23, 1940, p. 19; Douglas W. Churchill, "Hollywood Wire, Katharine Hepburn's Persuasive Sales Technique," *New York Times*, July 27, 1941, p. X3; "Katharine Hepburn Shatters Precedent," *Washington Post*, October 18, 1941, p. 18.

37. Abbott and Costello have attracted less scholarly attention than either the Marx brothers or Katharine Hepburn. Nonetheless, the usual biographies and other sources exist, such as Chris Costello with Raymond Strait, *Lou's on First* (New York: St Martins, 1991); Jeffrey S. Miller, *The Horror Spoofs of Abbott and Costello* (Jefferson, NC: McFarland, 2004); Lawrence Jeffrey Epstein, *Mixed Nuts: America's Love Affair with Comedy Teams* (New York: Public Affairs, 2004), pp. 129–50; Thomas Schatz, *The Genius of the System: Hollywood Filmmaking in the Studio Era* (New York: Henry Holt, 1986), p. 342.

38. "Jean Bedini and His Own Show Enter Gayety Today," *Washington Post*, September 9, 1934, p. M2.

39. Nelson B. Bell, "'The Last Gangster' and a Gay Revue Comprise Outstanding Bill at Capitol," *Washington Post*, January 1, 1938, p. X4; "Judy Garland at Loew's State," *New York Times*, February 11, 1938, p. 27.

40. John Dunning, *On the Air: The Encyclopedia of Old-Time Radio* (New York: Oxford University Press, 1998), pp. 2–3; "Today on the Radio," *New York Times*, March 3, 1938, p. 37; R. W. Stewart, "The 'Hokiest of the Hoke,' Stepping Out of the Old Joke Book, Abbott and Costello Clown on the Air in Unrestrained Fashion," *New York Times*, August 11, 1940, p. 110.

41. Theodore Strauss, "News of Night Clubs," *New York Times*, November 6, 1938, p. 174; Leonard Lyons, "The New Yorker," *Washington Post*, November 12, 1938, p. X14; "Bud Abbott Picketed as 'Unfair' to Nephew," *New York Times*, February 21, 1939, p. 21.

42. Brooks Atkinson, "The Play, 'The Streets of Paris' Moves to Broadway," *New York Times*, January 20, 1939, p. 29.

43. Leonard Lyons, "The New Yorker," *Washington Post*, August 23, 1939, p. 8; "The Fair Today," *New York Times*, September 6, 1939, p. 24; Leonard Lyons, "The New Yorker," *Washington Post*, December 25, 1939, p. 4.

44. Louella O. Parsons, "Close-Ups and Long-Shots of the Motion Picture Scene," *Washington Post*, July 30, 1940, p. 4.

45. "Today on the Radio," *New York Times*, August 14, 1940, p. 35.

46. Edwin Emery, *The Press and America: An Interpretative History of Journalism*, second edition (Englewood Cliffs: Prentice Hall, 1962), pp. 550–56; Robert J. Brown, *Manipulating the Ether: The Power of Broadcast Radio in Thirties America* (Jefferson, NC: McFarland and Company, 1998), pp. 136–85; Stanley Cloud and Lynne Olson, *The Murrow Boys: Pioneers on the Front Lines of Broadcast Journalism* (Boston: Houghton Mifflin, 1996).

47. Hedda Hopper, "In Hollywood," *Washington Post*, November 8, 1940, p. 14; Nelson B. Bell, "'One Night in the Tropics' Proves Almost a Blackout, at the Earle," *Washington Post*, December 6, 1940, p. 26; Bosley Crowther, "The Screen," *New York Times*, December 20, 1940, p. 33.

48. Douglas W. Churchill, "Screen News Here and in Hollywood," *New York Times*, November 12, 1940, p. 33; John Sforza, *Swing It!: The Andrews Sisters Story* (Lexington: University Press of Kentucky, 2004), pp. 55–56.

49. Douglas W. Churchill, "Hollywood Reports," *New York Times*, November 17, 1940, p. 141; Churchill, "Hollywood Dilemmas," *New York Times*, February 2, 1941, p. X5.

50. Versions of the "Who's on First?" routine have been reprinted countless times, such as in George Plimpton, ed., *The Norton Book of Sports* (New York: WW Norton, 1992), pp. 461–63.

51. Louella O. Parsons, "Close-Ups and Long-Shots of the Motion Picture Show," *The Washington Post*, February 3, 1941, p. 9; "The Screen," *New York Times*, February 14, 1941, p. 15.

52. Hedda Hopper, "In Hollywood," *Washington Post*, May 8, 1941, p. 14; Theodore Strauss, "Two Straws in the March Wind," *New York Times*, March 23, 1941, p. X5; R.W. Stewart, "Radio News and Gossip," *New York Times*, March 30, 1941, p. X12; Leonard Lyons, "Broadway Medley," *Washington Post*, June 16, 1941, p. 14; Frank S. Nugent, "Loco Boys Make Good," *New York Times*, August 24, 1941, p. 112.

53. Bosley Crowther, "The Screen in Review," *New York Times*, June 12, 1941, p. 29; Nelson B. Bell, "'In the Navy,' at Keith's, A Faster and Funnier Hit," *Washington Post*, June 27, 1941, p. 8; Bosley Crowther, "Low Comedy of a High Order," *New York Times*, June 15, 1941, p. X3; TMP, "At the Capitol," *New York Times*, August 8, 1941, p. 13; Nelson B. Bell, "Abbott and Costello Do It Again at RKO-Keiths," *Washington Post*, August 16, 1941, p. 10; Bosley Crowther, "The Screen," *New York Times*, November 27, 1941, p. 29.

54. "Abbott, Costello Top at Box Office," *New York Times*, December 26, 1942, p. 12; "Gossip of Radio Row," *New York Times*, November 5, 1944, p. X7; Hedda Hopper, "Minstrel in Reverse," *Washington Post*, December 10, 1943, p. B9; Bosley Crowther, "The Screen," *New York Times*, December 3, 1942, p. 35.

55. "Abbott to Quit Air Till Costello Regains Health," *Washington Post*, March 20, 1943, p. 4; "Costello Baby Drowns," *New York Times*, November 5, 1943, p. 23.

56. Bosley Crowther, "Way of All Flashes," *New York Times*, December 6, 1942, p. X3; Crowther, "Abbott-Costello, Inc.," *New York Times*, August 20, 1944, p. X1.

57. See Miller, *The Horror Spoofs of Abbott and Costello*.

5. Bogie, Bob, and the Boys at War

1. "And She Can Cook!" *Washington Post*, January 7, 1943, p. B6.

2. Quoted in Aljean Harmetz, *The Making of Casablanca: Bogart, Bergman and World War II* (New York: Hyperion Books, 2002), p. 113.

3. Thomas Schatz, *The Genius of the System* (New York: Henry Holt, 1986), p. 298; Harmetz, *Making of Casablanca*, p. 66.

4. Louella O. Parsons, "Some Changes Have Been Made," *Washington Post*, January 18, 1942, p. L3.

5. Bosley Crowther, "Movies Without Gables," *New York Times*, September 13, 1942, p. SM14; "An Ounce of Prevention," *New York Times*, June 7, 1942, p. X4.

6. "U.S. Missed Chance By Having Only White Movie Stars in Bond Drive," *Chicago Defender*, September 12, 1942, p. 7.

7. "Screen News Here and in Hollywood," *New York Times*, September 24, 1942, p. 23; Clayton Koppes and Gregory Black, "What to Show the World: The Office of War Information and Hollywood, 1942–1945," *Journal of American History* 64 (June 1977), pp. 87–105.

8. Jennifer R. Jenkins, "'Say It with Firecrackers': Defining the War Musical of the 1940s," *American Music* 19 (Autumn 2001), pp. 315–39.

9. Brianca Freire-Medeiros, "Hollywood Musicals and the Invention of Rio de Janeiro, 1933–1953," *Cinema Journal* 41 (Summer 2002), pp. 52–67.

10. Bosley Crowther, "One More Year," *New York Times*, December 27, 1942, p. X3.

11. Dorothy B. Jones, "The Hollywood War Film: 1942–1944," *Hollywood Quarterly* 1 (October 1945), pp. 1–19.

12. Harmetz, *The Making of Casablanca*, provides a good introduction to the movie and the circumstances under which it was made.

13. Hedda Hopper, "Fighters Come First!" *Washington Post*, November 17, 1942, p. B8.

14. Nelson B. Bell, "The Earle Theatre Takes Time by the Forelock," *Washington Post*, January 28, 1943, p. B6; Bell, "'Casablanca' at the Earle, Topflight, Romantic Melo," *Washington Post*, February 6, 1943, p. 4.

15. "Screen News Here and in Hollywood," *New York Times*, April 9, 1942, p. 25.

16. Among many biographies see A. M. Sperber and Eric Lax, *Bogart* (New York: William Morrow and Company, 1997).

17. "Theatrical Notes," *New York Times*, January 1, 1937, p. 18; Stark Young, "The Play, 'Nerves' Is Interesting," *New York Times*, September 2, 1924, p. 22; "The Play, 'Cradle Snatchers' Brings Laughter," *New York Times*, September 8, 1925, p. 28. On that same day in 1925 James Cagney opened in Maxwell Anderson's *Outside Looking In*, and the critic called him "sullen and imaginative."

18. "Helen Menken to Wed Humphrey Bogart," *New York Times*, May 20, 1936, p. 25; "Helen Menken Wed to Humphrey Bogart," *New York Times*, May 21, 1926, p. 21; "Miss Menken Asks Divorce," *New York Times*, November 13, 1927, p. 7; "Humphrey Bogart to Wed," *New York Times*, April 3, 1928, p. 33.

19. "Fox Engineers Second Raid on Ranks of Broadway Aces," *Washington Post*, April 27, 1930, p. A4.

20. Mordaunt Hall, "The Screen, Romantic War Fliers," *New York Times*, March 14, 1931, p. 23; Hall, "The Screen," *New York Times*, March 30, 1931, p. 29; Hall, "The Screen, War Women and Wine," *New York Times*, May 30, 1931, p. 17; J. Brooks Atkinson, "The Play, Thicker Than Water," *New York Times*, December 4, 1931, p. 28.

21. Brooks Atkinson, "The Play," *New York Times*, January 8, 1935, p. 26; Ed Sullivan, "Broadway," *Washington Post*, January 17, 1936, p. 19.

22. Sidney Skolsky, "Hollywood," *Washington Post*, January 17, 1936, p. 19.
23. Frank S. Nugent, "The Screen, Heralding the Warner Brothers Film Version of 'The Petrified Forest,' at the Musical Hall," *New York Times*, February 7, 1936, p. 14.
24. "News of the Screen," *New York Times*, December 20, 1937, p. 23.
25. Frank S. Nugent, "The Screen," *New York Times*, July 21, 1938, p. 14; Nugent, "The Screen," *New York Times*, November 26, 1938, p. 18; "The Screen," *New York Times*, August 11, 1938, p. 13; Mary Harris, "Rackets Film, At Earle, Hits Hard and Well," *Washington Post*, September 10, 1938, p. 8.
26. Parsons, "Close-Ups," *Washington Post*, July 20, 1940, p. 4.
27. "Hollywood Stars Accused as Reds Before Grand Jury," *New York Times*, August 15, 1940, p. 1; "Dies Clears Four Accused as Reds," *New York Times*, August 21, 1940, p. 21; Thomas Brady, "Hollywood Heckles Its Hecklers," *New York Times*, August 25, 1940, p. 111.
28. Bosley Crowther, "The Screen, 'High Sierra,' at the Strand, Considers the Tragic and Dramatic Plight of the Last Gangster," *New York Times*, January 25, 1941, p. 11; Nelson B. Bell, "'High Sierra' Is the High in Gangster Melodramas," *Washington Post*, March 1, 1941, p. 9.
29. Hedda Hopper, "On the Gentle Art of Kissing," *The Washington Post*, July 2, 1941, p. 18; "Bogart Reforms; Becomes Detective," *Washington Post*, July 31, 1941, p. 11.
30. Bosley Crowther, "The Screen, 'The Maltese Falcon,' a Fast Mystery-Thriller with Quality and Charm at the Strand," *New York Times*, October 4, 1931, p. 18; Crowther, "Nil Desperandum," *New York Times*, October 12, 1941, p. X5; Leonard Lyons, "Doctor's Dilemma," *Washington Post*, October 14, 1941, p. 18.
31. Quoted in Sperber and Lax, *Bogart*, p. 193; Bosley Crowther, "The Screen, 'Across the Pacific,' Featuring Humphrey Bogart and Sydney Greenstreet in a Tingling Thriller, Arrives at Strand," *New York Times*, September 5, 1942, p. 9.
32. Dee Lowrance, "Battling Bogarts," *Washington Post*, December 14, 1941, p. L1.
33. "Jack Benny to Play in 'The Horn Blows at Midnight," *New York Times*, May 11, 1943, p. 17; "News of the Screen," *New York Times*, June 7, 1943, p. 9; "Miss Grable Voted Leading 1943 Star," *New York Times*, December 25, 1943, p. 19; "Movie Award Goes to Jennifer Jones," *New York Times*, March 3, 1944, p. 17.
34. "$9,081,280 Raised in Red Cross Drive," *New York Times*, March 19, 1944, p. 23; C. J. Stewart Named to Help Fund Drive," *New York Times*, April 12, 1944, p. 14; Sperber and Lax, *Bogart*, p. 252.
35. Thomas M. Pryor, "Success Story, and News," *New York Times*, February 22, 1942, p. X4; "Tom Taggart Sells $2,250,000 Bonds," *New York Times*, August 17, 1942, p. 4; "17,000 in Park Hear War Bond Appeals," *New York Times*, August 27, 1942, p. 17; "Film Stars Due in Capital Today for Bond Rally Monday," *Washington Post*, August 29, 1942, p. B1.

36. "Scores Publicity for Bond Sellers, Morgenthau Denounces Use of Selling Drive to Promote Personal Affairs," *New York Times*, July 17, 1942, p. 11; "Abbott and Costello Crowned by Mayor," *New York Times*, February 4, 1943, p. 27.

37. Bob Hope has not received the biography he deserves, but see William Robert Faith, *Bob Hope: A Life in Comedy* (New York: Da Capo Press, 2003).

38. "News from Hollywood," *New York Times*, August 5, 1937, p. 19; "Bob Hope May Look Lazy But a Comedian's Life Is Hard," *Washington Post*, November 6, 1938, p. TS1; "A Hit Comedy Heads Bill at Columbia," *Washington Post*, December 17, 1938, p. X18; Hedda Hopper, "In Hollywood," *Washington Post*, November 2, 1938, p. X6; Kay Green, *Broadway Musicals: Show by Show* (New York: Hal Leonard Corporation, 1996), p. 1933; Dunning, *The Encyclopedia of Old-Time Radio*, pp. 105–09.

39. Alice Hughes, "A Woman's New York," *Washington Post*, August 11, 1939, p. 19; "Queen Mary Brings 2,231 Here Safe," *New York Times*, September 5, 1939, p. 14.

40. Frank S. Nugent, "The Screen," *New York Times*, March 14, 1940, p. 33.

41. Bosley Crowther, "The Screen, Bing Crosby, Bob Hope in 'Road to Zanzibar' at Paramount," *New York Times*, April 10, 1941, p. 29; "Film Crowds Set Week-End Marks," *New York Times*, April 15, 1941, p. 27.

42. "Crosby Tops Box Office," *New York Times*, December 29, 1944, p. 12; Nelson B. Bell, "A National Poll Picks Top Screen Favorites," *Washington Post*, November 17, 1945, p. 10.

43. Jenkins, "Say It with Firecrackers," pp. 328–32.

44. Dunning, *The Encyclopedia of Old-Time Radio*, p. 108.

45. "Hope for Humanity"(cover story), *Time Magazine*, September 20, 1943; Lowell Matson, "Theatre for the Armed Forces in World War II," *Educational Theatre Journal* 6 (March 1954), pp. 1–11.

46. Hedda Hopper, "'Rags to Riches' Fulfills Hope,' *Washington Post*, August 19, 1942, p. 8.

47. Bosley Crowther, "The Screen," *New York Times*, October 12, 1944, p. 24.

48. Bogdanovich, *Who the Devil Made It*, pp. 326–33.

49. Hedda Hopper, "Loneliness Is Tragic," *Washington Post*, October 26, 1944, p. 7; Charlie Cherokel, "National Grapevine," *Chicago Defender*, October 28, 1944, p. 15; "Campaign on the Radio," *New York Times*, October 28, 1944, p. 10; Hedda Hopper, "The Bottom Fell Out," *Washington Post*, November 8, 1944, p. 9; Hopper, "This King Business," *Washington Post*, February 6, 1945, p. 7; "Wife Divorces Humphrey Bogart," *New York Times*, May 11, 1945, p. 22; "Lauren Bacall Wed to Humphrey Bogart," *New York Times*, May 22, 1945, p. 13.

6. The Postwar Movie Scene

1. Mary Spargo, "Reds Tried to Ruin Him, Disney Says," *Washington Post*, October 25, 1947, p. 1; Gladwin Hill, "Stars Fly to Fight Inquiry into Films," *New York Times*, October 27, 1947, p. 1. A standard source is Larry Ceplair and Steven Englund, *The Inquisition in Hollywood: Politics in the Film Community, 1930–1960* (Urbana: University of Illinois Press, 2003). See also

Bud and Ruth Schultz, *It Did Happen Here: Recollections of Political Repression in America* (Berkeley: University of California Press, 1990).

2. Thomas Schatz, *The Genius of the System: Hollywood Filmmaking in the Studio Era* (New York: Henry Holt, 1986), p. 435; Tino Balio, *United Artists: The Company that Changed the Film Industry* (Madison: University of Wisconsin Press, 1987), p. 125.

3. Richard Schickel, *Elia Kazan: A Biography* (New York: Harper Collins, 2005), p. 285; "War Boom in Films Over, Says Warner," *New York Times*, August 6, 1947, p. 26.

4. Darryl Zanuck to All Producers and Executives, March 12, 1953, in Rudy Behlmer, ed., *Memo from Darryl F. Zanuck: The Golden Years at Twentieth Century-Fox* (New York: Grove Press, 1993), pp. 233–34.

5. Balio, *United Artists*, p. 87; Schatz, *The Genius of the System*, p. 437.

6. Scott Eyman, *Lion of Hollywood: The Life and Legend of Louis B. Mayer* (New York: Simon and Schuster, 2005), p. 443.

7. Thomas M. Pryor, "Observations on the Past Year in Hollywood, Industry Faces Future with Confidence in a Changing Motion Picture Scene," *New York Times*, December 30, 1951, p. X5; "Poll Lists Stewart Film Box-Office King," *New York Times*, December 29, 1955, p. 14; Marc Eliot, *Jimmy Stewart: A Biography* (New York: Harmony Books, 2006), pp. 247–55.

8. Schickel, *Elia Kazan*, pp. 296–317.

9. Earl J. Hess and Pratibha A. Dabholkar, *Singin' in the Rain* (Lawrence: University Press of Kansas, 2009).

10. Quoted in Ed Sikov, *On Sunset Boulevard: The Life and Times of Billy Wilder* (New York: Hyperion, 1998), p. 367.

11. Marilyn Monroe has inspired countless biographies, novels, and other books. Among them, see Carl Edward Rollyson, *Marilyn Monroe: A Life of the Actress* (New York: Da Capo Press, 1993); Barbara Leaming, *Marilyn Monroe* (New York: Crown Publishing, 1990); and Donald Spoto, *Marilyn Monroe: The Biography*. Even celebrated author Norman Mailer wrote a biography, *Marilyn: A Biography* (New York: Grosset and Dunlap, 1973).

12. Sikov, *On Sunset Boulevard*, p. 366; Charlotte Chandler, *Nobody's Perfect* (New York: Hal Leonard Corporation, 2004); Richard Alleman, *New York: The Movie Lover's Guide* (New York: Random House, 2005), pp. 355–56; Megan Gressor and Kerry Cook, *All for Love* (New York: Murdoch Books, 2005), pp. 283–89.

13. Sikov, *On Sunset Boulevard*, p. 426.

14. Tony Curtis with Peter Golenbock, *American Prince: A Memoir* (New York: Random House, 2008).

15. Will Holtzman, *Jack Lemmon* (New York: Pyramid, 1977).

16. Sikov, *On Sunset Boulevard*, pp. 428–52.

7. Make Room for TV

1. "Obviously Self-Defense," *New York Times*, October 21, 1952, p. 31.

2. Orrin E. Dunlap Jr., "Seeing a Telecast," *New York Times*, November 15, 1936, p. X10.

3. David Bianculli, *Teleliteracy: Taking Television Seriously* (New York: Simon and Schuster, 1992), p. 42; "News Around the Studios," *New York Times*, August 27, 1939, p. X10; "News Notes and Gossip," *New York Times*, July 21, 1940, p. X10.

4. Harry Castleman and Walter J. Podrazik, *The TV Schedule Book: Four Decades of Network Programming from Sign-On to Sign-Off* (New York: McGraw-Hill, 1984), pp. vii, 1.

5. Castleman and Podrazik, *The TV Schedule Book*, pp. vii, 2; Abel Green and Joe Laurie Jr., *Show Biz from Vaude to Video* (New York: Henry Holt and Company, 1951), pp. 532–33; Eric Barnouw, *Tube of Plenty: The Evolution of American Television* (New York: Oxford University Press, 1982), p. 102.

6. Castleman and Podrazik, *The TV Schedule Book*, pp. 3, 43.

7. James L. Baughman, *Same Time, Same Station: Creating American Television, 1948–1961* (Baltimore: Johns Hopkins University Press, 2007), pp. 51, 74.

8. Barnouw, *Tube of Plenty*, p. 112.

9. Douglas Gomery, "Rethinking Television History," in Gary R. Edgerton and Peter C. Rollins, eds., *Television Histories: Shaping Collective Memory in the Media Age* (Lexington: University Press of Kentucky), p. 293.

10. David Weinstein, "Capitalizing on the Capital: WMAL-TV," in Michael D. Murray and Donald G. Godfrey, eds., *Television in America: Local Station History from Across the Nation* (Ames: Iowa State University Press, 1997), pp. 61–70.

11. Russell A. Jenisch and Yasue Kuwahara, "The Nation's Station: WLWT-TV, Cincinnati," and William James Ryan, "'In the Heartland' WDAF-TV, Kansas City," in Murray and Godfrey, eds., *Television in America*, pp. 156–62, 282–84. It is worth noting that before the Eastern hookup, the Midwest stations were tied to Chicago, where NBC and CBS ran a live Midwest network. About the only show to survive the shift to New York production was *Kukla, Fran, and Ollie*, which featured the puppets of Burr Tillstrom. I am indebted to an anonymous reader of this manuscript for this point.

12. Barnouw, *Tube of Plenty*, p. 103.

13. James N. Miller, "Vaudeville on Video," *New York Times*, October 24, 1948, p. X11.

14. Donna McCrohan, *Prime Time, Our Time: America's Life and Times Through the Prism of Television* (Rocklin, CA: Prima Publishing, 1990), pp. 22–29; on Milton Berle, Sid Caesar, and the other stars of early television, see Frank Wertheim, "The Rise of Milton Berle," in John O'Connor, ed., *American History/American Television* (New York: Frederick Ungar, 1983), p. 56; Susan Murray, "Ethnic Masculinity and Early Television's Vaudeo Star," *Cinema Journal* 42 (Autumn 2002), pp. 97–119; Baughman, *Same Time, Same Station*, pp. 49–51; "The Child Wonder," cover story, *Time Magazine*, May 16, 1947; Gilbert Milstein, "Bring Things to a Berle," *New York Times*, April 8, 1951, p. 77; Larry Gelbart, *Laughing Matters* (New York: Random House, 1998); James Robert Parish, *It's Good to Be the King: The Seriously Funny Life of Mel Brooks* (Hoboken, NJ: John Wiley

and Sons, 2007); Neil Simon, *Rewrites: A Memoir* (New York: Simon and Schuster, 1996); Neil Simon, *The Play Goes On: A Memoir* (New York: Simon and Schuster, 1999); David Marc, *Comic Visions: Television Comedy and American Culture* (Boston: Unwin Hyman, 1989), pp. 70–72; Ginny Weissman and Connie Steven Sanders, *The Dick Van Dyke Show* (New York: St. Martin's Press, 1993); Tim Brooks and Earle Marsh, *The Complete Directory to Prime Time Network and Cable Shows, 1946–Present*, sixth edition (New York: Ballantine Books, 1995), pp. 1160–61; "Decline of the Comedians," *Time Magazine*, May 27, 1957.

15. "Sunday Night Scramble," *Time Magazine*, December 6, 1948; "Paley's Comet," *Time Magazine*, February 21, 1949.

16. "How Many Grains of Sand," *Time Magazine*, January 24, 1949.

17. Thomas F. Brady, "Benny Returning to Screen at R.K.O.," *New York Times*, December 11, 1950, p. 31.

18. In this description of Jack Benny's television career, I rely heavily on James L. Baughman, "Nice Guys Last Fifteen Seasons: Jack Benny on Television, 1950–1965," in Edgerton and Rollins, *Television Histories*, pp. 309–34.

19. Arthur Marx, "No 1 Master of Timing," *New York Times*, February 13, 1955, p. 207.

20. "Joan Benny Married," *New York Times*, March 10, 1954, p. 30.

21. Bill Davidson, "Buck$ Benny Rides Again," *Saturday Evening Post* 236 (March 2, 1963), pp. 26–31.

22. Bosley Crowther, "The Screen," *New York Times*, July 12, 1947, p. 7.

23. "The News of the Radio: Groucho Marx and Opie Cates Will Head Consecutive Shows on ABC Mondays," *New York Times*, October 23, 1947, p. 50; Jack Gould, "Programs in Review," *New York Times*, December 7, 1947, p. 93; Louis Calta, "'April Fool' Trial Will Be on Coast," *New York Times*, July 24, 1948, p. 9; Sam Zolotow, "Krasna-Marx Play Will Open Tonight," *New York Times*, September 27, 1948, p. 26; Brooks Atkinson, "At the Theatre," *New York Times*, September 28, 1948, p. 32.

24. Val Adams, "Groucho in Mufti," *New York Times*, April 23, 1950, p. X9; "Radio and Television, Groucho Marx Signs 8-Year Contract with N.B.C.," *New York Times*, May 29, 1950, p. 19.

25. Jack Gould, "TV Debut Is Made by Groucho Marx," *New York Times*, October 6, 1950, p. 34.

26. Jack Shanley, "TV – Groucho Marx Returns," *New York Times*, September 28, 1956, p. 55.

27. Val Adams, "Sponsor Asks to Quit," *New York Times*, January 13, 1958, p. 49; Val Adams, "C.B.S. Buys Show by Groucho Marx," *New York Times*, November 13, 1961, p. 63; Jack Gould, "TV: Groucho on C.B.S.," *New York Times*, January 12, 1962, p. 48.

28. Stefan Kanfer, *Groucho: The Life and Times of Julius Henry Marx* (New York: Alfred Knopf, 2000), pp. 374–94.

29. McCrohan, *Prime Time, Our Time*, pp. 50–52.

30. For biographical details of Lucille Ball's life, see Stefan Kanfer, *Ball of Fire: The Tumultuous Life and Times of Lucille Ball* (New York: Alfred Knopf, 2003); for contemporary coverage of her life and career, see "Sassafrassa,

the Queen," *Time Magazine*, May 26, 1952. For an academic take on Lucille Ball, see Alexander Doty, "The Cabinet of Lucy Ricardo: Lucille Ball's Star Image," *Cinema Journal* 29 (Summer 1990), pp. 3–22.

31. James Baughman, *Same Time, Same Station*, pp. 129–30.

32. "Unaverage Situation," *Time Magazine*, February 18, 1952; "The First 10 Million," *Time Magazine*, May 12, 1952.

33. "Birth of a Memo," *Time Magazine*, January 26, 1953.

34. "Lucy's $8,000,000," *Time Magazine*, March 2, 1953.

35. "Lucy and the Gifted Child," *Time Magazine*, June 28, 1954.

36. Of course New York did not simply close as a television production center. Among the New York productions was the *Phil Silvers Show* on film and the *Ed Sullivan* and *Perry Como* shows broadcast live, in addition to various game shows and live dramas. On Phil Silvers and his character Ernest Bilko, see David Everitt, *King of the Half Hour: Nat Hiken and the Golden Age of TV Comedy* (Syracuse: Syracuse University Press, 2001), pp. 98–123; "Old Army Game," *Time Magazine*, December 12, 1955; Baughman, *Same Time, Same Station*, p. 133. On Ed Sullivan, see James Maguire, *Impresario: The Life and Times of Ed Sullivan* (New York: Billboard Books, 2006). On Perry Como and his head writer Goodman Ace, see "Salvatore Mondello, "Perry Como," *American National Biography Online*, October 2001 Update (http://www.anb.org/articles/18/18-03652); "Hubba, Hubba, Hubba," *Time Magazine*, March 18, 1946; "Blue Chip," *Time Magazine*, June 29, 1953; Maurice Zolotow, "King of the Gag Men," *Saturday Evening Post*, April 19, 1958, pp. 44–45, 138–42.

37. "Who Pays the Alimony?" *Time Magazine*, April 25, 1955.

38. Barnouw, *Same Time, Same Station*, pp. 169–70.

39. Erik Barnouw, *Tube of Plenty – The Evolution of American Television* (New York: Oxford University Press, 1975), p. 197; James L. Baughman, *Same Time, Same Station*, p. 169.

40. Brooks and Marsh, *The Complete Directory*, pp. 701–04; Baughman, *Same Time, Same Station*, p. 177; Barnouw, *Tube of Plenty*, p. 151.

41. Aljean Harmetz, "The Man with No Name Is a Big Name Now," *New York Times*, August 10, 1969, p. D9.

42. "A. Hitchcock Taking TV Plunge Tonight," *Washington Post*, October 2, 1955, p. J3; John Crosby, "Merry TV From Macabre Hitchcock," *Washington Post*, November 16, 1955, p. 54.

43. Holly George-Warren, *Public Cowboy No. 1: The Life and Times of Gene Autry* (New York: Oxford University Press, 2007).

44. Robert W. Phillips, *Roy Rogers* (Jefferson, NC: McFarland, 1995).

45. "High in the Saddle," *Time Magazine*, March 4, 1957; Barnouw, *Tube of Plenty*, p. 195; Leonard H. Goldenson (with Marvin J. Wolf), *Beating the Odds: The Untold Story Behind the Rise of ABC* (New York: Charles Scribner's Sons, 1991), p. 129; *Have Gun, Will Travel*, like many of the 1950s TV shows, can be seen on DVD; Donna McCrohan, *Prime Time, Our Time: America's Life and Times Through the Prism of Television* (Rocklin, CA: Prima Publishing, 1990), p. 108.

46. Tim Brooks and Earle Marsh, *The Complete Directory to Prime Time Network and Cable TV Shows, 1946–Present,* sixth edition (New York: Ballantine Books, 1995), pp. 424–25, 592–93.

47. Gay Talese, "The Case of Erle Stanley Gardner," *New York Times,* September 13, 1959, p. BR51; Val Adams, "TV Series Slated for Perry Mason," *New York Times,* February 7, 1956, p. 62.

48. Lawrence Laurent, "Perry Mason Assaults Perry Como Popularity," *Washington Post,* September 21, 1957, p. C16; Laurent, "Perry Mason Isn't Afraid of Losing His Identity," *Washington Post,* June 25, 1959, p. D10; Ona L. Hill, *Raymond Burr: A Film, Radio, and Television Biography* (Jefferson, NC: McFarland, 1999); Michael Seth Starr, *Hiding in Plain Sight: The Secret Life of Raymond Burr* (Milwaukee: Hal Leonard Corporation, 2008).

49. "Ray Collins, 'Lt. Tragg' of 'Perry Mason" Series," *Washington Post,* July 3, 1965, p. C2.

50. Herbert Mitgang, "Raymond Burr, Clean Cases Only," *New York Times,* August 5, 1962, p. 97.

51. Val Adams, "Perry Versus the Ponderosa," *New York Times,* August 15, 1965, p. X13; Adams, "TV Career Ending for Perry Mason," *New York Times,* November 18, 1965, p. 95.

52. Lawrence Laurent, "Raymond Burr Proves He's Perry Mason's Match," *Washington Post,* August 31, 1960, p. C8.

53. Barnouw, *Tube of Plenty,* p. 306.

54. James Gilbert, *A Cycle of Outrage* (New York: Oxford University Press, 1986).

55. Val Adams, "Two 'Physicians on TV Next Fall," *New York Times,* May 18, 1961, p. 71.

56. Midge Decter, "Who Killed Dr. Kildare?" in T. William Boxx and Gary M. Quinlivan, eds., *Culture in Crisis and the Renewal of Civic Life* (Lanham, MD: Rowan and Littlefield, 1996), pp. 49–56.

57. Robert Easton, *Max Brand* (Norman: University of Oklahoma Press, 1970).

58. Rick Shale, "Image of the Medical Profession in the Popular Film," in Paul Loukides and Linda K. Fuller, eds., *Stock Characters in American Popular Film,* Volume 1 of *Beyond the Stars: Studies in American Popular Films* (Popular Press, 1990), distributed by University of Wisconsin Press, Madison, p. 162.

59. Jack Gould, "TV: N.B.C. and C.B.S. Offer Medical Melodramas," *New York Times,* October 5, 1962, p. 49; Val Adams, "TV Doctor Shows Expected to End," *New York Times,* November 19, 1965, p. 79.

8. Putting It Together: Walt Disney Introduces the Baby Boom to Television

1. "Most Important Persons Listed in Joint Opinions," *Los Angeles Times,* September 20, 1935, p. 2; "Yale Gives Honor Degrees to Disney and Tweedsmuir," *Los Angeles Times,* June 23, 1938, p. 3; "Hedda Hopper's Hollywood," *Los Angeles Times,* August 4, 1940, p. C3.

2. For biographical details related to Walt Disney and his career, I rely on Neal Gabler, *Walt Disney: The Triumph of the American Imagination* (New York: Alfred Knopf, 2006), and Michael Barrier, *The Animated Man: A Life of Walt Disney* (Berkeley: University Press of California, 2007).

3. Gary Wills, *Reagan's America: Innocents at Home* (New York: Doubleday, 1986).

4. Mickey Mouse, "The Mouse Mimes the Masters," *Saturday Evening Post* 250 (November 1978), p. 82.

5. Lee Shippey, "The Lee Side O' L.A.," *Los Angeles Times*, November 30, 1930, p. A4.

6. Kathy Merlock Jackson, "Mickey and the Tramp: Walt Disney's Debt to Charlie Chaplin," *Journal of American Culture* 26 (December 2003), pp. 439–44.

7. Edwin Schallert, "Original Music Scores Best," *Los Angeles Times*, November 10, 1929, p. 15; Phillip K. Scheuer, "A Town Called Hollywood," *Los Angeles Times*, November 13, 1932, p. 15; Jacob Cooper, "Comics Mean Hard Labor," *Los Angeles Times*, April 13, 1930, p. B11.

8. John Scott, "Three Little Pigs and Big, Bad Wolf Clean Up Millions," *Los Angeles Times*, October 8, 1933, p. A1; Arthur Miller, "Disney's Artistry Explains Silly Symphony Popularity," *Los Angeles Times*, November 5, 1933, p. A1; "Mickey Mouse Getting Ritzy," *Los Angeles Times*, December 13, 1933, p. 4.

9. "Disney Gets Gold Key," *Los Angeles Times*, January 23, 1937, p. A3; Edwin Schallert, "'Ballet of Flowers' to Renew High Art of Disney 'Symphonies'," *Los Angeles Times*, May 15, 1937, p. 13.

10. Edwin Schallert, "Walt Disney Preparing to Start Production on His First Feature-Length Cartoon," *Los Angeles Times*, July 4, 1934, p. 6; Sheilah Graham, "Mickey Mouse Growing Up; He's Eight Years Old," *Los Angeles Times*, September 28, 1936, p. 13; Dale Armstrong, "Snow White's Debut Listed," *Los Angeles Times*, December 21, 1937, p. 6; "Snow White Premiere Due Tonight," *Los Angeles Times*, December 21, 1937, p. 10; "Publicity Record Attributed to Disney Subject," *Los Angeles Times*, April 5, 1938, p. 10.

11. Edwin Schallert, "'Snow White' Achievement in Film Art," *Los Angeles Times*, December 22, 1937, p. 11; "'Snow White' Sets Records at Cathay," *Los Angeles Times*, January 5, 1938, p. A17; "'Snow White' Shatters Circle Theatre Record," *Los Angeles Times*, April 8, 1938, p. 9; "Praise Heaped on 'Snow White'," *Los Angeles Times*, January 28, 1938, p. 10.

12. "The Amazing Life of 'Snow White'," *New York Times*, December 24, 1962, p. 5.

13. *Ibid.*

14. Edwin Schallert, "'Pinocchio' Remarkable Cartoon Achievement," *Los Angeles Times*, February 10, 1940, p. 12; Read Kendall, "Fans Arrive Early to See Celebrities," *Los Angeles Times*, February 10, 1940, p. 12; Richard Griffith, "'Pinocchio' Flawless to Gothamites," February 9, 1940, *Los Angeles Times*, p. 12; Edwin Schallert, "'Pinocchio' New Movie Milestone for Disney," *Los Angeles Times*, January 30, 1940, p. 12.

15. Hedda Hopper, "In Hollywood," *Washington Post*, February 7, 1941, p. 18.
16. Richard Griffith, "Critics of 'Fantasia' at Loggerheads," *Los Angeles Times*, November 26, 1940, p. 15; "Public Hails 'Fantasia' as New Thrill" and "Fantasound Equipment Limits Engagements," both *LA Times*, February 2, 1941, p. 4; Read Kendall, "Celebrities Attend Film Premiere," *LA Times*, January 30, 1941, p. 9.
17. Edwin Schallert, "Disney Surpasses Earlier Fantasies with New Magic," *Los Angeles Times*, December 20, 1941, p. 9; Richard Griffith, "East Takes 'Dumbo' to Its Heart," *LA Times*, November 4, 1941, p. 13.
18. Westbrook Pegler, "Fair Enough," *LA Times*, December 5, 1941, p. 1A.
19. "Disney Tells Union Threat," *LA Times*, April 30, 1941, p. 5.
20. Gabler, *Walt Disney*, p. 357.
21. "N.L.R.B. Hits Film Union," *Los Angeles Times*, May 7, 1941, p. 11; "New Bargaining Unit Formed for Cartoonists of Screen," *Los Angeles Times*, May 17, 1941, p. 2.
22. "Walt Disney Cartoonists Strike in Bargaining Dispute," *Los Angeles Times*, May 29, 1941, p. A1; "Cartoon Strikers Get No Day Off," *Los Angeles Times*, May 31, 1941, p. A1; "Cartoonists Plan Pickets for Theaters," *Los Angeles Times*, June 1, 1941, p. 2; "Disney Artists Defy Strike," *Los Angeles Times*, June 3, 1941, p. 4; "Effigy Hanged at Disney Plant," *Los Angeles Times*, June 6, 1941, p. 16; "Striking Cartoonists File Disney Wage-Hour Charges," *Los Angeles Times*, June 25, 1941, p. 18; "Disney Studio Strike Ends; Unionists Back to Jobs Today," *Los Angeles Times*, July 29, 1941, p. A3; "Walt Disney Studios Resume Production," *Los Angeles Times*, September 16, 1941, p. A1.
23. "Dewey Will Speak in Bowl Tonight," *Los Angeles Times*, September 24, 1948, p. 1.
24. "Disney Issues Annual Report," *Los Angeles Times*, December 31, 1940, p. A8; Hedda Hopper, "Disney Outlines Postwar Plans," *Los Angeles Times*, February 20, 1944, p. C1.
25. Richard Shale, *Donald Duck Joins Up: The Disney Studio During World War II* (Ann Arbor: UMI Research Press, 1982).
26. Thomas M. Pryor, "Disney Is Saluted by the President," *New York Times*, February 19, 1957, p. 35.
27. "Disney Does It Again." *Washington Post*, February 15, 1953, p. S10.
28. *Time Magazine*, March 1954.
29. "The Busy Air," *Time Magazine*, April 12, 1954.
30. Thomas M. Pryor, "Disney Is Ending Ties with R.K.O," *New York Times*, September 21, 1954, p. 24.
31. "Exploitation," *Time Magazine*, January 1, 1951; Walter Ames, "Disney to Unveil Secrets in High Christmas Program; Model Train Show Debuts," *Los Angeles Times*, November 4, 1950, p. B4; Walter Ames, "Steve Allen Leaving for N.Y. Video Show; Disney Is Jittery Over TV Initiation," *Los Angeles Times*, November 16, 1950, p. 30; Walter Ames, "'One Hour in Wonderland' Is Top-Rate Fare," *Los Angeles Times*, December 23, 1950, p. A5.

32. Cecil Smith, "Disney Bows in Tonight with Salute to Mickey Mouse," *Los Angeles Times*, October 27, 1954, p. 28.

33. Louella O. Parsons, "And Just What Kind of Man Is This Disney," *Washington Post*, January 9, 1955, p. H6.

34. "The Week in Review," *Time Magazine*, November 8, 1954; "Disney, ABC Ready to Sign TV Contract," *Los Angeles Times*, March 30, 1954, p. A1; Walter Ames, "Disney Signs Agreement for TV," *Los Angeles Times*, April 3, 1954, p. A5; Cecil Smith, "Disneyland Is ABC Entry in Next Fall's TV Sweepstakes," *Los Angeles Times*, July 21, 1954, p. 26.

35. John Crosby, "Disney Puts TV to Work Exploiting His Movies," *Washington Post*, December 13, 1954, p. 37.

36. "Father Goose," *Time Magazine*, December 27, 1954.

37. Barbara Berch Jamison, "Amazing Scripts by Animals," *New York Times*, July 18, 1954, p. SM16.

38. Bosley Crowther, "Disney's Nature," *New York Times*, August 22, 1954, p. X1. Disney's famous critics include Richard Schickel, *The Disney Version*, third edition (Chicago: Elephant Paperbacks, 1997).

39. Val Adams, "2nd Disney Series Will Start Oct. 3," *New York Times*, February 23, 1955, p. 35.

40. Jack Gould, "TV: Disney's 'Mickey Mouse Club,'" *New York Times*, October 4, 1955, p. 71.

41. "Screen: Disney and the Coonskin Set," *New York Times*, May 26, 1955, p. 36.

42. Richard Griffith, "Disney's 'Davy Crockett' Hit on Television Screen," *Los Angeles Times*, June 3, 1955, p. B6.

43. Walter Ames, "Unknown Gets Disney Role in TV Film," *Los Angeles Times*, August 14, 1954, p. A5; Hedda Hopper, "Science-Fiction Bit Starts 'Davy' on Way," *Los Angeles Times*, May 18, 1955, p. A6; Hedda Hopper, "Ebsen on Top After Long Haul," *Los Angeles Times*, October 2, 1955, p. E1.

44. Bosley Crowther, "Screen: Dogs and Lovers," *New York Times*, June 24, 1955, p. 17.

45. "Disney Acquires Site for $9,000,000 Wonderland," *Los Angeles Times*, May 2, 1954.

46. "Disneyland Gets Ready for Gala Opening July 18," *Los Angeles Times*, May 5, 1955, p. 16.

47. Walter Ames, "Splash TV Opening Set for Disneyland," *Los Angeles Times*, June 18, 1955, p. A5.

48. Walter Ames, "Fans Await Debut of Disneyland Via TV Screens Today," *Los Angeles Times*, July 17, 1955, p. D11.

49. Ed Ainsworth, "Disneyland Readied by 'Mr. Magic,'" *Los Angeles Times*, June 23, 1955, p. A1.

50. John Crosby, "Another Fellow Agrees Disney Wasn't 'On,'" *Washington Post*, July 10, 1955, p. 44; "Dream Comes True in Orange Grove, Disneyland, Multimillion Dollar Magic Kingdom, to Open Tomorrow," *Los Angeles Times*, July 17, 1955, p. A1. The broadcast of Disneyland's opening, like many Disney features, is available on DVD.

51. "Disneyland Opens Gates to Thousands," *Los Angeles Times*, July 19, 1955, p. 2; "Disneyland Hosts 3,642,597 in Year," *Los Angeles Times*, July 21, 1956, p. 9.
52. Robert W. Rydell, *All the World's a Fair* (Chicago: University of Chicago Press, 1987).
53. Val Adams, "A.B.C. Signs Pact for Disney Series," *New York Times*, January 21, 1957, p. 38.
54. "Disney to Try N.Y. Stage Show, *Washington Post*, January 31, 1962, p. C5.
55. Bob Thomas, "Disney Puts New Life in Animals," *Washington Post*, August 11, 1963, p. G2.
56. "Disney Profits Set Record High," *New York Times*, January 9, 1963, p. 10.
57. Peter Bart, "The Golden Stuff of Disney Dreams," *New York Times*, December 5, 1965, p. X13.
58. Gabler, *Walt Disney*, p. xii; "Walt Disney, 65, Dies on Coast; Founded an Empire on a Mouse," *New York Times*, December 16, 1966, p. 1.

9. The End of an Era?

1. Marc Fisher, *Something in the Air: Radio, Rock, and the Revolution That Shaped a Generation* (New York: Random House, 2007), p. 66.
2. *Ibid.*, p. 68.
3. John Gambling, *Rambling with Gambling* (Englewood Cliffs, NJ: Prentice Hall, 1972).
4. Jonathan Schwartz, *All in Good Time: A Memoir* (New York: Random House, 2004).
5. Eric Lax, *Woody Allen: A Biography* (New York: Alfred Knopf, 1991); Marion Meade, *The Unruly Life of Woody Allen: A Biography* (New York: Scribner, 2000); John Baxter, *Woody Allen: A Biography* (New York: Carroll and Graf, 1998).
6. http://www.guardian.co.uk/film/2001/sep/27/woodyallen.guardianinterviewsatb fisouthbank.
7. Marion Meade, *The Unruly Life of Woody Allen*, p. 40.
8. "Y.M.H.A. Presents 2D Jazz Concert, Allen, Comedian, Heard with Evans and Mann Groups," *New York Times*, May 19, 1962, p. 37.
9. Arthur Gelb, "Young Comic Rising in 'Village,'" *New York Times*, November 21, 1962, p. 26.
10. Joanne Stang, "'Verbal Cartoons': They Happen When Woody Allen Talks of Life, Death and Why His Toaster Hates Him," *New York Times*, November 3, 1963, p. SM61.
11. John S. Wilson, "Woody Allen 'Copes' at the Royal Box," *New York Times*, January 22, 1966, p. 18.
12. Jack Gould, "Viewer's Notebook, Talented Guests Share Spotlight with Johnny and Judy," *New York Times*, December 15, 1963, p. 139.
13. Bosley Crowther, "The Screen: What's New Pussycat," *New York Times*, June 25, 1965, p. 49.
14. A. H. Weiler, "On the Run Toward the 'Money,'" *New York Times*, December 19, 1965, p. X13.

15. Neal Gabler, "FILM VIEW; Chaplin Blazed the Trail, Woody Allen Follows," *New York Times*, September 27, 1992.
16. Mark Harris, *Pictures at a Revolution: Five Movies and the Birth of the New Hollywood* (New York: Penguin Press, 2008), p. 45.
17. Helen Markel, "The Girl Friend," *New York Times*, November 21, 1954, p. 75.
18. Arthur Gelb, "Two Stars Weigh Roles in Musical," *New York Times*, March 21, 1955, p. 20.
19. Leo Friedman, "Accent on Stardom: Julie Andrews," *New York Times*, March 17, 1956, p. 11; Louis Calta, "Critics Doff Hats to 'My Fair Lady,'" *New York Times*, March 17, 1956, p. 11.
20. Harris, *Pictures at a Revolution*, p. 42.
21. Neil Gabler, *Walt Disney: The Triumph of the American Imagination* (New York: Alfred Knopf, 2006), pp. 597–600.
22. James Spada, *Streisand: Her Life* (New York: Crown Publishers, 1995).
23. Vincent Canby, "Hello Dolly," *New York Times*, December 18, 1969, available at http://movies.nytimes.com/movie/review?res=9807E2D6123CEE34BC4052DFB4678382679EDE.
24. James L. Baughman, *The Republic of Mass Culture* (Baltimore: Johns Hopkins University Press, 1992), p. 142.
25. Peter Lev, *American Films of the 70s: Conflicting Visions* (Austin: University of Texas Press, 2000), p. 185.
26. Edward Berkowitz, *Something Happened: A Political and Cultural Overview of the 1970's* (New York: Columbia University Press, 2006), p. 198.
27. "Quotation of the Day," *New York Times*, February 28, 2009, p. A15.
28. Timothy Hollins, *Beyond Broadcasting: Into the Cable Age* (London: BFI Publications, 1984), p. 261.
29. Tim Arango, "Broadcast TV Faces Struggle to Stay Viable," *New York Times*, February 28, 2009.
30. *Ibid.*
31. Michael Cieply and Brooks Barnes, "In Downturn, Americans Seek Silver-Screen Lining," *New York Times*, March 1, 2009.

Movie, Radio, and TV Listings

Movies

Across the Pacific [1942], 89
Air Force [1943], 80
Alice in Wonderland [1951], 142
The Amazing Dr. Clitterhouse [1938], 87
An American in Paris [1951], 102
Angels With Dirty Faces [1938], 87
Animal Crackers [1930], 27–28
Annie Hall [1977], 159–60
The Apartment [1960], 107–09
At the Circus [1938], 31
Bambi [1942], 136
Ben Hur [1907], 7
The Big Broadcast [1932], 39, 40
The Big Broadcast of 1938 [1938], 91
The Big Store [1941], 32
A Bill of Divorcement [1932], 58–59
Birth of a Nation [1915], 9
Bonnie and Clyde [1967], 163
Break of Hearts [1935], 60
Bringing Up Baby [1938], 61, 62, 65
Broadway Melody of 1936 [1936], 55
Buck Privates [1941], 72–73, 85
Butch Cassidy and the Sundance Kid
    [1969], 162
Casablanca [1942], 80–84
Caught in the Draft [1941], 71
Christopher Strong [1933], 59
Cinderella [1950], 142
The Circus [1928], 11–12
City Lights [1931], 12
The Cocoanuts [1929], 27
Copacabana [1947], 117

Davey Crockett, King of the Wild Frontier
    [1955], 147–48
A Day at the Races [1936], 30–31
Dial M for Murder [1954], 102
Duck Soup [1933], 29
Dumbo [1941], 136, 137–38
Fantasia [1940], 133, 136
Flying Down to Rio [1933], 34
42nd Street [1933], 18, 59
Funny Girl [1968], 162
The Gay Divorcee [1934], 35–36
Gentlemen Prefer Blondes [1953], 104
Go West [1940], 31–32
Going My Way [1944], 93
Goldiggers of 1933 [1933], 18
Gone with the Wind [1939], 63
The Graduate [1967], 163–64
Grand Hotel [1932], 98
The Great Dictator [1940], 12
The Great O'Malley [1937], 86
The Great Train Robbery [1905], 4, 5
The Greatest Show on Earth [1952], 102
Hello, Dolly! [1969], 161, 162–63
High Sierra [1941], 88
Holiday Inn [1942], 93
Hollywood Hotel [1938], 41
The Hollywood Revue [1929], 51–52
Horse Feathers [1932], 29
How to Marry a Millionaire [1953], 124–25
I Am a Fugitive from a Chain Gang [1932],
    22, 87
The Jazz Singer [1927], 12

Lady and the Tramp [1955], 148
Limelight [1951], 12
The Little Minister [1935], 60
Little Women [1933], 59
The Maltese Falcon [1941], 88–89
Mary Poppins [1964], 151, 161
Mister Roberts [1955], 106
Modern Times [1936], 12, 133
Monkey Business [1931], 28, 33
Morning Glory [1933], 60
Mr. Smith Goes To Washington [1939], 164
My Fair Lady [1964], 161
My Man Godfrey [1936], 61
Niagara [1953], 104
A Night at the Opera [1935], 30, 33, 85
On the Waterfront [1954], 101
Peter Pan [1953], 143
The Petrified Forest [1936], 86
The Philadelphia Story [1940], 63–64
Pinocchio [1940], 136
Public Enemy [1931], 105
Quo Vadis [1951], 102
Racket Busters [1938], 87
The Road to Singapore [1940], 91, 92–93
The Road to Utopia [1946], 92
The Road to Zanzibar [1941], 93
Room Service [1938], 31, 119
Scarface [1932], 105
The Seven Year Itch [1955], 103
The Shaggy Dog [1959], 151
Silly Symphonies [1933], 134
Singing in the Rain [1952], 102
Sleeper [1973], 159
Snow White and the Seven Dwarfs [1937], 131, 134–36
Some Like it Hot [1958], 104–06
The Sound of Music [1965], 160
Spitfire [1934], 60
Stage Door [1937], 119
Steamboat Willie [1928], 132
Swing Time [1936], 37
Sylvia Scarlet [1936], 60
Take the Money and Run [1969], 159
The Thin Man [1934], 61
To Have and Have Not [1944], 95
Too Many Girls [1940], 120

Top Hat [1935], 36–37, 85, 119
Transatlantic Merry Go Round [1934], 55
Treasure Island [1950], 142
Twenty Thousand Leagues Under the Sea [1954], 143, 145
The Vanishing Prairie [1954], 145
Wake Island [1942], 80
The Way We Were [1973], 162
We're Not Dressing [1934], 39
What's New Pussycat [1965], 158
What's Up, Doc? [1972], 162
Whoopee [1929], 17
Wild Boys of the Road [1933], 22
The Wizard of Oz [1939], 164
Woman of the Year [1940], 66–67
You Were Never Lovelier [1942], 79
You'll Never Get Rich [1941], 79

Radio Programs

Amos 'n' Andy [1928], 47–50, 69
The Goldbergs [1931], 69
Hollywood Hotel [1934], 41
The Jack Benny Show [1932], 52–56
My Favorite Husband [1948], 120
Sam 'n' Henry [1926], 48

TV Shows

Ben Casey [1961], 129
The Beverly Hillbillies [1962], 128
Disneyland [1954], 144–45
Dr. Kildare [1961], 129
Father Knows Best [1954], 124
Gomer Pyle [1964], 116
Gunsmoke [1957], 125–26
Have Gun Will Travel [1957], 125
I Love Lucy [1951], 110
Mickey Mouse Club [1955], 146–47
Our Miss Brooks [1952], 124
Perry Mason [1957], 126–27
Saturday Night at the Movies [1961], 124
The Tonight Show [1962], 118, 158
Wagon Train [1957], 125
You Bet Your Life [1950], 117–18

Index

Abbott, Bud, 57, 67–74
  Broadway career, 69
  Buck Privates, 72–73, 85
  early career of, 68
  film career of, 70–74
  Marx brothers and, comparisons to,
    71–72
  personal problems, 74
  radio appearances, 68–69
  slapstick films of, 70–73
  "Who's on First," 71
Abbott and Costello. *See* Abbott, Bud;
  Costello, Lou
ABC. *See* American Broadcasting Company
Across the Pacific (film) [1942], 89
advertising. *See also* sponsors, radio
  on *Amos 'n' Andy* show, 49–50
  on commercial radio, 46
Aherne, Brian, 60
air conditioning, in movie houses,
  7–8
Air Force (film) [1943], 80
Alber, David, 157
Alice in Wonderland (film) [1951], 142
Allen, Fred, 69
Allen, Woody, 2, 119, 156–60
  Annie Hall, 159–60
  childhood, 156
  film career, 158–60
  film persona of, 159
  influences for, 156
  as joke writer, 156–57
  Marx brothers as influence on, 159

  as standup comedian, 157–58
  Take the Money and Run, 159
AM radio, 155
The Amazing Dr. Clitterhouse (film)
  [1938], 87
American Broadcasting Company (ABC)
  Ben Casey, 129
  Disneyland and, 144–45
American Federation of Labor Cartoon
  Guild, 139
An American in Paris (film) [1951], 102
American Society of Screen Cartoonists, 139
American Telegraph & Telephone (ATT),
  42–43
  transistor technology, 154
Amos 'n' Andy (radio) [1928], 47–50, 69
  advertising and, 49–50
  character backstories, 50
  cultural impact of, 47–48
  on television, 114
Anderson, Eddie, 53, 78
Andrews, Julie, 151, 152, 160–61
  Broadway career of, 160–61
  Mary Poppins, 151, 161
  My Fair Lady, 161
  The Sound of Music, 160
The Andrews Sisters, 73
Angels With Dirty Faces (film) [1938], 87
Animal Crackers (play), 26
Animal Crackers (film) [1930], 27–28
animated films. *See also* Disney, Walt
  critical reception for, 134
  Fantasia, 133, 136

animated films *(cont.)*
  as full-length features, 134–38
  during postwar period, 141–43
  production values under Disney, 133–34
  Snow White and the Seven Dwarfs, 131,
    134–36
  Steamboat Willie, 132
Annie Hall (film) [1977], 159–60
anti-trust regulations, against film industry
  during postwar period, 98–99
  during wartime, relaxation of, 77
The Apartment (film) [1960], 107–09
  corporate themes in, 107–08
  dark tone of, 108–09
Arbuckle, Fatty, 11
Arden, Eve, 124
Arnaz, Desi, 119–22
  Ball and, personal and professional
    relationship with, 119–22
  Desilu Studios, 124
  early career, 119–20
  I Love Lucy, 110
Arness, James, 126
Arthur, Jean, 164
Arzner, Dorothy, 59
Ashby, LeRoy, 177
Astaire, Adele, 33–34
Astaire, Fred, 1, 20, 32–38, 79, 175
  cultural impact of, 36–37
  early career of, 33
  film career of, 34–37
  The Gay Divorcee, 35–36
  Rogers as dance partner, 34–37
  sister as partner, 33–34
  Swing Time, 37
  Top Hat, 36–37, 85, 119
Astor, Mary, 88
At the Circus (film) [1938], 31
Atkinson, Brooks, 26, 64, 69
Austin, John, 171
Autry, Gene, 125
Ayres, Lew, 129

Babbitt (Lewis), 8
baby boom generation, *I Love Lucy*
  and, 122
Bacall, Lauren, Bogart and, 94–96
Balio, Tino, 169, 170, 172, 174, 187
Ball, Lucille, 2, 130
  Arnaz and, personal and professional
    relationship with, 119–22

  Desilu Studios, 124
  early career, 119
  I Love Lucy, 110
  radio career of, 120
"The Ballad of Davey Crockett," 147
Bambi (film) [1942], 136
The Band Wagon (play), 34
Bara, Theda, 7, 9
Barbas, Samantha, 176
Barber, Roland, 172
Barnouw, Eric, 188, 190, 191
Barry, Phillip, 57, 63–64
Barrymore, John, 3
Barrymore, Lionel, 52, 129, 140
Basinger, Jeanine, 170
Baughman, James L., 188, 190, 196
Behlmer, Rudy, 187
Bellush, Bernard, 172
Ben Casey (TV) [1961], 129
  lasting impact of, 129
Benchley, Robert, 28, 93
Benny, Jack, 1, 50–56, 91, 178
  Broadway career of, 51
  early career, 50–51
  film career of, 51–52, 55
  The Jack Benny Show, 52–56
  musical skills of, 50–51
  radio career, 50–56, 68–69, 114
  social status of, within Hollywood, 116
  transition to television, 114, 115–16
Benny, Joan, 178
Benny, Mary Livingstone, 178
Benton, William, 49
Berg, A. Scott, 171, 172, 179
Bergen, Edgar, 114, 135
Bergman, Ingrid, 81–82
Berkeley, Busby, 17–18, 41
  early career, 17–18
  personal scandals, 18
Berle, Milton, 115
Berlin, Irving, 26, 30, 36, 93
Bernhardt, Sarah, 9
The Beverly Hillbillies (TV) [1962], 128
Bianculli, David, 188
The Big Broadcast (film) [1932], 39, 40
The Big Broadcast of 1938 (film) [1938], 91
The Big Store (film) [1941], 32
A Bill of Divorcement (film) [1932], 58–59
Birth of a Nation (film) [1915], 9
blackface, performers in, 48–49
Blake, George Gascoigne, 176

Blanc, Mel, 55
Boasberg, Al, 51
Bogart, Humphrey, 2, 80–90, 100
  accusations of being Communist
    sympathizer, 87
  Bacall and, 94–96
  Broadway career, 84–86
  Casablanca, 80–84
  directors and, relationship with, 89
  early film career, 85
  early life of, 84
  rise to stardom for, 87–89
  social responsibility of, use of fame and,
    89–90
  as spokesman for war effort, 90
  at Warner Brothers, 86–89
Bogdanovich, Peter, 162, 186
Bolger, Ray, 164
Bonnie and Clyde (film) [1967], 163
Boone, Pat, 157
Bow, Clara, 9
Boyer, Charles, 92
Brand, Max, 129
Brando, Marlon, 100, 109
Brandt, Harry, 65
Break of Hearts (film) [1935], 60
Brennan, Walter, 95
Brent, George, 87
Bringing Up Baby (film) [1938], 61, 62, 65
Broadway
  Abbott and Costello on, 69
  Andrews' career on, 160–61
  backstage musicals and, 17
  Benny's career on, 51
  Bogart's career on, 84–85
  exodus of writers from, to Los
    Angeles, 28
  Hepburn, Katharine, career on, 58, 60
  Hope's career on, 91
  Marx brothers and, 24–25
  as source for films, 16–17, 160–63
  Streisand's career on, 162
  transition of performers to Hollywood, 37
Broadway Melody of 1936 (film) [1936], 55
Bromfield, Louis, 96
Brooks, Tim, 190, 191
Brown, Joe E., 106
Brown, Robert J., 182
Buck Privates (film) [1941], 72–73, 85
Burr, Raymond, 126, 127
"But Not For Me," 35

Butch Cassidy and the Sundance Kid (film)
  [1969], 162
Butsch, Richard, 169

cable television, 165
Cagney, James, 86, 105
  accusations of being a Communist
    sympathizer, 87
Cantor, Eddie, 1, 16, 17, 18–19, 39
  "de-semitization" of, 18–19
Capra, Frank, 164
Carson, Johnny, 118, 158
Cartoon Guild. *See* American Federation of
  Labor Cartoon Guild
cartoons. *See* animated films
Casablanca (film) [1942], 80–84
  early production of, 84
  political neutrality as metaphor in, 83–84
  political timeliness of, 81
  viewing of as generational rite of
    passage, 82
Castleman, Harry, 188
Caught in the Draft (film) [1941], 71
CBS. *See* Columbia Broadcasting System
Chaplin, Charles, 1, 9–13, 170
  artistic development of, 10–11
  City Lights, 12
  contract history, 10
  early life of, 9–10
  in Keystone comedies, 10
  as Little Tramp, 10
  Mickey Mouse as homage to, 133
  Modern Times, 12, 133
  personal scandals, 11–12
  as political exile, 12–13
  on sound in film, 15
  vaudeville origins of, 9
Chicago Defender, 78
Chicago Tribune, 48
children's programming, on television,
  146–47
Christopher Strong (film) [1933], 59
Churchill, Winston, 12
Cinderella (film) [1950], 142
Cinemascope, 100
The Circus (film) [1928], 11–12
City Lights (film) [1931], 12
Clark, Mae, 105
Cloud, Stanley, 182
The Cocoanuts (play), 26
The Cocoanuts (film) [1929], 27

Colbert, Claudette, 135
Collins, Ray, 127
Colman, Ronald, 115, 164
Colonna, Jerry, 94
Columbia Broadcasting System (CBS), 45
    early programming, 114–15
commercial radio, as industry, 39–56
    Abbott and Costello as performers, 68–69
    after advent of television, 154–55
    AM/FM formatting regulations for, 155
    Amos 'n' Andy, 47–50, 69
    Ball's career on, 120
    Benny as performer, 50–56, 68–69, 114
    CBS, 45
    Crosby, Bing, as performer, 39
    cultural impact of, 45
    decline of ethnic characters on, 55, 72
    "drive time," 154–55
    early development of, 42
    Federal Radio Commission, 44
    Hoover influence on, 44
    Hope on, 91
    The Jack Benny Show, 52–56
    media technology and, advancements in, 153
    music on, early beginnings of, 42
    NBC, 43–44
    networks, 42–43, 44–47
    news commentators on, 70
    as news source, 69–70
    origins of, 41–44
    political debates on, 70
    Radio Act of 1927, 44
    radio sales and, 42
    record sales influenced by, 46–47
    singing styles tailored to, 40
    sponsors and, 45–46, 47
    technical infrastructure, 40–41
    television and, performers' transition to, 114–16
    transistor technology as influence on, 154
Communism
    Bogart accused of, 87
    Cagney accused of, 87
    within film industry, government fears of, 99
A Connecticut Yankee in King Arthur's Court (play), 17
Copacabana (film) [1947], 117
Correll, Charles, 48–50. *See also Amos 'n' Andy*
    in blackface, 48–49
    early career, 48

Cosby, Bill, 119
Costello, Chris, 182
Costello, Lou, 57, 67–74, 91
    Broadway career, 69
    Buck Privates, 72–73, 85
    early career of, 68
    Marx brothers and, comic comparisons to, 71–72
    personal setbacks for, 74
    radio appearances, 68–69
    slapstick films of, 70–73
    "Who's on First," 71
Cotton, Joseph, 104
Craig, Douglas B., 177
Crawford, Joan, 34, 52, 62
Cristillo, Lou Francis. *See* Costello, Lou
Crockett, Davey, as cultural phenomenon, 147–48
Crosby, Bing
    public image of, 93
    radio career of, 39
    "road" pictures with Hope, 91, 92–93
    singing style of, 40
Crosby, John, 145
Crowther, Bosley, 65, 74, 79–80, 88
Cukor, George, 59, 63, 64, 179
Curtis, Tony, 100, 109, 187
    early career of, 105
    Some Like it Hot, 104–06

Dabholkar, Pratibha A., 187
Davey Crockett, King of the Wild Frontier (film) [1955], 147–48
Davies, Marion, 52
Davis, Bette, 86, 95
Day, Dennis, 53
Day, Doris, 108
A Day at the Races (film) [1936], 30–31
Dean, James, 100
Decter, Midge, 191
Desilu Studios, 124
Detroit News, 42
Dewey, Thomas, 140
Dewey Theater, 7
Dial M for Murder (film) [1954], 102
Dies, Martin, 87
Disney, Walt, 131–52. *See also* Disneyland; labor strikes, against Disney; Mickey Mouse
    artistic control of, for films, 134

artistic v. commercial aspirations of, 136–38
cartoon production under, 133–34
children's programming from, 146–47
as commercial artist, 132
cultural impact of, 131, 152
Disneyland, 143, 148–51
Dumbo, 136, 137–38
early career, 131–32
empire expansion by, 151–52
Fantasia, 133, 136
Ford and, similarities to, 140–41
international popularity of, 145
labor strikes against, 138–41
live action features, 142, 143
Mickey Mouse, creation of, 132–33
Mickey Mouse Club, 146–47
Pinocchio, 136
postwar animated films, 141–43
profits for, 151
as Republican, 138–39, 152
Snow White and the Seven Dwarfs, 131, 134–36
Steamboat Willie, 132
television as cross-marketing tool for, 144, 145
television production under, 143–45
True Life Adventure series, 143, 145–46
wartime propaganda films, 141
Disneyland (theme park), 143, 148–51
audio-animatronic animation in, 151
expansion of, 152
as idealization of small town America, 150
publicity and marketing for, 149
themes within, 150
Disneyland (TV) [1954], 144–45
ABC and, 144–45
Davey Crockett phenomena, 147–48
Disney as host, 144
as marketing tool for Disney feature films, 145
Dodd, Jimmie, 147
Doty, Alexander, 179
Douglas, Kirk, 101
Douglas, Susan J., 176
Dr. Kildare (TV) [1961], 129
in films, 129
lasting impact of, 129
origins of, 129
"drive time" radio, 154–55

Duck Soup (film) [1933], 29
critical response, 29
Dumbo (film) [1941], 136, 137–38
Dumont, Margaret, 26, 30, 31
Dunne, Irene, 149
Dunning, John, 176, 177, 182, 186

Earl Carroll's Vanities (play) [1930], 52
Easton, Robert, 191
Eastwood, Clint, 125
Ebsen, Buddy, 148
Edison, Thomas, 9
Eisenhower, Dwight, 127, 141
Eliot, T. S., 131
Ely, Melvin Patrick, 177
"Embraceable You," 35
Emery, Edwin, 182
Epstein, Joseph, 175
Epstein, Lawrence Jeffrey, 174, 178
ethnicity and race, in popular culture
on commercial radio, decline of ethnic characters, 55, 72
on *The Jack Benny Show*, 54–55
in *The Jazz Singer*, 13–14
performers in blackface, 48–49
in war movies, 80
World War II as influence on, in film industry, 78
Eyman, Scott, 169, 187

Fantasia (film) [1940], 133, 136
artistic v. commercial aspirations in, 136–37
critical praise for, 136
"Fascinating Rhythm," 34
Father Knows Best (TV) [1954], 124
Faulkner, William, 95, 131
Faust, Frederick Schiller, 129
Federal Radio Commission, 44
Fein, Irving, 178
Fields, Lew, 43
Fields, W. C., 91
films, as industry. *See also* animated films; Disney, Walt; musical films; sound era, of film; war movies
anti-trust regulations, during postwar period, 98–99
anti-trust regulations, during wartime, 77
attendance decline, during Great Depression, 20–21
attendance increase, during wartime, 77

films, as industry *(cont.)*
  audience participation in, 3
  Broadway as source, 16–17
  Broadway performers' transition to, 37
  Christian ideals in, 6–7
  comedians in, 32
  cutbacks on long-term performer
    contracts, 100
  development of, early, 4
  financial impact of, 21
  government regulation of, 21–23
  during Great Depression, 20–21
  independent theater owners and, 62
  Internet sources for, 2
  Jewish influence on, 6–7
  lack of respectability for, 6
  links to Communism within, government
    fears of, 99
  major production companies, 4
  of Marx brothers, 25
  media technology for, advancements
    in, 153
  as morale booster, during wartime, 77
  movie houses, early, 7–8
  movie publicity during WW II, 76–77
  movie stars, early, 8–17
  movie stars in military service and,
    influence on, 78
  under New Deal, 22–23
  during postwar period, 98–109
  productions for television, 124
  radio's performers' transition to, 39
  response to television, 100–01
  under Roosevelt, 22–23
  sound era, 3–19
  stockpiling of movies, during wartime, 78
  television and, collaboration with, 124–25
  as trade association, 21
  vaudeville as early entertainment
    partner, 5
  Westerns on television and, 125–26
  during World War II, 76–97
Firestone, Leonard, 92
Fischer, James, 171
Fisher, Marc, 195
Flying Down to Rio (film) [1933], 34
Flynn, Errol, 86
FM radio, 155
Fonda, Henry, 78
Ford, Henry, similarities to Disney, 140–41
Fortune Magazine, 45

42nd Street (film) [1933], 18, 59
Fox, William, 7
Frawley, William, 120
Fred and Ginger. *See* Astaire, Fred; Rogers,
  Ginger
Freed, Arthur, 102
Freedland, Michael, 171
Freund, Karl, 123
Friedrich, Otto, 170
Fuller, Linda K., 191
Funicello, Annette, 147
Funny Face (play) [1927], 34
Funny Girl (film) [1968], 162

Gable, Clark, 34, 78, 100
Gabler, Neil, 169, 170, 192, 196
Gallafent, Edward, 175
Gambling, John, 195
Garbo, Greta, 62
Gardner, Erle Stanley, 126
Garfield, John, 80
Garland, Judy, 68, 103, 164
Garner, James, 125
The Gay Divorce (play) [1932], 34
The Gay Divorcee (film) [1934], 35–36
GE. *See* General Electric
Gehring, Wes D., 172, 174, 180
Gelbart, Larry, 157
General Electric (GE)
  radio and, 41
  RCA and, 41
Gentlemen Prefer Blondes (film) [1953], 104
George-Warren, Holly, 190
Gershwin, George, 28, 33, 102
Gershwin, Ira, 28, 102
Giddins, Gary, 176
Gilbert, Douglas, 169
Gilbert, James, 191
Go West (film) [1940], 31–32
Godfrey, Donald G., 188
Going My Way (film) [1944], 93
The Goldbergs (radio) [1931], 69
Golden, Eve, 169
Goldiggers of 1933 (film) [1933], 18
Goldman, Herbert G., 171
Goldstein, Malcolm, 174
Goldwater, Barry, 152
Goldwyn, Samuel, 17, 22
  on introduction of sound in film, 15
Golenblock, Peter, 187
Gomer Pyle (TV) [1964], 116

Gomery, Douglas, 188
Gone with the Wind (film) [1939], 63
Goodman, Benny, 41
Goodman, Theodosia, 7. *See also* Bara,
    Theda
Gosden, Freeman, 48–50. *See also Amos 'n'*
    Andy
    in blackface, 48–49
    early career, 48
Gould, Jack, 117, 118
Grable, Betty, 17
The Graduate (film) [1967], 163–64
Grand Hotel (film) [1932], 98
Grant, Cary, 62, 64–65, 94, 100
Grauman's Chinese Theater, 8
Great Depression
    film industry during, 20–21
    movie attendance during, 20–21
The Great Dictator (film) [1940], 12
The Great O'Malley (film) [1937], 86
The Great Train Robbery (film) [1905], 4, 5
The Greatest Show on Earth (film)
    [1952], 102
Green, Abel, 170, 172
Greenstreet, Sydney, 89
Gruedel, John, 118
Gunsmoke (TV) [1957], 125–26

Hackett, Buddy, 157
Hanks, Tom, 125
Harmetz, Aljean, 183, 184
Harris, Mark, 196
Harris, Phil, 53
Hart, Lorenz, 17
Hart, Moss, 30
Have Gun Will Travel (TV) [1957], 125
Hawks, Howard, 89, 95, 104
Hawley, Ellis W., 172
Hayes, Helen, 85
Hays, Will, 3, 21–22
Hayworth, Rita, 76, 79
Heatter, Gabriel, 70
Hello, Dolly! (film) [1969], 161, 162–63
Hemingway, Ernest, 131
Hepburn, Audrey, 161
Hepburn, Katharine, 2, 57–67, 179
    as "box office deterrent," 62
    Bringing Up Baby, 61, 62, 65
    Broadway career, 58, 60
    career revival of, 63–67
    career setbacks of, 60–63

    change in public image, self-imposed,
        62–63
    early box office success of, 59–60
    early life of, 57–58
    film career, 58–63, 64–65
    gender-bending dress of, 60–61
    Hughes and, 63
    during 1940s, 66–67
    The Philadelphia Story (film), 57, 63–65
    The Philadelphia Story (play), 57, 63–64
    public popularity of, 65–66
    in screwball comedies, 61–62
    Tracy and, 66–67
    Woman of the Year, 66–67
Hess, Earl J., 187
High Sierra (film) [1941], 88
Higham, Charles, 169
Hilmes, Michele, 176, 177
Hirschorn, Clive, 169
Hitchcock, Alfred, 102
    use of television as promotional
        medium, 125
Hoffman, Dustin, 163
Holden, William, 101
Holiday Inn (film) [1942], 93
Hollins, Timothy, 196
Hollywood. *See also* films, as industry;
        movie studios; television
    production by, 123–24
Hollywood Hotel (radio) [1934], 41
Hollywood Hotel (film) [1938], 41
The Hollywood Revue (film) [1929], 51–52
Holtzman, Will, 187
Hoover, Herbert, 21
    regulation of radio industry under, 44
Hope, Bob, 2, 32, 71, 90–94
    Broadway career, 91
    film career, 91–93
    radio career, 91
    "road" pictures with Crosby, Bing, 91,
        92–93
    as spokesman for war effort, 93–94
    wartime tours, 94
Hopper, Hedda, 63, 64, 81, 91, 94, 95–96,
        131, 148
    on Disney films, 136
Horse Feathers (film) [1932], 29
House Un-American Affairs Committee, 101
How to Marry a Millionaire (film) [1953],
        124–25
Howard, Leslie, 85–86

Hudson, Rock, 108
Hughes, Howard, 63
Huston, John, 89
Huston, Walter, 89

I Am a Fugitive from a Chain Gang (film)
    [1932], 22, 87
I Love Lucy (TV) [1951], 110
    baby boom generation and, 122
    blurring of TV show and real life, 120–21
    cultural politics of, 121–22
    production of, 122–23
    ratings for, 121
    reruns of, 123
    writing for, 121
Iger, Robert, 165
I'll Say She Is (play), 26
independent theater owners, 62
Internet
    film history from, as source, 2
    television dominance challenged by, 165
Iskowitz, Israel, 16. *See also* Cantor, Eddie
The Jack Benny Show (radio) [1932], 52–56
    development of show, 53–54
    ethnic aspects of, 54–55
    move to West Coast, 55
    stock company for, 53
Jackson, Gail, 127
The Jazz Singer (play) [1925], 13
The Jazz Singer (film) [1927], 12
    as Broadway play, 13–14
    ethnic immigration as backdrop for,
        13–14
    as transformative experience, 14
Jenisch, Russell A., 188
Jessel, George, 13, 171
Jewish immigrants, film history influenced
        by, 6–7
    Christian ideals and, 6–7
Johnson, Andrew, 78
Johnson, Malcolm, 101
Jolson, Al, 1, 14–15, 39
    in blackface, 48–49
    The Jazz Singer (film), 12
    The Jazz Singer (play), 13
    as musical comedy star, 15
    vaudeville history of, 14–15

Kaltenborn, H. V., 70
Kanfer, Stefan, 172, 173, 174, 189
Kanin, Garson, 179

Kaufman, George, 26, 28, 30
Kazan, Elia, 101
    House Un-American Affairs Committee
        testimony, 101
Keaton, Buster, 13, 52
Keaton, Diane, 159
Kelly, Gene, 102
Kelly, Grace, 101
Kennedy, John F., 128
Kennedy, Myrna, 18
Kern, Jerome, 33, 37
Kitross, John M., 176
Krushchev, Nikita, 152
Kubelsky, Benjamin. *See* Benny, Jack
Kubelsky, Meyer, 50
Kuwahara, Yasue, 188

labor strikes, against Disney, 138–41
    Disney-created company union, 138–39
    fights against Cartoon Guild, 139
Lady and the Tramp (film) [1955], 148
Lady Be Good (play) [1924], 33–34
LaGuardia, Fiorello, 69
The Lake (play) [1933], 60
Lamour, Dorothy, 92
Lancaster, Burt, 101
Langford, Frances, 94
Lasker, Albert, 49
Laurie, Joe, Jr., 170, 172
Lax, Eric, 195
Leaming, Barbara, 179
Lee, Sammy, 26
legal dramas, on television, 126–27
Leigh, Janet, 105
Lemmon, Jack, 98, 101, 109
    The Apartment, 107–09
    early career of, 105–06
    Some Like it Hot, 104–06
Lenneah, Michael, 178
LeRoy, Mervyn, 23
"Let's Face the Music and Dance," 36
Lev, Peter, 196
Lewis, Sinclair, 8
Limelight (film) [1951], 12
Lindbergh, Charles, 14
Linkletter, Art, 149
The Little Minister (film) [1935], 60
Little Women (film) [1933], 59
Lloyd, Harold, 13
Loew, Marcus, 6
Loew, Nicholas, 7

Lombard, Carole, 62
Long, Robert Emmet, 179
Lorre, Peter, 89
Los Angeles Times, 149
Loukides, Paul, 191
Louvish, Simon, 172
Loy, Myrna, 62
Lynd, Helen Merell, 177
Lynd, Robert Staughton, 177
Lynn, Kenneth Scuyler, 170

MacLaine, Shirley, 108–09, 164
MacMurray, Fred, 108–09, 151
"made for television" movies, 125
The Maltese Falcon (film) [1941], 88–89
Mann, William J., 179
March, Frederic, 87
Marconi, Guglielmo, 41
Marks, Sadie, 53
Marsh, Earle, 190, 191
Marx, Adolph "Harpo," 24, 172. *See also*
    Marx brothers
Marx, Arthur, 173
Marx, Hilliard, 178
Marx, Julius "Groucho," 1, 20, 172 *See also*
    Marx brothers
  career decline, 116–17
  career revival, 117, 118–19
  early career of, 23–24
  as product spokesman, 118
  transition to television, 116–19
  You Bet Your Life, 117–18,
Marx, Leonard "Chico," 24. *See also* Marx
    brothers
Marx, Minnie, 23–24, 51
Marx, Sam, 23
Marx brothers, 23–32
  Abbott and Costello and, comparisons to,
    71–72
  Allen, Woody, influenced by, 159
  Animal Crackers, 27–28
  on Broadway, 24–26
  character development for, 24
  The Cocoanuts (film), 27
  The Cocoanuts (play), 26
  A Day at the Races, 30–31
  decline in popularity of, 31–32
  Duck Soup, 29
  early career of, 23–24
  in films, 25
  at MGM, 30–31

  move to Los Angeles, 28
  A Night at the Opera, 30, 33, 85
  at Paramount Studios, 27–30
  on vaudeville circuit, 24
Mary Poppins (film) [1964], 151, 161
May, Elaine, 157
Mayer, Louis B., 6, 22, 31, 100
McCann, Graham, 181
McCarthy, Todd, 180
McCrohan, Donna, 188, 189
McGranery, James, 12
McQueen, Steve, 125
Meade, Marion, 195
media technology, advancements in, 153
  structural platforms for, 166
medical dramas, on television, 128–29
Melnick, Jeffrey Paul, 171
Meredith, Scott, 173, 180
Methot, Mayo, 89, 95
Metro Goldwyn Mayer (MGM), 6
  Marx brothers at, 30–31
  Mayer departure from, 100
  musical films at, during postwar period,
    102
MGM. *See* Metro Goldwyn Mayer
Mickey Mouse, 132–33
  Chaplin and, resemblance to, 133
  marketing of, 132–33
  Steamboat Willie, 132
Mickey Mouse Club (TV) [1955], 146–47
Mickey Mouse Club Magazine, 147
Milland, Ray, 164
Miller, Arthur, 101
Mills, Hayley, 151
Milner, Cork, 169
miltary draft, films about, 71
Minow, Newton, 128
Mister Roberts (film) [1955], 106
Mitchell, Margaret, 63
Modern Times (film) [1936], 12, 133
Monkey Business (film) [1931], 28, 33
Monroe, Marilyn, 101, 102–06, 109, 115
  early life of, 103
  Gentlemen Prefer Blondes, 104
  public perception of, 103
  The Seven Year Itch, 103
  Some Like it Hot, 104–06
  at Twentieth Century Fox, 103–04
  Wilder on working with, 103, 104
Montgomery, Robert, 78
Moore, Gary, 157

Morgan, Dennis, 84
Morgan, J. P., 92
Morgan, Michele, 84
Morgenthau, Henry, 92
Morning Glory (film) [1933], 60
Motion Picture Herald, 90
Motion Pictures Producers and Distributors
     Association, 21, 22
movie houses. *See* theaters, for film
movie stars
     early, 8–17
     in military service, influence on film
          production, 78
     studio development of, 9
     on television, failure of, 164
movie studios. *See also* Metro Goldwyn
     Mayer; Paramount Studios; RKO
     Studios, Fred and Ginger films at;
     Twentieth Century Fox Studios,
     Monroe at; Warner Brothers
     divestiture of theater holdings by, 99
     "made for television" movies, 125
     television and, collaboration with, 124–25
     television production by, 124
Mr. Smith Goes To Washington (film)
     [1939], 164
Muir, Esther, 18
Muni, Paul, 23, 86, 87, 88, 90
Murray, Michael D., 188
musical films
     as backstage story, 17
     Berkeley and, 17–18
     Broadway as source for, 16–17, 160–63
     early, 15–17
     at MGM, as second Golden Age of, 102
     during postwar period, 102
     during WW II, 79–80
My Fair Lady (play) [1956], 161
My Fair Lady (film) [1964], 161
My Favorite Husband (radio) [1948], 120
My Man Godfrey (film) [1936], 61

Nachman, Gerald, 177
Nasaw, David, 169, 170
National Broadcasting Company (NBC),
     43–44
     company mission, 43–44
     early television programming, 117–18
     television development and, 111
National Industrial Recovery Act (U.S.), 22
nature films. *See* True Life Adventure series

NBC. *See* National Broadcasting Company
New Deal, 22–23
New York Times, 3, 59, 114
The New Yorker, 26
Niagara (film) [1953], 104
Nichols, Mike, 157
     The Graduate, 163–64
nickelodeons, 5–6
"Night and Day," 34
A Night at the Opera (film) [1935], 30,
     33, 85
Niven, David, 159
Novak, Kim, 101

Obama, Barack, 37
     inauguration of, expansion of media
          outlets for, 165
O'Brien, Pat, 86, 105
Olderman, Stuart, 170
Olsen, George, 52
Olson, Lynne, 182
On the Waterfront (film) [1954], 101
     political themes in, 101
Oppenheimer, Jess, 121
O'Toole, Peter, 158
Our Miss Brooks (TV) [1952], 124

Paley, William, 114
Paramount Studios
     Marx brothers at, 27–30
Parker, Dorothy, 28
Parker, Fess, 148, 149
Parsons, Louella, 41, 64, 69, 73, 87
     on Disney, 144
Pegler, Westbrook, 137
Pendleton, Nat, 85
Perelman, S. J., 28
Perry Mason (TV) [1957], 126–27
     background history of, 126
     character adjustments for television, 127
     cultural impact of, 127
     in films, 126
     international popularity of, 127
Peter Pan (film) [1953], 143
The Petrified Forest (play) [1935], 85–86
The Petrified Forest (film) [1936], 86
The Philadelphia Story (play) [1939], 57,
     63–64
     critical success of, 64
The Philadelphia Story (film) [1940], 57,
     63–65

Phillips, Robert W., 190
phonographic records, decline in sales as
  result of commercial radio, 46–47
Picasso, Pablo, 131
Pickford, Mary, 9
Pinocchio (film) [1940], 136
  Hollywood support for, 136
Plimpton, George, 183
Podrazik, Walter J., 188
Porter, Cole, 33
Potter, Phyllis Livingston, 34
Powell, Dick, 41, 124
Powell, William, 61–62
Present Arms (play), 17
Presley, Elvis, 100
propaganda films
  by Disney, 141
  war movies as, 80
Public Enemy (film) [1931], 105
Purdy, Jim, 172
Pygmalion. See My Fair Lady

Quo Vadis (film) [1951], 102

race. *See* ethnicity and race, in popular
  culture
Racket Busters (film) [1938], 87
radio. *See also* commercial radio, as industry
  ATT and, 42–43
  in automobiles, 154
  early uses of, 41
  GE and, 41
  invention of, 41
  media technology for, advancements
    in, 153
  transistor technology, 154
radio, sales of, 42
  increase in, 44–45
  as part of home entertainment center, 44
  transistor technology as influence on, 154
Radio Act of 1927 (US), 44
Radio Corporation of America (RCA), 41
  television development and, 111
radio sponsors. *See* sponsors, radio
Raft, George, 89, 92, 105
RCA. *See* Radio Corporation of America
Reagan, Ronald, 78, 84, 88, 152
records. *See* phonographic records, decline
  in sales as result of commercial radio
Red Scare. *See* Communism; House Un-
  American Affairs Committee

regulation, of film industry, 21–23
  under Roosevelt, 22–23
Reich, Leonard S., 176
reruns, of television programs, 123
Reynolds, Debbie, 164
RKO Studios, Fred and Ginger films at,
  35–37
The Road to Singapore (film) [1940], 91,
  92–93
The Road to Utopia (film) [1946], 92
The Road to Zanzibar (film) [1941], 93
The Robe (1953), 100
Roberta (play), 91
Robeson, Paul, 90
Robinson, David, 170
Robinson, Edward G., 86
Roffman, Peter, 172
Rogers, Ginger, 2, 20, 175
  Astaire as dance partner, 34–37
  cultural impact of, 36–37
  early career of, 34–35
  The Gay Divorcee, 35–36
  as Republican, 140
  Swing Time, 37
  Top Hat, 36–37, 85, 119
Rodgers, Richard, 17, 28
Rogers, Will, 43
Room Service (film) [1938], 31, 119
Rooney, Mickey, 129
Roosevelt, Franklin D., 22–23
  on films as morale booster during
    wartime, 77
  New Deal under, 22–23
Ross, Shirley, 91
Roxy Theater, 8
Rubin, Martin, 171
Rubin, Rachel, 171
Ruh, Evelyn, 18
Ruth, Babe, 14
Rydell, Robert W., 195
Ryskind, Morrie, 26, 30

Saint, Eva Marie, 101, 109
Sam 'n' Henry (radio) [1926], 48
  Amos 'n' Andy and, 47–50, 69
  as franchised characters, 49
  as immigrant saga, 49
  racial aspects of, 48
Sandrich, Mark, 35
The Saturday Evening Post, 5, 45
Saturday Night at the Movies (TV) [1961], 124

Scarface (film) [1932], 105
Schatz, Thomas B., 169, 172, 183, 187
Schickel, Richard, 170, 187
Schwartz, Bernard, 105. *See also* Curtis,
   Tony
Schwartz, John, 195
Screen Cartoon Guild, 139
screwball comedy, 61–62
   conventions of, 61
   origins of, 61
Selective Service Act (U.S.), 71
Sellers, Peter, 158
Selznick, David, 34, 63
Sennett, Max, 10
The Seven Year Itch (film) [1955], 103
   production of, 104
Sforza, John, 183
The Shaggy Dog (film) [1959], 151
Shale, Richard, 191, 193
Shearer, Norma, 40, 91–92
Sheridan, Ann, 84, 86
Sherwood, Robert, 85
Sikov, Ed, 187
silent films, production decline of, 17
Silly Symphonies (film) [1933], 134
Silverman, Fred, 164
Singin' in the Rain (film) [1952], 102
Skelton, Red, 114
Sklar, Robert, 61, 169, 170, 180
slapstick films, 70–73
Sleeper (film) [1973], 159
Smith, Kate, 52, 68
Snow White and the Seven Dwarfs (film)
   [1937], 131, 134–36
   critical reviews for, 135
   production process for, 134–35
   publicity and marketing for, 135
   re-releases for, 136
   as template for future productions,
   135–36
Some Like it Hot (film) [1958], 104–06
   cross-dressing theme in, 105
sound era, of film, 3–19
   ambivalence of artists, in early period, 15
   Berkeley and, 17–18
   Broadway as influence on, 16–17
   Chaplin on, 15
   decline of silent films, 17
   early examples, 3
   early musicals, 15–17
   Goldwyn on, early introduction of, 15

The Jazz Singer and, 12
   vaudeville during, decline of, 4–6, 8
   Warner Brothers and, 3–4
The Sound of Music (film) [1965], 160
Sothern, Ann, 17
Spada, James, 196
Sperling, Cass Warner, 169
Spitfire (film) [1934], 60
sponsors, radio, 45–46, 47
Stage Door (film) [1937], 119
Steamboat Willie (film) [1928], 132
Stearns, Marshall Winslow, 175
Sterling, Christopher H., 176
Stewart, James (Jimmy), 64, 115, 164
   military service of, 78
Stokowski, Leopold, 137
Stone, Lewis, 129
Strait, Raymond, 182
Stravinsky, Igor, 131
The Street of Paris (play) [1939], 69
Streisand, Barbra, 161–63
   Broadway career, 162
   childhood, 161–62
   film career, 162–63
   Funny Girl, 162
   Hello, Dolly!, 161, 162–63
strikes. *See* labor strikes
Sullivan, Ed, 52
Swing Time (film) [1936], 37
"S'Wonderful," 34
Sylvia Scarlet (film) [1936], 60

Take the Money and Run (film) [1969], 159
Taurog, Norman, 39
Taylor, Robert, 140
television, 110–30. *See also* Columbia
   Broadcasting System; Disney, Walt;
   Westerns, on television
   Amos 'n' Andy on, 114
   as bad influence on youth, 128
   Benny, and transition to, 114, 115–16
   cable, 165
   CBS, 114–15
   children's programming, 146–47
   comedians on, film career as result of, 156
   daytime programming, 146–47
   Desilu Studios, 124
   diffusion of, as popular medium, 110–13
   Disney on, 143–45
   early development of, 110–12
   early service, 111–12

early variety acts, 114
as entry point for film work, 125
failure of movie stars on, 164
film industry and, collaboration with, 124–25
film industry response to, 100–01
films produced for, 124
Hollywood as production center for, 123–24
I Love Lucy, 110
infrastructure improvements, 112, 113
Internet as influence on, 165
legal dramas on, 126–27
licensing freeze for stations, 112–13
live productions, 123
"made for television" movies, 125
Marx, Groucho and, transition to, 116–19
media technology for, advancements in, 153
medical dramas, 128–29
movie studios as producers, 124
NBC and, 111
New York City as production center for, 190
after 1960s, 164–65
Perry Mason, 126–27
political climate as influence on, 127–28
political crusades against violence on, 128
radio performers on, 114–16
rapid expansion of, outside of urban areas, 112–13
RCA and, 111
reruns, 123
seasonal lineups, 164–65
in Washington D.C. area, 113
Westerns, 125–26
Thalberg, Irving, 30, 31, 40
"Thanks for the Memories," 91
theater chains, early, 7–8
theaters, for film
air conditioning technology in, 7–8
audience attendance, 8
development of, 7–8
Dewey Theater, 7
early, 7–8
early chains, 7–8
Grauman's Chinese Theater, 8
vaudeville shows in, 7
theme parks. *See* Disneyland
The Thin Man (film) [1934], 61

Thomas, Danny, 149
Thomas, Lowell, 70
Time Magazine, 94
To Have and Have Not (film) [1944], 95
The Tonight Show (TV) [1962], 118, 158
Too Many Girls (film) [1940], 120
Top Hat (film) [1935], 36–37, 85, 119
Tracy, Spencer, 66–67, 100
Transatlantic Merry Go Round (film) [1934], 55
transistor technology, for radio, 154
ATT development of, 154
radio sales increases as result of, 154
Travolta, John, 125
Treasure Island (film) [1950], 142
True Life Adventure series, 143, 145–46
Twentieth Century Fox Studios, Monroe at, 103–04
Twenty Thousand Leagues Under the Sea (film) [1954], 143, 145

Vallee, Rudy, 40, 69
Vance, Vivian, 120
The Vanishing Prairie (film) [1954], 145
vaudeville, 4–6
Chaplin origins in, 9
creation of, 5
decline of, during sound era of film, 4–6, 8
early film partnership with, 5
in film theaters, 7
Marx brothers in, 24
Vaughn, Stephen, 176

Wagon Train (TV) [1957], 125
Wake Island (film) [1942], 80
Walsh, Frank, 110
war movies. *See also* propaganda films
Casablanca, 80–84
ethnic variety within, 80
as propaganda, 80
during World War II, 80
Warner, Jack, 4
Warner, John L., 89
Warner, Rose, 4
Warner Brothers
Bogart's career at, 86–89
Casablanca, 84
family history, 3–4
The Jazz Singer (film), 14
sound era and, introduction of, 3–4
The Warrior's Husband (play) [1932], 58

Washington, Denzel, 125
Washington Post, 52
Washington Star, 113
The Way We Were (film) [1973], 162
"The Way You Look Tonight," 36–37
Wayne, John, 140
Weber, Joe, 43
Weinstein, David, 188
Welles, Orson, 159
Wells, H. G., 12
We're Not Dressing (film) [1934], 39
Wertheim, Arthur, 178
West, Mae, 62
Westerns, on television, 125–26
  adults as main audience for, 125
  children as main audience for, 125
What's New Pussycat (film) [1965], 158
What's Up, Doc? (film) [1972], 162
"White Christmas," 93
Whoopee (play) [1928], 16, 52
Whoopee (film) [1929], 17
"Who's on First," 71
Wild Boys of the Road (film) [1933], 22
Wilder, Bllly
  The Apartment, 107–09
  on Monroe, working with, 103, 104
  Some Like it Hot, 104–06
Williams, Tennessee, 101
Wills, Gary, 192
Wilson, Don, 53
Winchell, Walter, 120, 156
The Wizard of Oz (film) [1939], 164
Woman of the Year (film) [1940], 66–67

Woolcott, Alexander, 28, 33
World War II
  anti-trust regulations during, against
    movie studios, 77
  Bogart as spokesman for war effort, 90
  ethnic and racial sensitivities during, in
    film industry, 78
  film content influenced by, 78
  film industry during, 76–97
  films as escapist entertainment, 96
  Hope as spokesman for war effort,
    93–94
  movie musicals, 79–80
  movie publicity during, 76–77
  patriotism during, 76–77
  stockpiling of films during, 78
  war movies, 80

Yale, Paul, 24
You Bet Your Life (TV) [1950], 117–18
"You Took Advantage of Me," 17
You Were Never Lovelier (film) [1942], 79
You'll Never Get Rich (film) [1941], 79
Young, Robert, 124

Zanuck, Darryl, 100
Ziegfeld, Florenz, 16
Zorro (TV) [1957], 151
Zucker, Jeff, 165
Zukor, Adolph, 5, 7. *See also* Paramount
    Studios
  development of movie stars by, 9
Zurawik, David, 178